Contemporary Britain

D0421110

Contemporary States and Societies Series

This series provides lively and accessible introductions to key countries and regions of the world, conceived and designed to meet the needs of today's students. The authors are all experts with specialist knowledge of the country or region concerned and have been chosen also for their ability to communicate clearly to a non-specialist readership. Each text has been specially commissioned for the series and is structured according to a common format.

Contemporary Britain

Fourth Edition

John McCormick

© John McCormick 2003, 2007, 2012, 2018

All rights reserved. No reproduction, copy or transmission of this publication may be made without written permission.

No portion of this publication may be reproduced, copied or transmitted save with written permission or in accordance with the provisions of the Copyright, Designs and Patents Act 1988, or under the terms of any licence permitting limited copying issued by the Copyright Licensing Agency, Saffron House, 6–10 Kirby Street, London EC1N 8TS.

Any person who does any unauthorized act in relation to this publication may be liable to criminal prosecution and civil claims for damages.

The author has asserted his right to be identified as the author of this work in accordance with the Copyright, Designs and Patents Act 1988.

First edition 2003
Second edition 2007
Third edition 2012
Fourth edition published 2018 by
PALGRAVE

Palgrave in the UK is an imprint of Macmillan Publishers Limited, registered in England, company number 785998, of 4 Crinan Street, London, N1 9XW.

Palgrave® and Macmillan® are registered trademarks in the United States, the United Kingdom, Europe and other countries.

ISBN 978–1–137–57679–8 hardback
ISBN 978–1–137–57678–1 paperback

This book is printed on paper suitable for recycling and made from fully managed and sustained forest sources. Logging, pulping and manufacturing processes are expected to conform to the environmental regulations of the country of origin.

A catalogue record for this book is available from the British Library.

A catalog record for this book is available from the Library of Congress.

Printed and bound by CPI Group (UK) Ltd, Croydon, CR0 4YY

Contents

List of Illustrative Material

Illustrations

Maps

Figures

Tables

Boxes

Preface and Acknowledgements

This is a book about Britain, written for anyone looking for a brief and accessible guide to this remarkable country. Like others in the *Contemporary States and Societies* series, it makes no assumptions about prior knowledge: it provides the key facts and figures that are needed to place Britain in context with other countries – especially its European neighbours – but it also ties the facts together with explanatory analysis. It is deliberately short and concise, the goal being to help its readers better appreciate the key themes and concepts in British political, social and economic life, dispel some of the myths that too often interfere with an understanding of the country and its people, and offer a guide through the confusing changes now taking place in Britain.

I am a political scientist, but I have tried to make sure that all the key dimensions of life in Britain are covered, from history to geography, economics, society, culture and politics. My background and credentials will shed light on the approach, and on my arguments and conclusions. I was born in Britain and am still a British citizen, but I have spent most of my life living somewhere else. I was brought up in Kenya, went to school in Britain, attended university in South Africa and then lived in London from the winter of discontent in early 1979 to the height of Thatcherism in 1986. Since then I have lived in the United States, although I return to Britain regularly, and still closely follow its political, economic and social developments. I see Britain both from near and from far, and because I come and go I have a different perspective on the changes that have come to Britain than if I lived there full-time. My approach is also inevitably coloured by my experiences in the United States, by the fact that I specialize in comparative politics and by my interest in the European Union.

The first edition of this book was published in 2003 and was used by readers in many countries around the world, especially in Europe and North America. The second edition came out in 2007 and the third edition in 2012. The challenge of writing this fourth edition has been deepened by the uncertainties imposed by the fallout from Brexit and the 2017 general election; as this book went to press it was hard to know what the future held for Britain. It is sailing through uncharted waters, and no one can know with any confidence where the country will be in five or ten years from now, or even if it will still exist in its present form. As a result, many of the conclusions in the chapters that follow must be speculative. These are deeply uncertain times for Britain, and those uncertainties are reflected throughout this new edition.

I would like to thank Lloyd Langman at Palgrave for his usual excellent judgement and guidance, Tuur Driesser and Chloe Osborne for their professional support, Cathy Tingle for her work on the editing, and several anonymous reviewers for their comments and suggestions. And my thanks and love as ever to Leanne, Ian and Stuart for their support and happy distractions.

The author and publishers are grateful to the following for permission to use copyright material: PA Photos for Illustrations 1.2, 2.2, 3.1, 3.2, 4.1, 5.1, 5.2, 6.1, 6.2, 7.2 and 8.2. Illustrations 1.1, 2.1 and 8.1 are by the author, and Illustration 7.1 by Leanne McCormick. Every effort has been made to trace all copyright holders of third-party materials included in this work, but if any have been inadvertently overlooked the publishers will be pleased to make the necessary arrangement at the first opportunity.

List of Abbreviations

BBC	British Broadcasting Corporation
CAP	Common Agricultural Policy
EEC	European Economic Community
EFTA	European Free Trade Association
ESDP	European Security and Defence Policy
EU	European Union
GDP	gross domestic product
IRA	Irish Republican Army
ITV	Independent Television
MP	Member of Parliament
NATO	North Atlantic Treaty Organization
NHS	National Health Service
OECD	Organisation for Economic Co-operation and Development
PR	proportional representation
RUC	Royal Ulster Constabulary
SDP	Social Democratic Party
SDR	Strategic Defence Review
SNP	Scottish National Party
TUC	Trades Union Congress
VAT	value added tax
WTO	World Trade Organization

Notes:

For convenience, the terms 'Britain' and 'British' are used throughout, even though the book is about the United Kingdom.

Currency conversions are made at the rate of €1.15 and $1.20 to £1, the prevailing figures in mid-2017.

Unless otherwise indicated, most national statistics used in this book come from the website of the Office for National Statistics at www.ons.gov.uk.

Introduction

Britain is one of those few countries that has quite literally changed the world. Out of a small cluster of islands off the north-west coast of the European continent came three developments with global impact: the industrial revolution, the parliamentary system of government and the English language. It is impossible to talk of economic change without referring back to the inventions that spawned the industrial revolution, and the impact of the writings of Adam Smith on our ideas about capitalism. It is impossible to talk of political change without referring back to the origins of the British democratic model, and the impact of the writings of Thomas Hobbes, John Locke, John Stuart Mill and others. And it would be difficult for the citizens of different countries to exchange their views without the help of English, the international language of business, communications, diplomacy and – increasingly – everyday conversation.

For these reasons alone, Britain is an important subject of study. But there are other motives as well: life is all about change, and few societies have seen such dramatic changes in the last 200 years as Britain. It has one of the oldest continuously functioning political systems in the world, yet the character of that system has been altered in response to philosophical and popular pressures. It once had the world's biggest economy, yet has found itself having to adapt to a post-imperial economic environment coloured by competition from the United States, Japan and its bigger European neighbours. It has a long history of relative social stability, yet British society has undergone a fundamental reordering in the last two generations.

Two recent events have underlined the place of change in Britain. On 23 June 2016, British voters took part in a referendum on the continued membership of their country in the European Union and changed the course of British history by opting to leave. Few predicted such an outcome, which sent shockwaves through Britain, the rest of the European Union and around the world. The government of the day resigned, markets fell before recovering, the value of the British pound fell, critics of the EU crowed at their victory, supporters of the EU were stunned and saddened by the outcome and the so-called Brexit vote threw the short-term future of Britain into confusion. Even its

1

long-term future became uncertain, as calls were renewed for independence for Scotland (which had voted to remain in the EU), troubling questions were raised over what might happen in Northern Ireland (which had also voted to remain), uncertainties hung over the heads of EU residents of the UK and Britons living or working in other parts of the EU, and speculation grew about the reaction of business and the potential effects on London as a global financial centre. Overnight, a country that had built its political and economic structures on engagement with the rest of the world seemed to have turned in on itself.

As though this did not create enough uncertainties, the new government of Conservative Prime Minister Theresa May decided to capitalize on a 20-point lead in opinion polls by calling an early 'snap' general election. The next election had not been due until 2020, but the May administration argued that it needed to be in a strong position in order to negotiate the best possible Brexit deal with the other 27 EU member states, so a vote was pushed through Parliament arranging for the snap election on 8 June 2017. The Conservatives ran a poor election campaign, the troubled Labour party ran a surprisingly strong campaign, and the result was a hung Parliament; the Conservatives lost 13 seats and fell eight short of the 325 needed for an absolute majority, forcing them into an uncomfortable alliance with the socially conservative Democratic Unionist Party of Northern Ireland. Questions now hung over not just the likely path of the Brexit negotiations, but also over the future of the government.

The broader signs of change in Britain continue to be found everywhere:

- In the growing racial, religious, national and cultural diversity of British society.
- In the redefinition of the class system that for so long determined how Britons related to each another, but which has been diluted by improved education, the rise of the middle class, the growth of the consumer society and by new levels of affluence and social mobility.
- In demographic shifts as the British live longer, as the idea of the family is redefined and as Britons move away from the old assumptions of the welfare state towards a stakeholder society in which benefits are determined by the extent to which individuals have played by the rules.
- In the altered balance of power among government institutions as the executive becomes more powerful and Britain now prepares for the legal changes that will result from its decision to leave the EU.
- In the new attitudes of voters towards government, in the questions raised about the nature of the electoral system and the balance among the major political parties, and in the rise of alternative channels through which citizens can express their views on politics.

- In dramatic developments in communications technology, with satellite, cable and digital options changing the character of television, and the internet revolutionizing the way that people communicate.
- In shifts in the direction of economic policy, from the interventionist approaches of the postwar years to the free-market approaches introduced in the 1980s by the Thatcher government and perpetuated by her successors, who have recently faced the additional problems of having to respond to the global financial crisis, the troubles in the eurozone, and now the post-EU adjustments.
- In the redefinition of Britain's place in the world as it has moved from being a global and imperial power to a regional and European one and must wonder how its changing relationship with the EU will change its global role.

In the chapters that follow, the causes and effects of these changes will be examined and an attempt made to understand the effects on contemporary Britain. Along the way, the book explores three key themes. First, it asks whether or not claims of the decline of Britain hold up. Since the 1960s and 1970s, there has been a bandwagon effect among academics, journalists and political leaders, who often bemoan the loss of Britain's pre-eminent economic position in the world, complain that the British political system has failed to meet the needs of the citizens of a modern democracy and find evidence of decline in everything from lowered educational standards to inefficient public services, challenges to law and order, threats to the environment and even the failure of British sports teams to win international competitions. Studies of postwar Britain are littered with words such as *angst, melancholy* and *discontent*, and the concerns have been both renewed and deepened as a result of recent political, economic and social developments.

The second key theme is how Britain will change in the wake of Brexit. Britain was slow to appreciate the possibilities of European integration, was late joining what was then the European Economic Community, and developed a reputation – not always deserved – as a reluctant European. The sentimental British attachment to its global past has not gone away, a phenomenon well described by Hugo Young (1999) when he noted that Britain had struggled for two generations 'to reconcile the past she could not forget with the future she could not avoid'. Whatever happens to its relationship with the rest of Europe, Britain will continue to remain torn indefinitely between its European interests, its remaining ties with its former colonies and dominions, and its 'special relationship' with the United States.

The third theme explored in the book is the meaning of Britain and the dynamics of the relationship between its parts. It has long been unusual in the sense of being a union of four countries: England, Scotland, Wales and Northern

Ireland. That union has not always been a happy or a stable one, the relationship among the parts having been shaken in recent decades by the rebirth of Scottish, Welsh, Irish and even English nationalism, which has redefined the meaning of 'Britain' and 'Britishness'. The different results of the Brexit referendum in the four parts added new stresses, as did the increasingly uncomfortable place of London – one of the world's leading global cities – within the context of the relative introspection of small-town and rural England (Table 0.1).

Table 0.1   Quick facts about Britain

Official name:	United Kingdom of Great Britain and Northern Ireland
Capital:	London
Area:	244,103 sq. km (94,249 square miles)
Population:	64.6 million
Population density:	265 per sq. km (690 per square mile)
Population growth rate:	0.6%
Languages:	Overwhelmingly English, with some regional languages (Welsh, Gaelic)
Religions:	Predominantly Christian (mainly Anglican, Catholic and Presbyterian), with growing Muslim and Hindu minorities
GDP (2015):	$2,900 billion (€2,520 billion, £2,400 billion)
Per capita GNP:	$43,900 (€38,200, £36,600)
Distribution of GNP:	70% services, 29% industry, 1% agriculture
Urban population:	89%
Literacy:	99%
Infant mortality:	5 per 1,000 live births
Life expectancy:	81 years
Government type:	Parliamentary democracy with a constitutional monarchy
Administration:	Unitary
Head of state:	Hereditary monarch
Executive:	Prime Minister and Cabinet
Legislature:	Bicameral Houses of Parliament; appointed/hereditary House of Lords and elected House of Commons (650 members). MPs are elected for renewable terms of a maximum of five years
Party structure:	Multi party, with two dominant parties (Labour and Conservative) and several smaller parties
Judiciary:	Supreme Court

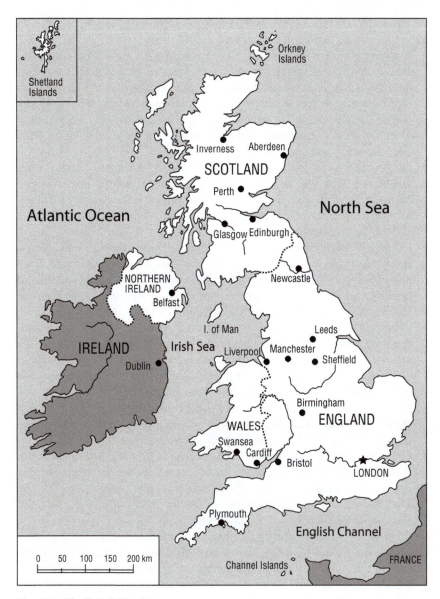

Map 0.1   The United Kingdom

These and other themes are explored in the chapters that follow:

- *Chapter 1* provides the historical background. Beginning with the early invasions from the continent, it surveys the rise and fall of feudalism, the rise of the United Kingdom, political and economic changes and the rise and fall of the Empire. It focuses in particular on postwar history, looking at key political, economic, social and cultural developments, notably the impact of Thatcherism, of membership of the EU, of the changes brought by the Blair administration, and the implications of Brexit.
- *Chapter 2* assesses the geography and resources of Britain – both natural and human. The first half discusses the geography, natural resources and environment of Britain and the second half looks at the people of Britain, focusing on recent demographic changes, and on the impact of immigration, nationalism, regionalism and race.
- *Chapter 3* looks at the British social system, beginning with a discussion about the evolution of the class system, then looking at the changing structure of the family. It examines the welfare system, the structure and state of British education, and ends with a review of the performance of the criminal justice system in maintaining law and order.
- *Chapter 4* examines the British system of government and its major institutions: the monarchy, the Prime Minister and Cabinet, Parliament, the judiciary, the bureaucracy and local government. It explains how they relate to each other, assesses their relative influence over the political process and offers a critical review of the nature of British democracy.
- *Chapter 5* looks at politics and civil society in Britain, beginning with a discussion of the main features of British political culture, then looking at how Britons engage in politics through elections, political parties, interest groups and the media.
- *Chapter 6* turns to the structure and performance of the British economy. It begins with an overview of the structure of the economy, then assesses economic developments since 1945, examining the changes wrought by Thatcherism, assessing the renewed economic successes of the 1990s and speculating on the potential economic effects of Brexit.
- *Chapter 7* provides a survey of British culture, beginning with a general outline and an analysis of the meaning of 'Britishness'. It then examines the state of the arts in Britain, with an emphasis on theatre, film, television and popular music. It looks at how the British spend their spare time and ends with an examination of the role of sports and religion in national life.
- *Chapter 8* looks at Britain's changing place in the world. It examines key relationships, including those with the Commonwealth, within the Atlantic Alliance and with the European Union, and argues that the first is weak, the second is troubled and the third is undergoing change. It finishes with an assessment of the changing status of the British military.

1

Historical Context

The history of Britain – like the history of most European countries – is one of layers upon layers of change, and of new influences mixing with old to create new identities. For a small country, Britain's history is surprisingly complex: in order to understand its modern boundaries, its social system, and its place in Europe and the wider world, we need to dig down through nearly 2,000 years of history. That history encapsulates elaborate social change, ongoing political struggles, internal and external imperialism, and economic revolutions, which continue today. Unusually within Europe, Britain is an island state, and this has impacted both its view of itself and its view of the world. And – again unusually – change in Britain has been driven more by evolution than by revolution. The British have mainly been able to avoid sudden departures and changes of course, which is part of the reason why so many of them have found the changes that have come since 1945 so hard to digest.

Through all the complexity, there are five themes that hold the story together:

- The ebb and flow of the relationship among the four members of the United Kingdom: England, Scotland, Wales and Northern Ireland. This is today ebbing once again as powers are devolved from London to regional assemblies, as the prospect arises once again of independence for Scotland, and questions are raised about the meaning of 'Britishness'.
- Relations with the European mainland. These have always played a critical role in the development of Britain, whether through the effects of alliances and royal marriages, threatened or actual invasions, or Britain's dilatory approach to European integration.
- The changing character of the British system of government. The adjustments continue as the powers of the Prime Minister are redefined, as the role of Parliament changes and as the electoral system evolves.

- The waxing and waning of Britain's economic fortunes. Where Britain once stood astride the world, it has seen postwar crisis, allegations of decline, reinvigoration as the state has retreated from the marketplace, and new economic problems in the wake of the global financial crisis, problems within the eurozone, and Brexit.
- Britain's changing place in the world, from being first a European and then a global power, then having to adjust to its place in the European Union (EU) and now having to adjust to the fallout from its 2016 vote to leave the EU.

This chapter provides a brief survey of British history. Beginning with the Roman era, it works through the Saxon, Viking and Norman invasions; the rise and fall of feudalism; the break with the Catholic Church; the changing relationship among England, Scotland, Wales and Ireland; the emergence of the parliamentary system; the rise of the British Empire; the agricultural and industrial revolutions; and the pressures leading up to two world wars. The chapter then looks in more detail at developments since 1945, including the construction of the welfare state, the end of empire, the cultural changes of the 1960s, the economic problems of the 1970s, the advent and effects of Thatcherism, the impact of membership of the EU, Britain's changing view of itself, its changing relationship with the world and – most recently – the effects of its decision to leave the EU. Change has always been part of life in Britain, but the speed of that change has accelerated since 1945 and even more so since 2016. The destination to which the British people today find themselves travelling is unclear.

The Emergence of Britain

When the Romans under Julius Caesar first arrived in Britain in 55–54 BC, they found it peopled by Celts who had arrived there between 800 and 200 BC, the latest in a long line of immigrants from Northern Europe and the Iberian peninsula. The Celts – ancestors of the Irish, Scots and Welsh of today – were less a race than a disparate group of peoples who shared a language, religious patterns and social norms (Roberts, 2015). When the Romans came again in AD 43 (this time to stay), they occupied most of what is now England, Wales and southern Scotland, pushing the Celts west and north. As a result, England developed a distinctive social and political system: it had roads, planned towns, a centralized economy, a thriving commercial system, and for 300 years was mainly at peace. Signs of the Roman occupation are still evident, notably in many place names, including

London (Londinium during Roman times) and any cities with the Latin termination for camp (*castra*), such as Winchester, Lancaster and Worcester.

The departure of the Romans at the beginning of the fifth century left behind a political vacuum into which later moved several more waves of invaders, notably Germanic tribes such as the Angles and the Saxons, who arrived in about 500–700. While the Irish Celts were converted to Christianity in the early fifth century by St Patrick, the arrival in 597 of the monk Augustine – on a mission from the Pope in Rome – brought a different form of Christianity to England: at a conference of bishops in 664 (the Synod of Whitby), it was decided to adopt the Roman rather than the Celtic form.

In the eighth century the first Viking and Danish raids took place, turning into a full-blown invasion by the mid-ninth century; the attempt to drive out the native population and to settle permanently was only prevented by the resistance of King Alfred of Wessex. By the time of the last successful invasion of Britain – by William, Duke of Normandy, in 1066 – the British Isles had become divided into two zones, one predominantly Celtic and the other predominantly Anglo-Saxon (see Morris, 2012). Although England was now united under the Normans, cultural and religious divisions persisted, England continuing to be distinguished from the Celtic regions by a more stable and centralized system of government. At the same time, England and France were bound together under the Angevins, whose rule peaked between 1150 and 1220, and whose lands stretched from the Scottish border to the Pyrenees (Gillingham, 2001).

Like the rest of Europe, England was a feudal society. Sovereign power lay in the hands of the monarch, who owned the land managed by aristocrats, who in turn bought access to that land with military service and used landless peasants as labour. Monarchs also claimed to rule by divine right, arguing that they were answerable only to God, exercised religious power on earth, and might even have been gods themselves. But the powers of the monarch began their long decline in 1215 when the despotic King John was forced by his barons – with the support of the Church – to sign the contract known as Magna Carta. Under its terms he was obliged to consult with his aristocrats before levying taxes and to agree that he could not arbitrarily arrest or seize property from his subjects. Magna Carta did little more than confirm the privileges of the Church and the barons, but it was the first critical step in the redistribution of political power in Britain.

More change came in 1265 when the Norman baron Simon de Montfort – exploiting the political weaknesses of King Henry III (1216–72) – convened the first British Parliament. It was unelected and met only sporadically, but it included both commoners and aristocrats, monarchs came to rely on it for political support and it provided an alternative focus of political power. Magna Carta and the creation of Parliament marked the beginning of the long and complex process by which democracy was to come to Britain.

Meanwhile, the supremacy of England over the British Isles was established as wars and attrition led to the incorporation of its Celtic neighbours, and as nationalism superseded feudalism as the driving force in politics. The Normans conquered Wales in 1285 but did not fare so well in Scotland – they invaded in 1296, meeting resistance first from William Wallace and then from Robert Bruce, who routed the invaders at the Battle of Bannockburn in 1314. The Normans now looked to expand outside the British Isles, setting off the Hundred Years' War against France in 1337. Revenue from estates was not enough to pay for the war, so the king – Edward III – looked to Parliament for help. It began meeting more regularly and the House of Commons began sitting separately from the barons. The war started well, with notable victories at Crécy and Poitiers, but then the Black Death in 1348–49 halved the population of England. Another victory over the French at Agincourt in 1415 marked the end of the war for the English, who now became diverted by their own Wars of the Roses (1455–85), in which two factions – the Lancastrians and the Yorkists – fought for control of the throne. The Lancastrians prevailed at the Battle of Bosworth in 1485, and King Henry VII became the first member of the Tudor dynasty.

To the ethnic, cultural and linguistic divisions of Britain, religious differences were added when King Henry VIII – aiming to curb the power of the church – dissolved England's ties with the Roman Catholic Church in 1534 and created the Church of England. The break with the Catholic Church was followed by a series of Acts of Parliament in 1536–42 by which Wales was formally integrated with England. The reign of Elizabeth I (1558–1603) saw England developing new power, prosperity and cultural wealth. Sir Francis Drake embarked on his voyages of discovery, William Shakespeare and Christopher Marlowe penned their plays, Ben Jonson and John Donne wrote their poems, and Thomas Morley and William Byrd composed their music. When Elizabeth's successor James I came to the throne, Scotland and England shared a common monarch, and in 1707 a political union took place, creating Great Britain. Meanwhile, Ireland was steadily subjugated, beginning with attacks in the thirteenth century and eventually making it to all intents and purposes part of the British state by the late eighteenth century.

The dominant influence in British politics continued to be the struggle for power between the monarchy and Parliament, which boiled over in 1642 with

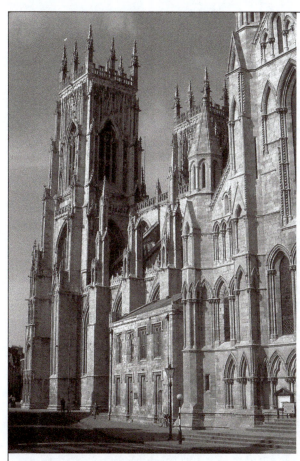

York Minster in northern England, symbolic of the impact of the church on the historical development of Britain, and on the evolution of a distinctive English architectural style. York is the seat of one of the two archbish-oprics of the Church of England.

Illustration 1.1   York Minster

the outbreak of a civil war. This led to the execution in 1649 of King Charles I and the declaration of a brief republic (1649–60) under the military dictatorship of Oliver Cromwell (see Ackroyd, 2014). The monarchy was restored in 1660, but when King James II (1685–88) tried to win back the divine right of monarchs, and to rule without Parliament, he was forced to flee the country in the Glorious Revolution. His place was taken by William of Orange, who – as William III – became Britain's first constitutional monarch. In 1689 a Bill of Rights was drawn up which confirmed the supremacy of Parliament over the monarch.

Box 1.1   Britain or the United Kingdom: what's in a name?

Something that routinely confuses and puzzles people – even sometimes the British themselves – is the correct name of the country. The problem stems from the fact that the United Kingdom is four countries in one: a union of England, Scotland, Wales and Northern Ireland. Each has its own separate identity, its own history and culture, its own 'national' sports teams and – in the case of Scotland – its own separate legal and educational system.

Formally, the full name is the United Kingdom of Great Britain and Northern Ireland. Great Britain consists of England, Scotland and Wales, while Northern Ireland is physically separate but is part of the union with Great Britain. However, while the term 'United Kingdom' is used at government conferences and in diplomatic dealings, in everyday conversation most Britons use the terms 'Britain' and 'British' as shorthand, even though it is technically incorrect to refer to all four countries together as anything but the United Kingdom. If this is a forgivable sin, it is more unforgivable to use the term 'England' when referring to the United Kingdom, as (for example) many Americans and some continental Europeans persist in doing. It would be the same as describing all Americans as 'Texans' or all Germans as 'Bavarians', and is akin to the mistake of referring to the Netherlands as Holland.

The complications do not end there. The Isle of Man in the Irish Sea and the Channel Islands to the south of England – consisting of Jersey, Guernsey and their neighbours – are usually assumed to be part of the United Kingdom. Their inhabitants speak English and their ways of life are almost indistinguishable from those of people on the mainland. Yet the islands are not part of the United Kingdom, nor are they even members of the EU. Instead they are dependencies of the British Crown. They each have their own legislatures and system of law (the Tynwald on the Isle of Man claims to be the oldest continuously functioning legislature in the world), and the British government is responsible for their foreign and defence policies. The free movement of services and people that applies to the EU does not apply to the islands, making it difficult even for someone living in mainland Britain to move permanently to one of the islands.

New complications have been added by growing nationalism in England and Scotland, and by the fallout from Brexit. Scotland held a referendum on independence in 2014, and while the outcome was a decision to remain part of the UK, Scotland (unlike England) voted in 2016 against leaving the EU, and the pressure immediately grew for a second referendum on independence. Were Scotland ever to become independent, the meaning of the *United Kingdom* and *Britain* would change.

The definition of 'England' was also tightened by its success in fighting off invasion, and by its critical interventions in struggles for power on the European continent, which altered the course of English, British and European history. There had been the defeat of the Spanish Armada in 1588, the defeat of an Irish–French army at the Battle of the Boyne in 1690 and the English intervention in the War of the Spanish Succession (1701–14), in which France and Austria vied for the Spanish Empire: the Duke of Marlborough waged ten campaigns, won every battle he fought and – at Blenheim in 1704 – ended 40 years of French military dominance on the Continent. Attempted uprisings in Scotland in 1715 and 1745 failed, and Britain later made decisive interventions in the war against Napoleon. The French navy was defeated in 1805 at Trafalgar, and Napoleon's aspirations for European domination were finally brought to an end in 1815 at the Battle of Waterloo.

Industrialization and Empire

With its military and political power growing, Britain also underwent a social and economic revolution (see Horrox and Ormrod, 2006). Organized agriculture had taken root with the Saxons, who cleared forests, introduced new methods of farming and established the open-field system that was to remain in place until the late eighteenth century. The enclosure movement – begun in Tudor times – saw landowners gradually consolidating their property, clearing wasteland, reducing common pasture and woodland and denying peasants access to land. The peasantry began to shrink as small landowners were squeezed out by large estates. In 1800, the vast majority of the British population was poor and lived off the land, while barely 10 per cent lived in towns and cities. But this was all to change with the rise of industry, which led to the expansion of towns and cities and the creation of factories, such that by 1900 the population had tripled in size – to about 38 million – and had also become more urbanized. Less than a quarter of the population lived in the rural areas, and more than 40 per cent lived in large towns and cities, usually in overcrowded and unsanitary conditions. By 1900 industrial workers outnumbered rural workers by nine to one.

At the heart of the economic changes were developments in the coal-mining industry, where improvements in extraction methods had allowed a 300 per cent increase in production during the eighteenth century alone. Manufacturing industries grew, and Britain became part of the trading system that brought together communities across Europe, and encouraged immigration, emigration and the transfer of new technologies. New and more efficient processes for smelting iron and making steel were developed by Abraham Darby and others, which sparked the beginning of the industrial revolution (see Osborne, 2013). Weaving and spinning were improved by the flying shuttle (invented by John Kay in 1733), the spinning jenny (James Hargreaves, 1765) and the water frame (Richard Arkwright, 1767). The steam engine was invented by James Watt (1769), George Stephenson developed the first railway engine (1829), and industry was mechanized and large-scale business enterprises emerged.

These technological changes encouraged improvements in transport. Major roads, previously badly maintained by local parishes, were taken over by private companies, and engineers such as Robert Macadam and Thomas Telford developed new methods of building roads with harder surfaces and better drainage. The introduction of the railway made it possible for people and goods to be transported more quickly and in greater quantities, and huge new fortunes were made by entrepreneurs. Commerce and markets grew, and Britain was forged into the world's first and most powerful industrial state. By the mid-nineteenth century it had become the 'workshop of the world', producing two-thirds of the world's coal, half its steel, half its cotton goods and virtually all its machine tools.

With its industry growing, Britain's priority was to find new markets and sources of raw materials, and to build on its competitive advantage over its European rivals, particularly Spain, France and the Netherlands. After centuries during which other Europeans had immigrated into Britain, the British began to emigrate to Europe and further afield. England's acquisitive impulses dated back to the earliest attempts to subjugate the Scots, Welsh and Irish, and to the expansion of English control over parts of France during the reigns of Henry II (1154–89), Edward II (1307–27) and Henry V (1413–22). In 1583 the first English colony in the new world was established at Newfoundland, and the settlement of North America began with the foundation of Virginia in 1607. So was born what would eventually grow into the British Empire (see Box 1.2).

Meanwhile, political change came as the balance of power between the monarch and Parliament continued to shift. George I (1714–27) had little interest in politics, so Parliament and the executive became more influential, and when Robert Walpole became the King's First Minister in 1721 he had enough power to be later acclaimed as Britain's first Prime Minister (although it was under William Pitt the Younger (1783–1801, 1804–06) that the office really took form (see Hague, 2004)). The House of Lords was made up of unelected aristocrats, while the House of Commons was elected by only a small fraction of the population, in contests that were subject to bribery, fraud and intimidation, and often from districts that had only a handful of voters. The new middle class of industrialists and entrepreneurs railed against the domination of Parliament by wealthy merchants and landowners, and the pressure for change grew. The Great Reform Act of 1832 began a transformation that included the elimination of corrupt electoral districts, extension of the vote, the creation of single-member parliamentary districts and the rise of mass-membership political parties.

Box 1.2   The British Empire

Britain's global impact rests mainly on the legacy of the British Empire. Tracing their origins to the tradition of mercantilism and seafaring that emerged in the late fifteenth century, Britain's global aspirations saw their first significant expression in the reconquest of Ireland, in the first settlements in North America and in trade with the Asian subcontinent.

The defeat of the French at Quebec in 1759 preceded the Peace of Paris in 1763 by which France ceded Canada and all its territory west of the original 13 English colonies to Britain (Baugh, 2011). Robert Clive's victory at the Battle of Plassey in 1759 gave Britain direct or indirect control over much of India, and in 1770 Captain James Cook landed at Botany Bay on the newly discovered east coast of Australia. The loss of the 13 American colonies in 1781 may have dampened enthusiasm for colonialism, and may have brought an end to what is sometimes described as the 'first British Empire', but a new focus on other parts of the world led to the development of the 'second British Empire', which was eventually to include Canada, Australia, New Zealand, parts of western Africa, most of southern and eastern Africa, parts of the Middle East, many Caribbean and Pacific islands, parts of South East Asia and – of course – India, the 'jewel in the crown' of the Empire, over which Queen Victoria was declared Empress in 1877. At its height during the late nineteenth century, the Empire included about a quarter of the world's population.

Empire meant not only political influence for Britain, but also economic power. Britain required that all trade with its colonies be conducted using British ships, and that the colonies could buy manufactured goods only from Britain. Thus, goods imported into Britain were often re-exported to the Continent at a profit, and British ports began doing considerable trade with their colonial counterparts. When the Great Exhibition was held in London in 1851, it confirmed that Britain led the world in almost every field of human endeavour (for details, see Roberts *et al.*, 2009: Chapter 23).

The Empire was brought to an end by a combination of two world wars in the twentieth century, revised opinions about the merits of imperialism and agitation in many British colonies for greater self-determination or independence: between 1945 and 1965 the Empire was largely dismantled and generally in an orderly fashion (see Douglas, 2002). But the influence of empire continues to linger in the British psyche: at least part of the concern that Britons have with the place of their country in the world is driven by conscious or subconscious comparisons with the heyday of British global power. Scholars remain divided over the historical legacy of empire (see Kwarteng, 2012, for example).

With the introduction of pensions and national health and unemployment insurance in 1908–11, government spending grew, as did the need to generate revenue, more of which now came from direct taxes, particularly on income.

The First World War (1914–18) sparked a massive transformation of government, society, the economy and of Britain's place in the global system. The cream of a generation of young Britons died in one of the most brutal and mismanaged conflicts in the history of warfare: more than 800,000 were killed or went missing and 1.4 million were injured. After the war, competing political ideologies grew in the face of disillusionment with the old options (see Reynolds, 2014), women finally won the right to vote, and labour disputes became more common, peaking with the General Strike of 1926.

Nationalist movements had meanwhile begun to emerge in Ireland, India and other parts of the Empire. Events in Ireland had the most immediate impact, beginning with calls in the 1880s for home rule. These were accepted in 1914, but were delayed by the outbreak of war. Impatient revolutionaries staged the Easter Rebellion of 1916, which failed, and might have had no lasting impact were it not for the aggressive British response, beginning with the execution of 15 rebel leaders. A struggle for independence broke out in 1918, leading to a peace treaty in December 1921 under which Ireland was partitioned the following year; the 26 southern (and predominantly Catholic) counties became the independent Irish Free State, while the six northern (and predominantly Protestant) counties remained part of the United Kingdom.

The economic slump that followed the Wall Street crash of October 1929 brought widespread unemployment, and emphasized the impact of the growing power of the United States, Japan, Germany and the Soviet Union. Britain entered the war in September 1939 as the world's biggest creditor nation, but emerged six years later as one of the world's biggest debtor nations. Its wartime record was heroic: it stood virtually alone in the fight against Nazi Germany between 1939 and 1941, rebuffed preparations for a German invasion during the Battle of Britain in 1940, withstood the aerial bombing of its major cities, scored the first major defeat over German forces at El Alamein in the North African desert in October 1942, and then played the leading role alongside the United States in invading the Continent in June 1944 and finally defeating Nazism. But the rigours of war left its economy devastated, its political influence diminished, its export earnings and merchant shipping fleet halved and many of its colonies agitating for independence.

Postwar Adjustment, 1945–79

Within weeks of the end of the war in Europe in May 1945, voters went to the polls in a general election at which the character of postwar Britain would be decided. It was widely assumed that Winston Churchill – Prime Minister

Table 1.1   Key dates in British history

1066	Norman Conquest
1215	Magna Carta signed
1265	Parliament founded
1534	Creation of the Church of England
1536–42	Union with Wales
1642–49	Civil war leads to the deposition of the monarchy
1649–60	Cromwell's republic; ends with restoration of the monarchy
1707	Union with Scotland
1801	Legislative union with Ireland
1832	Great Reform Act
1914–18	First World War
1922	Irish independence
1928	All women given the right to vote
1939–45	Second World War
1947	Independence of India and Pakistan
1957–70	Independence of most of Britain's colonies
1973	Britain joins the European Economic Community
1979	Margaret Thatcher wins first of three elections
1982	War with Argentina over the Falklands (Malvinas)
1991	British forces participate in Gulf War
1997	(May) Tony Blair wins first of three elections; (July) Hong Kong is returned to China; (August) death of Diana, Princess of Wales; (September) referendums in Scotland and Wales approve regional assemblies
1998	(April) Northern Ireland peace agreement approved by public referendum
2001	(September) nearly 70 Britons killed in 9/11 terrorist attacks in New York; (November) British forces participate in US-led invasion of Afghanistan
2003	(March) British forces participate in US-led invasion of Iraq
2005	(July) 52 people killed in terrorist bombings in central London
2007	Gordon Brown succeeds Tony Blair as Prime Minister; first signs emerge of global financial crisis
2010	(May) general election results in Conservative–Liberal Democratic coalition government
2011	(May) referendum turns down proposal for change to British electoral system; (August) civil disturbances shake several English cities
2012	Queen Elizabeth celebrates her diamond jubilee; (July–August) London hosts summer Olympics
2014	(September) referendum turns down Scottish independence
2016	(June) referendum supports proposal to leave the European Union
2017	(March–June) 36 people killed and more than 200 injured in terrorist attacks in Manchester and London

since 1940 in a government of national unity, and the hero of Britain's wartime resistance – would be rewarded by being elected to lead a new government of his own. But there was instead a convincing mandate for the socialist Labour Party, which was elected into power in its own right for the first time. Many explanations were offered for the change, including criticism of the leadership of the prewar Conservative Party, which had shown a lack of sympathy for working people. When war came, the experience had brought the British closer together, obliging them to share the sacrifices of conscription, rationing and austerity, blurring class differences and convincing many that government intervention could be helpful and useful. Finally, Labour politicians had served the country well during the war, managing home affairs and removing doubts that socialists could govern effectively and fairly (Roberts *et al.*, 2009: 825).

The new Labour government set out to put into practice its vision of a new society and a 'land fit for heroes'. Much of its thinking was prompted by the findings of a 1942 government report authored by William Beveridge, an adviser to Winston Churchill. Warning of the dangers of want, ignorance and poverty, Beveridge had recommended the introduction after the war of a universal social security system, a national health service and policies aimed at preventing mass unemployment. His report was followed in 1944 by an Act of Parliament providing universal free education up to the age of 15. Now, under the leadership of Prime Minister Clement Attlee, the new Labour government embarked on a programme based on three foundations:

- Completion of the welfare state. The National Insurance Act of 1946 provided pensions for the retired, payments to the ill and the unemployed and grants to mothers and widows. Two years later, the National Health Service (NHS) was created, providing free medical and dental care for all.
- The development of a planned economy that would prevent depressions and end unemployment. Adopting the philosophy of economist John Maynard Keynes (1883–1946), Labour directed economic activity using monetary and fiscal controls, running budget deficits to pay for its programmes, taxing luxuries and controlling imports, and imposing austerity measures to help deal with Britain's financial crisis.
- Expanded public ownership of key services, with nationalization of the coal, gas, electricity, iron and steel industries, the railways, the Bank of England, civil aviation and the road transport system.

Hopes for a rapid return to a peacetime quality of living were dashed, and criticisms of Labour resulted in a small majority at the 1951 general election for the Conservatives under the leadership of Winston Churchill. He left intact most of the changes made by Labour, and British politics in the 1950s was driven by a consensus on the maintenance of the welfare system and a mixed economy with a view to sustaining full employment. (Critics of the consensus thesis argue that there was more disagreement over policy than most analysts suggest (see, for example, Kerr, 2001).)

Another of the legacies of the postwar Labour government was the end of empire, the economic and military costs of which were increasingly difficult to bear. The 1931 Statute of Westminster recognized the independence of the dominions (Australia, Canada, Ireland, Newfoundland, New Zealand and South Africa), and the future of India had been the subject of much parliamentary debate in 1932–35 (Tanner, 2002). After the war there was growing pressure for decolonization from the new United Nations, from a segment of the Labour government, and from nationalist movements within many British colonies. The biggest step was taken in August 1947 when independence came to the newly partitioned India and Pakistan. In 1948, independence came to Burma and Ceylon, and negotiations were soon opened that would lead to the independence of most of Britain's remaining African and Asian colonies; the Gold Coast (now Ghana) became independent in March 1957; and in February 1960 Prime Minister Harold Macmillan made his famous 'wind of change' speech, acknowledging that the days of British colonialism in Africa were numbered.

If there was a single event that confirmed the changed global role of Britain it was the Suez crisis of 1956. It was sparked by the decision of Egyptian leader Gamal Abdel Nasser to nationalize the Suez Canal in order to raise the revenue needed to build a dam on the River Nile at Aswan. Conservative Prime Minister Anthony Eden felt that – if unanswered – the nationalization would represent an end to British influence in Asia and Africa, and responded by colluding with France and Israel to win the canal back. Israel launched an arranged attack on Egypt in October 1956, to which Britain and France responded with an insistence that both sides withdraw to a distance of 10 miles each side of the canal. When they did not, Egyptian airfields were bombed and British and French paratroopers were dropped into the Canal Zone.

The Eisenhower administration in the United States – just a week away from an election, and keen to criticize the Soviets for suppressing a democracy movement in Hungary – led the international opposition to the attack, thereby emphasizing the differences that had emerged between the Americans and the British over the new international order. The United States was hostile to the idea of colonialism, and was eager to see Britain tie itself more closely to its European neighbours. The British, by contrast, refused to view themselves as Europeans and saw their main interests lying outside Europe, notably in the white dominions: Australia, Canada and New Zealand. A ceasefire was quickly arranged, the last British troops left the Canal Zone in December, and in January 1957 Eden resigned, ostensibly on medical grounds, but reputedly at the insistence of Eisenhower. Britain's international prestige suffered, public opinion began to question Britain's role in the world, the process of decolonization moved into high gear and the focus of British interests shifted from the Empire to Europe (for details, see Kyle, 2011). In his 1977 obituary in *The Times*, Eden was described as 'the last Prime Minister to believe Britain was a great power and the first to confront a crisis which proved she was not'.

Meanwhile, the domestic economy was recovering: wartime rationing ended, workers' wages increased, agricultural production grew by 160 per cent between 1945 and 1957, Britain's share of the world export market returned to prewar levels (nearly 25 per cent of the world total), mass consumption escalated as middle class Britons bought new cars and consumer goods, industrial output and gross domestic product grew, and inflation and unemployment remained low; the British, claimed Harold Macmillan in a 1957 speech, had 'never had it so good'. But while the British economy prospered, it did not grow as quickly as those of many other industrialized countries, notably the United States, Japan and Germany. Britain was handicapped by class divisions, an education system that was prejudiced against business as a career, low levels of mobility within the labour force, inadequate investments in industry and in research and development, and high levels of government involvement in production and employment (Marr, 2017: Part One).

Where Britain had once been a global actor, it now began to be drawn into a closer relationship with its European neighbours. In a 1946 speech, Winston Churchill had encouraged European cooperation with France and West Germany at its core, but had argued that Britain was 'with Europe but not of it. We are interested and associated, but not absorbed' (Zurcher, 1958: 6). This view was widely supported by the British Establishment, so that when six continental nations led by France and West Germany created an experimental European Coal and Steel Community (ECSC) in 1952, Britain opted not to join. It also opted not to join the European Economic Community (EEC) launched in January 1958, instead creating its own looser model of cooperation in the form of the European Free Trade Association (EFTA), founded in May 1960.

Even as EFTA was under discussion, however, it was clear that the EEC was working, bringing down barriers to trade among its six member states and encouraging them to cooperate in a variety of policy areas. The impact of Suez had also finally hit home, shaking Britain's status as an independent great power. In 1961 the Macmillan government lodged Britain's first application to join the EEC, along with Denmark, Ireland and Norway. This was dismissed by President Charles de Gaulle of France, who saw Britain as a rival for leadership in the Community and felt that British membership would give the United States too much influence in Europe (Mangold, 2006). Britain applied again in 1967, and was vetoed by de Gaulle for similar reasons. Following the French leader's resignation in 1969, Britain applied for a third time, was accepted, and negotiations on the terms of membership opened. On 1 January 1973 Britain finally joined the EEC, along with Denmark and Ireland (for more details, see Geddes, 2013).

Meanwhile, Britain's empire had been all but dismantled. Malaysia and Singapore became independent in 1957, Nigeria and Cyprus in 1960, Kuwait and Tanzania in 1961, Jamaica and Trinidad in 1962, Kenya in 1963, Malta and Zambia in 1964, Barbados and Guyana in 1966, Mauritius and Swaziland in 1968, Fiji in 1970 and the Bahamas in 1973. The one holdout in Africa was Rhodesia, whose white minority unilaterally declared independence in November 1965, and was to be first ostracized and then battered by guerrilla warfare before becoming legally independent in 1980 as Zimbabwe. By the mid-1970s, little was left of the Empire beyond Hong Kong, the Falklands, Gibraltar and a few Caribbean and Indian Ocean islands. Where Britain had once committed its army and navy almost all over the world, it was now a second-ranking power with limited military interests. It was a key actor in the North Atlantic Treaty Organization (NATO), to be sure, was a nuclear power and was one of the five members of the UN Security Council with veto power. However, the British Empire had been replaced by the Commonwealth, whose interests were more cultural and economic than political.

One of the legacies of empire was the immigration into Britain of citizens from its ex-colonies (see Winder, 2013). Initially, these had come mainly from the white dominions of Australia, New Zealand and Canada, but a labour shortage in the 1950s encouraged an influx of immigrants from the so-called New Commonwealth, particularly the Caribbean, India and Pakistan. The government passed a number of Immigration Acts between 1962 and 1971 aimed at restricting immigration, but a new wave of mainly Asian immigrants from Kenya and Uganda arrived at the turn of the 1970s when they were expelled by the governments of those two countries. In 1951, there had been just 75,000 non-whites in Britain, or about 0.2 per cent of the population. By the early 1980s, the number had jumped to more than 2 million, or about 4 per cent of the population, and racial tensions had begun to mount (see Chapter 2).

More societal change came in the 1960s. Reacting to what they saw as the conformist and conservative 1950s, and fed by new injections of American culture, the easy availability of birth control and concerns about social and political problems, young people questioned old attitudes, reflected in their love of rock and roll, new fashions, the sexual revolution and support for mass movements targeted at nuclear weapons, gender discrimination, the war in Vietnam and threats to the environment. The musical revolution was led by the Beatles, the Rolling Stones, the Who, the Kinks, Cream and other musicians who took the music charts on both sides of the Atlantic by storm. The fashion revolution was led by designers such as Mary Quant and Biba, the introduction of the miniskirt and the images associated with Carnaby Street and 'swinging London' (Sandbrook, 2009). Cinema captured the spirit of the new Britain as Sean Connery's James Bond exuded panache and sophistication, Michael Caine's Alfie glorified anti-heroes and Lynn Redgrave's *Georgy Girl* emphasized changing sexual mores. England won the football World Cup in 1966 and the Beatles' *Sergeant Pepper's Lonely Hearts Club Band* shook the music world in 1967 – Britain's empire may have gone, but now it stood astride Western popular culture.

But then problems erupted in Northern Ireland. The province had governed itself since 1922, largely forgotten by national government. Protestants had maintained a policy of discrimination towards the Catholic minority on housing, jobs and political rights, ensured in particular by its control of the police, the Royal Ulster Constabulary (RUC). In 1968, a movement campaigning for equality for Catholics had been aggressively opposed by the RUC, which also broke up a civil rights march from Belfast to Londonderry in January 1969. Violence and rioting followed, the British army was sent in to restore order in August 1969 and from there the problems escalated. Internment without trial was introduced and terrorist groups representing the Protestant and Catholic causes brought death and destruction, while soldiers, members of the RUC and ordinary citizens were killed and injured in street violence and bombings. Direct rule from London was imposed in March 1972.

On the economic front, the growth of the 1950s began to falter, and commentators and political leaders began to talk of a 'British disease' that had come to afflict the country. The Right blamed 'creeping socialism' in the form of welfare, powerful and recalcitrant labour unions, high rates of taxation and the large public sector. The Left questioned this interpretation, asking why other countries with extensive welfare and high tax rates (such as France and Sweden) did not have similar problems. Their explanations focused less on workers and more on management, whom they blamed for failing to adjust to postwar economic competition. They also pointed to a class system that prevented management and workers from developing a constructive joint effort, and that gave more value to inherited 'old money' than to 'new money' earned by hard work and entrepreneurial innovation. Confrontation became more common than cooperation in relations between managers and workers, leading to bitterness, low productivity and a sense of 'Us versus Them'.

Meanwhile, the fabric of Britain came under new pressure with a revival of Scottish and Welsh nationalism. The Welsh nationalist party Plaid Cymru won its first seat in Parliament at a 1966 by-election and saw its share of the vote grow. In the case of Scotland, the neglect of central government, combined with declining support for the Labour Party and the development of North Sea oil (large reserves of oil and natural gas had been discovered in the early 1970s), boosted the fortunes of the Scottish National Party (SNP). Founded in 1928, it won its first seat in Parliament in 1967, its share of the Scottish vote growing from 11.4 per cent in 1970 to 21.0 per cent in February 1974. The Labour government responded with plans to devolve power to Scotland and Wales, and referendums were held in both countries in March 1970, a favourable vote of 40 per cent or more being required to proceed. Only 33 per cent were in favour in Scotland and only 12 per cent in Wales, so devolution was temporarily shelved.

A new low point in Britain's economic fortunes came at the end of the 1970s. Against a background of high unemployment, 16 per cent inflation and a record budget deficit, the Labour government of Harold Wilson was obliged in 1976 to ask the International Monetary Fund (IMF) for a loan to help offset a run on the pound and to help Britain service its debts. Then, during the 'winter of discontent' in 1978–79, public sector workers went on strike across Britain, almost shutting the country down. Clearly it was time for a new approach both to economic policy and to government. In 1979 there was a general election, which resulted in the return to power of the Conservative Party, led since 1975 by the crusading Margaret Thatcher.

The Thatcher Revolution, 1979–90

Alone among modern British Prime Ministers, Margaret Thatcher's name has been applied to a set of political ideas and a style of administration. Thatcher believed she had identified the critical elements of the 'British disease', and set out to give Britain the hard medicine that she believed must be applied if postwar economic problems were to be addressed. Above all, she felt, this meant an end to consensus politics and an abandonment of compromise, bargaining and the search for policies acceptable to the majority. In its place, Thatcher wanted a new kind of politics, variously labelled adversarial, confrontational or conviction politics (Evans, 2013).

The philosophy of Thatcherism revolved around a belief in the guidance of one's own passionately held beliefs, in markets, monetarism and authoritative government, and in the development of a strong state and a free economy. Writing at the time, Marquand (1988: 160–64) argued that Thatcherism had four dimensions: 'a sort of British Gaullism' born out of a growing sense of despair with Britain's difficulties, economic liberalism, traditional Toryism (including patriotism and a pride in tradition), and a style of politics that was both popu-list and charismatic. Thatcherism meant rolling back the state, privatizing busi-nesses and industries owned and operated by the government, reducing trade union power, promoting family values in order to ensure a 'higher' moral level in society and a strong British role in international affairs.

The impact of the Thatcher years on Britain is debatable. Her supporters argue that she sparked the changes needed to reverse Britain's relative economic decline by freeing up the marketplace, cutting the power of unions, reducing dependence on welfare and promoting a stakeholder culture in which more Britons became involved in creating their own wealth and opportunities. For her detractors, she heightened class tensions, failed to meet the needs of the underclass and allowed too many people to slip through the safety net of wel-fare. She also widened the gap between the 'haves' and the 'have-nots': the number of British millionaires grew as a result of her tenure, but so did poverty and homelessness, and many felt that Britain became a less caring society.

Thatcher was also criticized for her views on Europe, where she was fre-quently at odds with other European Community leaders. During her tenure, the 1986 Single European Act was signed, completing the final steps in the creation of a European market free of borders, within which there was free movement of people, money, goods and services. The Community also grew, with member-ship expanding to three poorer countries: Greece, Spain and Portugal. Finally, work had begun on the Channel Tunnel, which promised to remove an impor-tant psychological barrier between Britain and the Continent (it was opened in 1994). Despite these developments, Thatcher dragged her feet on Europe, most famously demanding (and receiving) a rebate on Britain's contributions to the Community budget.

Thatcher won three elections (1979, 1983 and 1987), but by the late 1980s had become widely unpopular, both within her party and with the broader elec-torate. Her insistence on seeking advice from outside the Cabinet, combined with differences over policy, led to resignations by key ministers in her govern-ment, emphasizing her weakness. Her attempt in 1989–90 to replace progres-sive local taxes (rates) with a poll tax to which rich and poor alike would be subject proved highly unpopular. Finally, a squabble between pro- and anti-European Conservatives (the latter led by Thatcher) revealed that her policies on Europe were becoming too divisive. In 1990, after a party leadership vote which she won, but not convincingly, Thatcher resigned the leadership and the Prime Ministership, and was replaced by John Major. He won his own mandate at the 1992 general election, but infighting continued among the Conservatives, mainly over Europe, and the opposition Labour Party in 1994 elected a new leader – Tony Blair – with his own brand of reforming zeal.

While Thatcher was controversial, her policies combined with the effects of membership of the EU to bring great change to Britain. It was visible in the renewal of cities, in the rise of a new entrepreneurial spirit that was transforming the attitudes of business and industry and in the growth of the middle class and the consumer society. The average Briton was healthier, better educated and more affluent than before, and there was a new spirit of liveliness and optimism, at least among the younger generations. Many even argued that Britain was being Americanized – not only had its economy rediscovered something of the competitive nature that made it so strong in the nineteenth century, but many aspects of politics (notably election campaigns) took on a more aggressive American character. But beneath the surface there was growing discontent; not all had benefited from Britain's new growth, and resentment against the political and economic elite was widening, as were fears for the effects of globalization and immigration.

From Blair to Brexit

The legacy of Thatcherism was reflected in the policies pursued after his May 1997 election victory by Tony Blair. Taking political analysts by surprise, the rejuvenated Labour Party swept the internally divided Conservative Party out of office after 18 years in power, winning a remarkable 177-seat majority in Parliament. Blair's 'New' Labour government underlined the importance of the free market and emphasized the need to improve education, rebuild the NHS, invest more heavily in Britain's human capital, build a society less dependent on government, take a tough stance on crime and work in a more constructive fashion with Britain's EU partners. Blair made much of his view that Britain should be 'repackaged' as a society that had deep roots in history and culture, but which was also forward-looking and economically dynamic.

During its first term (1997–2001), the Blair administration made far-reaching changes to the institutions of government:

- Sweeping reforms were made to the upper chamber of Parliament, the House of Lords, long criticized for being anachronistic and undemocratic. The right of hereditary aristocrats to sit in the House ended in 1999, and a commission was appointed to develop plans for the future of the chamber.
- Following referendums in 1997, regional assemblies were created for Wales and Scotland, completing the process of devolution first discussed in the

1970s. Elected mayors were also created for several major cities, including London.

- Proportional representation (PR) was introduced for the 1998–99 elections to the regional assemblies and for the 1999 elections to the European Parliament, the assumption being that PR might also eventually be introduced for the general election.
- The Bank of England was given independence in 1997.

Meanwhile, the monarchy was also changing. In an attempt to make it more open and relevant, Queen Elizabeth had allowed greater media access to the life of her family, which had become something of a feeding frenzy in the 1980s and 1990s as the failed marriages of her three eldest children – Charles, Anne and Andrew – attracted the attention of the tabloid press and its readers. In particular, the rather dry style of the royal family had been challenged by the fashionable and socially conscious Princess Diana, who in 1981 had married Prince Charles, the heir to the throne. In August 1997, Princess Diana – by then divorced from Charles – died in a car accident in Paris, an event that sparked a remarkable public outpouring of grief. Blair seemed to capture public sentiment by describing Diana as 'the people's princess'. There was a clear desire for the monarchy to catch up with a new set of public expectations about its status and role.

Meanwhile, there were developments in Northern Ireland. The conflict had worsened during the 1980s, with sectarian killings and bombings both in Northern Ireland and on the British mainland; by the mid-1990s more than 3,500 people had died and many more had been injured. The 'troubles' strained government resources, incurred additional costs for the military and tarnished Britain's reputation as a champion of civil rights and liberties: trial without jury was allowed, as was arrest for seven days without charge, and a ban was imposed on broadcasting interviews with terrorists. An attempt had been made on the life of Margaret Thatcher at the Conservative Party annual conference in Brighton in October 1984, and a mortar attack was made on the London residence of the Prime Minister in 1991.

A 1985 Anglo-Irish agreement pledged the British and Irish governments to work towards a solution, and the 1993 Downing Street Declaration committed the government to hold talks with any groups that renounced violence. Negotiations began in 1995, leading to the Good Friday Agreement of April 1998, which brought a ceasefire between the warring sides, founded a regional assembly for Northern Ireland in which Protestants and Catholics shared power, and created cross-border councils that would bring members of the new assembly together with members of the British and Irish parliaments (Mitchell, 2015). The new

Northern Ireland regional government met for the first time in November 1999. Unfortunately, ongoing disputes lead several times to the suspension of the Northern Ireland government and the threat of renewed violence. When a new power-sharing government took office in May 2007, and five years of direct rule from London ended, new hope was born for the troubled province.

On foreign policy, the Blair administration proved more willing to commit British troops to service overseas than were any of its Labour predecessors. Britain played an active role in the NATO attack on Serbia in 1999 and was quick to come to the support of the Bush administration following the terrorist attacks of September 2001 on targets in New York and Washington, DC. British troops also played a key role in operations in Afghanistan following the US-led attacks on the Taliban regime in late 2001 and early 2002. But then Blair went against public and political feeling in Britain and the EU in 2002–03 by refusing to oppose the plans of the Bush administration to remove Saddam Hussein from power in Iraq. Public opposition to the war was widespread, criticism of Blairite policy deepened, an anti-war demonstration in London in February 2003 became the largest such public protest in British history and Blair's government was accused of lying about the reasons behind British support for the March 2003 invasion (see Cox and Oliver, 2006: 178–84). Militant Islamic terrorism hit home in July 2005 when four suicide bombers took the lives of 52 people in central London.

Blair also found his government under attack for its failure to stem the decline in the quality of public services. Waiting lists for patients wanting operations under the NHS grew, several headline-making and deadly accidents underlined the declining state of Britain's railways and concerns were raised about the state of the British educational system. Regardless, Blair was returned to a second term in 2001 and a third term in 2005, but with reduced majorities and against a background of declining enthusiasm for his leadership. Iraq had dealt the first blow, but his government was also affected by charges of sleaze, with accusations that Blair had awarded peerages in the House of Lords in return for donations to the Labour Party. By 2006 Blair was widely unpopular and he left office in 2007 under a cloud.

Blair was replaced as Prime Minister by his Chancellor of the Exchequer Gordon Brown, but voters had tired of Labour, Brown was a lacklustre leader, and he took office just as the global financial crisis broke. It had its origins in the United States, where banks and financial companies, encouraged by growing home prices, had lent to low-income home buyers. The loans were turned into securities and sold off to other institutions, including many in Britain and other parts of Europe, so that when the US housing bubble burst in 2007 the value of assets held by banks and financial companies fell, stock prices plummeted, many financial institutions went bankrupt or turned to governments for help, and shrinking consumer demand led to recession.

The May 2010 general election was held against the background of severe economic woes, and while Labour was penalized with the loss of nearly 100 seats in the House of Commons the Conservatives were unable to win a majority (Kavanagh and Cowley, 2010). The result was the first coalition government in Britain since the wartime National Government, with the small and centrist Liberal Democratic Party reaching a deal with the Conservatives, and Conservative leader David Cameron becoming Britain's youngest Prime Minister since Lord Liverpool in 1812. His first order of business was to institute new austerity measures that included a wide-ranging series of public spending cuts aimed at reducing Britain's budget deficit. New challenges were then added by the breaking of a crisis in the eurozone in 2010 (see Chapter 6); while Britain had not adopted the euro, it could not avoid being caught up in the fallout. There was also continued political reform, with a bill introduced to Parliament to set fixed terms of five years between elections.

In July 2011, Cameron became embroiled in a controversy involving the media company News International, owner of the Sunday newspaper the *News of the World* (see Box 5.1). It was accused of hacking into the mobile phones of celebrities, politicians, relatives of British soldiers killed in Iraq and Afghanistan, victims of the 2005 London bombings and of Milly Dowler, a 13-year-old schoolgirl abducted and murdered in 2002. The *News of the World* had been edited between 2003 and 2007 by Andy Coulson, who then joined Cameron's staff as communications director, resigning in early 2011 in the face of continued media coverage of the phone-hacking affair. Cameron was obliged to publicly defend and explain his decision to employ Coulson, and at least briefly looked to be in deep political trouble.

Cameron faced more crisis in August 2011 when the police shooting of a suspect in north London sparked four days of riots in London and several other major English cities. Unlike riots in the 1980s and 1990s, which were often generated by charges of racism against the police, or had political motives, the 2011 riots seemed to have no clear political or social agenda, and were marked by widespread criminality, with vandalism, arson, looting and violent disorder (see Box 3.2).

Meanwhile, Europe continued to pose challenges. The British had long had a reputation for being lukewarm Europeans and a reaction against membership had been growing since the early 1990s. The Conservative Party continued to be internally divided on the question, and the rise of the eurosceptic UK Independence Party (UKIP) seemed to pose a threat to continued Conservative

Illustration 1.2   Brexit

Anti-Brexit campaigners take to the streets of Manchester to protest the decision by a majority of British voters to leave the European Union. The outcome of the Brexit referendum was enormously controversial, and found Britain divided by party, age, levels of education and wealth.

dominance. In 2013, David Cameron began hinting at plans for a referendum on continued UK membership of the EU, but this was less an exercise in democracy than an effort to put a stop to bickering within the Conservative Party and to head off the threat posed by UKIP. When the Conservatives won a majority in the 2015 general election, plans proceeded for the referendum, and campaigns were formed to Remain and to Leave.

Neither of the major parties (the Conservatives or Labour) made much of an effort to fight in favour of remaining, the assumption being that a win for Remain was a foregone conclusion. But then came the vote on 23 June 2016 and a shock win – by 52 per cent to 48 per cent on the basis of a 72 per cent turnout – for Leave. Cameron stepped down as Prime Minister and was replaced by Theresa May, who then became embroiled in a political struggle over how to proceed with the negotiations to leave. Hoping to strengthen her negotiating position, May called an early general election in June 2017, but her party lost seats in the face of an unanticipated challenge from Labour and she was forced into an uncomfortable alliance with the Democratic Unionist Party of

Northern Ireland. These political changes took place against a background of more terrorist concerns, with a May 2017 attack at a concert in Manchester that took 22 lives and injured 120, and a series of attacks in London in March and June that took 14 more lives and injured nearly 100 people.

More than at any time in its recent history, Britain today finds itself in a state of flux. The decision to depart the EU not only leaves important questions hanging over Britain's place in Europe and the world, but has also raised troubling questions about the future of a country that is deeply divided within itself. The definition of 'Britain' continues to be reviewed as the relationship between England, Scotland, Wales and Northern Ireland has continued to change, and how the relationship between Britain and its European neighbours will evolve remains to be seen. At the same time, the problem of social division continues to fester and the threat of militant Islamic terrorism has not gone away. As a result, talk of British decline – dismissed by optimists in the wake of signs of new economic growth and social change – has been dusted off and revisited.

Further Reading

Black, Jeremy (2017) *A History of Britain: 1945 to Brexit* (Indiana University Press). One of the first historical studies of Britain to take account of Brexit, placing this controversial decision within its post-1945 context.

Childs, David (2012) *Britain Since 1945*, 7th edn (Routledge), and Andrew Marr (2017) *A History of Modern Britain* (Pan Books). Two surveys of British history since 1945, offering contrasting academic and journalistic perspectives.

Clarke, Peter (2004) *Hope and Glory: Britain 1900–2000*, 2nd edn (Penguin). Provides a survey of the remarkable changes that came to Britain during the twentieth century.

Newton, Scott (2017) *The Reinvention of Britain 1960–2016: A Political and Economic History* (Routledge). Offers a focus on the political and economic transformation of Britain in the modern era.

The *Very Short Introduction* series published by Oxford University Press does not have a title covering all of British history, but individual titles offer useful surveys of different eras, ranging from the Romans and the Saxons to the twentieth century.

2

Land and People

Like most of its European neighbours, Britain is a small, crowded country. Its residents live in close proximity to one another, the physical dimensions of everything from homes to shops, offices, roads and parking spaces are small, and the landscape everywhere bears the imprint of human activity. It is difficult for Britons to escape each other or permanent human habitation, whether in the form of sprawling cities, small villages or isolated farmhouses. Similarly, it is impossible to ignore the physical changes made by humans; the conversion of land to agriculture has combined with the removal of forests and the use of hedgerows as plot dividers to create a landscape that is almost unique and instantly recognizable: an amalgam of winding roads, carefully maintained fields, patches of woodland, sprawling cities, compact towns and villages, landscaped parks and public footpaths.

This is a country where a large population must make the best possible use of limited resources. Britain has rich agricultural land and meets most of its own basic food needs. It has a wealth of energy resources, from the coal that drove the industrial revolution to the oil and natural gas that meet most of its needs today. But a growing population has placed increased pressure on those resources, and the changes wrought first by agriculture and then by industry have taken their toll on the environment, first with the air and water pollution that were once such grim features of Britain's cities, then with the threats posed to nature and wildlife by more 'efficient' agriculture. Environmental trends have become mainly positive in recent decades thanks to greater awareness of threats to the environment and a concerted EU response to problems such as climate change. But the weather of Britain is another matter, and some might argue that the British have been moulded by their country's mild temperatures and mythically persistent rain. It has certainly helped make Britons a phlegmatic people, provides a recurring topic of conversation and has driven many to leave for sunnier and drier parts of the world.

The people of Britain have also been influenced by important social divisions, the most fundamental of which stem from the cultural, historical, political and linguistic differences among the English, the Scottish, the Welsh and the Irish. The unity of the kingdom has loosened of late; nationalism first took Ireland out of the union, then brought violence and civil strife to Northern Ireland, then encouraged movements for greater local control in Wales and Scotland (and even for independence in the latter) and finally was a driving force behind the Brexit vote. The redefinition of the term 'British' has been further complicated by waves of immigration since the Second World War that helped push the issue of race up the political and social agenda, and have more recently added further fuel to the fires of Brexit.

This chapter looks at the land and people of Britain. The first half examines geography, climate and key natural resources and looks at the state of the British environment, the threats it faces and the policy responses it has prompted. While there have been advances in some areas, there are concerns about changes in energy needs and continuing threats to natural resources and nature, and new debates about the welfare of rural areas. The second half of the chapter looks at recent demographic trends in Britain, with a focus on population growth and some of the remarkable changes that have taken place in patterns of migration, including the large number of people who leave (or would like to leave) Britain. It then examines regionalism and national identity and the troubling trends in the area of race relations. Notable among these have been questions about multiculturalism arising out of a new debate about the place of Muslims in British national life.

The Geography of Britain

The most notable geographical facts about the United Kingdom are (a) it is an island state and (b) its dimensions are moderate in almost every way: there are no extremes of distance, size, height, length, climate, or variety of animal life and vegetation. It has no great mountain chains, no great rivers or estuaries, no large lakes, and no sweeping forests. Its highest mountain (Ben Nevis in Scotland) is less than one-sixth the height of Mount Everest and less than one-third the height of Mont Blanc, Europe's highest mountain. Its largest lake (Lough Neagh in Northern Ireland) could fit into Lake Superior more than 215 times and nearly 15 times into Europe's largest lake, Vänern in southern Sweden. And its longest river (the Severn in England) is barely one-twentieth the length of the Nile and only one-eighth the length of the Danube, Europe's longest river. It has just 420 animal species and 1,400 flowering plant species, few of which are unique to the British Isles.

At the same time, however, Britain is notable for the variety of its landscapes, which are the product of a combination of geological and climatic change and of centuries of human activity. Its geological history has seen the British landmass pushed from the southern hemisphere to the northern, and its landscape types have included tropical rainforests, deserts, freezing ice caps, high mountains and mudflats. The last great natural influence on its geology came with the last ice age that ended about 10,000 years ago, during which ice sheets and glaciers covered all but what are now the most extreme southern reaches of England. The result is that Britain today has – for its size – one of the richest and most diverse sets of geological features of any country in the world: examples of most of the different types of rock, soils, minerals and land forms found elsewhere in the world can be found somewhere in the British Isles (see Crane, 2016).

During the last ice age (about 110,000 to 11,700 years ago), Britain was connected to the European mainland, but the melting of the icecaps caused sea levels to rise, creating the island of Great Britain and many of its neighbouring smaller islands, such as the Isle of Wight off the southern coast of England, Anglesey off the northern coast of Wales, the Isle of Man in the Irish Sea and the islands of Arran, Islay, Mull, Skye and the Hebrides off the west coast of Scotland. Britain has since been divided from the Continent by the North Sea and by the English Channel, which is just 35 km (22 miles) wide at its narrowest point. Britain and Ireland, for their part, are divided by the Irish Sea, which is 21 km (13 miles) across at its narrowest point. The only land boundary that the UK has with another country is the 488-km (303-mile) border with Ireland.

The landscape continues to change even today. The long-term effects of the end of the Ice Age mean that Scotland is slowly rising, while southern England is slowly sinking and the sea is moving up its estuaries; at one of its lowest points in the Fens of East Anglia, wetlands prevail. The weather and the sea continue to exert their effects on the land, with wind and rain breaking down exposed rocks, rivers eroding the land and carrying debris downstream and the action of wind and the oceans breaking up coastal rocks and headlands. Added to these changes have been the effects of humans on the landscape, almost every accessible square metre of which has been remodelled by human activity. Physically (see Map 2.1), Britain today can be broadly divided into highland and lowland regions. The highest land is found in the south-west (Dartmoor and Exmoor) and the Pennine mountains of north-central England; the Cambrian mountains of Wales; the central areas of Northern Ireland; and the southern uplands, Grampian mountains and north-west highlands of Scotland. The rest of Britain consists of plains and lowlands interspersed with moorland and the gently undulating chalk downs of the south-east.

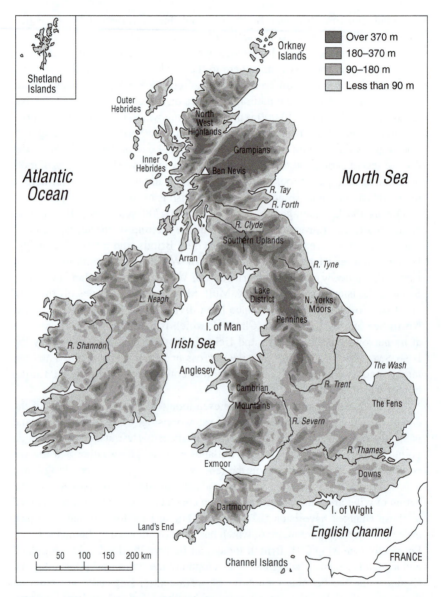

Over 370 m
180–370 m
90–180 m
Less than 90 m

Shetland Islands

Orkney Islands

Outer Hebrides

North West Highlands

Grampians

Inner Hebrides

△ Ben Nevis

R. Tay

R. Forth

R. Clyde

Southern Uplands

Arran

R. Tyne

Atlantic Ocean

North Sea

L. Neagh

Lake District

N. Yorks. Moors

Pennines

I. of Man

R. Shannon

Irish Sea

Anglesey

The Wash

R. Trent

Cambrian Mountains

The Fens

R. Severn

Exmoor

R. Thames

Downs

Dartmoor

I. of Wight

Land's End

0   50   100   150   200 km

English Channel

FRANCE

Channel Islands

Map 2.1   Physical features of the British Isles

The weather of Britain is notorious to residents and visitors alike. Climatologists describe it as 'moderate', a polite term for the cool and often wet summers and the mild and usually snowless winters, prompting the old joke that British summers consist of two fine days and a thunderstorm. In fact Britain – particularly England – is drier than most people think, a problem which – combined with the growing population, summertime droughts and excessive leakage from the ageing water distribution system – leads to frequent summertime bans on the use of hosepipes to water gardens or wash cars. And the experience of recent years suggests that climate change is helping make British summers warmer (see Kohn, 2010); in both 2005 and 2006 there were long spells of hot weather with little rain, leaving large parts of Britain dry and parched. Temperatures continue to rise, making 2015 and 2016 the warmest years globally since 1850.

The most telling influences on Britain's climate are surrounding seas (which act as a temperature buffer that keeps coastal areas cool when inland areas are warm and vice versa), the intersection between cool air moving down from the North Pole and warm air moving up from the tropics, and the Gulf Stream, which carries warmer water from the tropics to the Arctic and has a moderating effect on Britain's weather, making it much warmer than areas at similar latitudes in Asia or North America. January temperatures are generally in the range of 3–5°C (37–41°F) and July temperatures are in the range of 11–16°C (52–61°F). Rainfall is usually well distributed throughout the year and tends to be soft and steady rather than sharp and heavy, with few major storms. One of the results is the characteristic lush greenery of the British landscape, which usually lasts throughout the summer and the winter. Another result is that the British are often caught wrong-footed by more extreme weather, such as hot summers or heavy snow in winter. Whatever the conditions, weather is one of the standard topics of conversation among Britons (Fort, 2006; Woodward and Penn, 2007).

Natural Resources

Britain may not be well-endowed in land, and may have lost most of its natural forest cover to agriculture, but it has a wealth of commercial energy resources: it is one of the most fuel-rich countries in Europe, with significant supplies of coal, natural gas and oil, is rich in fisheries, has much productive agricultural land and is self-sufficient in almost every foodstuff that can be grown in its climate.

Coal was one of the foundations of the industrial revolution. It was the presence of vast coal resources in the midlands, the north of England and the south of Wales that offered the opportunity for the generation of steam power, which in turn allowed for the exploitation of seams of coal that had previously been out of reach. While coal is still an important source of energy, it accounted in 2014 for just 20 per cent of British energy consumption, down from 36 per cent in 1980; most is used to generate electricity at steam-powered generation plants. Coal has been superseded by three other sources of energy: natural gas (35 per cent of needs in 2014), oil (34 per cent) and nuclear power (8 per cent). For decades Britain has been self-sufficient in electricity generation, but the planned closure of nuclear and coal-fired power stations has led to projections that it this will change. Pressure has grown for greater investment in renewable sources of energy (such as solar, wind and geothermal power) and there has even been talk of reviving nuclear power as a key energy source; Calder Hall in northern England was the first nuclear reactor in the world to deliver electricity in commercial quantities, but most of Britain's 19 nuclear power reactors, which provided about 21 per cent of electricity needs in 2014, are due to be closed by 2023. International enthusiasm for nuclear power has waned since the earthquake and tsunami that caused damage to the Fukushima reactor in northern Japan in March 2011.

Following the discovery of oil in the North Sea in the 1960s, production quickly picked up momentum and Britain became a major oil producer. This increased government income, reduced Britain's dependence on imported oil and transformed the economic prospects of many coastal communities. But British North Sea oil output halved between 1999 and 2010, and after several heady decades of being an energy exporter Britain since 2004 has been a net importer, helping push its trade deficit to new record highs. Oil is still being drawn from the North Sea, but production levels are continuing their decline and there will be diminishing profits and returns as smaller and more expensive oil fields are exploited. This will mean less income for government, and oil will become an increasingly important security issue. The story is similar for natural gas, which is Britain's second biggest source of primary energy after petroleum. Britain is the world's fourth biggest producer, but production and consumption have both fallen steadily in recent years.

As an island nation, Britain is well-endowed with fisheries; by tonnage, it has the second biggest fishing fleet in the EU after Spain, it is one of the EU's largest fishing nations and it meets about half of its own domestic demand. But life has changed for the fishing industry; fish catches have dropped substantially as a result of changes in law and biology; access to waters outside the 20-km (12-mile) limit was opened up to fishing boats from other European countries in 1976, new technology has improved the efficiency of catching fish, and in spite of the quotas imposed under the EU's Common Fisheries Policy, overfishing and changes in the breeding patterns of fish have led to falling stocks, smaller catches and a 25 per cent reduction in the size of the British fishing fleet since 1996. The impact of these changes has been most obvious in Britain's traditional fishing communities, where fewer people work in fishing, and new jobs in other fields have not always been created to take up the slack.

Agriculture in Britain has long been among the most technologically innovative and productive in the world (see Soffe, 2003). Technical advances have allowed British farmers to exploit the limited land area of Britain to produce as much as is physically possible from a country with its climate. Farmland takes up just over three-quarters of the land area of Britain (much higher than the figure for the EU as a whole, which is just 42 per cent) and there are about 235,000 farm units, ranging in size from large industrial operations to small family farms. Barely 2 per cent of the workforce is employed in agriculture and it contributes just 1 per cent of Britain's GDP (figures which are similar to those in other European countries), but Britain's farmers provide two-thirds of the country's food needs, with much left over for export.

Half of Britain's farmers concentrate on dairy farming and on raising beef cattle and sheep; most of the beef and sheep farms are in the northern, western and south-western parts of the country and they account for about one-third of Britain's agricultural output. The other half focus on poultry and egg production (in which Britain is almost self-sufficient) and on raising arable crops such as wheat, barley, oats and vegetables; crop farms are found particularly in eastern and central-southern England. The agricultural industry has been heavily impacted by the EU's controversial Common Agricultural Policy (CAP), which long set minimum guaranteed prices for food products. While the CAP helped promote European agricultural production, standardized the quality of that production and increased productivity and efficiency, it swallowed up a large part of the EU's annual budget, promoted overproduction, encouraged farmers to rely more on chemical fertilizers and pesticides and upset the EU's major trading partners. Recent reforms have led to change, but the pressures remain for a review of the European agricultural regime.

British agriculture in recent years has been hit by two crises that have brought economic hardship to farmers, many of whom were put out of business. The first was the advent of mad cow disease (BSE, or Bovine Spongiform Encephalopathy). First identified in the mid-1980s, it led to controls on the use of cattle organs in animal feed in 1990. When the government announced a link between BSE and a human equivalent in 1996, the EU imposed a worldwide two-year ban on exports of all British beef. According to one assessment (Packer, 2006), the government response to the crisis was little more than a combination of informed guesswork and sheer good fortune. The second crisis was the outbreak in February 2001 of foot-and-mouth disease, which began in northern England and quickly spread to other parts of the country. Over the next seven months, in order to contain the disease, more than 3 million sheep, nearly 600,000 cattle and nearly 140,000 pigs were slaughtered.

Illustration 2.1   Exmoor, England

British agriculture is both productive and technologically innovative, and has also helped give the British landscape its characteristic look of small fields divided by hedgerows. Even national parks – such as Exmoor in south-west England, shown here – are still actively farmed.

The combined effects of BSE and foot-and-mouth disease meant significant hardship for Britain's rural areas. Ironically, though, the crises may actually have had long-term benefits for the countryside, because they emphasized the links between agriculture and other parts of the rural economy, such as tourism. There has also been more sympathy for those working and living in rural areas, and lobbying organizations with an interest in rural issues have become more active, leading – as Michael Woods (2005) puts it – to 'the strange awakening of rural Britain'. Many were mobilized by the decision of the Blair government to outlaw fox hunting with dogs in 2005 (hounds can still be used to chase and flush out foxes, which can still be shot, or killed by birds of prey – they cannot be killed by foxhounds). Long a controversial pastime, criticized as much for its mistreatment of foxes as for its elitism, fox hunting was defended by its supporters as both an important tradition and a key source of jobs in rural areas. One of the results of concerns about rural issues was the creation of the Countryside Alliance, a lobbying organization that has drawn new public attention to those issues.

The Environment

The state of the British environment has been determined by three major forces: Britain's long history of human settlement, the long-term effects of the industrial revolution and the size and density of its population. These have combined to leave every part of the country directly or indirectly impacted by human development, removing all true wilderness from Britain. In many ways, the British countryside is nothing more than a large human-made park, most of which is actively farmed and remodelled. Nature and agriculture have long had to coexist, with nature usually coming off worst. Industry and population growth have also combined to produce a society heavily impacted by the fallout from the use of fossil fuels, the growth of road-vehicle traffic and the spread of housing. British cities were once notorious for their smogs, and indeed the term *smog* was coined to describe the combination of smoke and fog that once polluted the air over major cities, notably London (Brimblecombe, 1989). Air and water in Britain are cleaner today than at any time since the rise of industry, but most of Britain's major environmental problems – like those of all post-industrial societies – still stem from transportation and the use of fossil fuels (petrol, oil, coal and natural gas).

The natural vegetation of the British Isles is deciduous woodland. Except for heaths and moors, most of Britain was once covered by forests dominated by oak, ash, beech, elm and – along the banks of rivers – water-loving species such as alder and willow. The first forest clearances were carried out by Neolithic humans beginning about 6,000 years ago, since when there has been an almost continuous process of change (Rackham, 2004). In the Middle Ages, forests still occupied about one-third of the land area, but today only about 7 per cent of land is covered by forest, and less than one-third of what remains consists of ancient woodlands and broadleaf forests. Visitors to Sherwood Forest, the New Forest and the Forest of Dean will find only the vestiges of once great natural forests. Government policies have allowed landowners to make more money from converting woodland to cornfields or to commercial conifer plantations, and an outbreak of Dutch elm disease in the 1960s and 1970s brought more change; by the 1990s there were few mature elms left in Britain (or in most of northern Europe). The result is that Britain today has less forest cover per square kilometre than any other country in Europe except Ireland. It has only been since the 1980s/1990s that there has been broader public awareness and concern about the loss of forests.

Wildlife and natural habitat in Britain is now found only in those areas not immediately impacted by human activity, or in isolated pockets surrounded by farmland or in the heart of cities. Agricultural intensification during and

after the Second World War combined with the spread of cities and the creation of new towns to bring marked changes to the landscape. Wetland, moorland, heathland and downs were 'reclaimed', hedgerows and woodland were
cleared to make way for bigger fields that were easier to plough and to crop, and
increasing quantities of chemical fertilizer were applied to the land. The resulting increase in agricultural yields has been remarkable, but the natural environment has suffered proportionately:

- Britain's growing population has combined with the rising price of property to encourage the steady conversion of agricultural land (or greenfield
  sites) to new development. Meanwhile, much old industrial land in cities (or
  brownfield sites) has been left derelict. Brownfield sites are more difficult to
  develop because they may be contaminated and because the owners of these
  sites often have inflated ideas about the value of the land.
- Nearly one-fifth of Britain's plant species and many of its animal species are
  threatened, mainly by loss of habitat: the draining of wetlands, the removal
  of hedgerows and forests, the expansion of development, and the use of
  chemicals in agriculture.

On the positive side of the ledger, the area of protected land has increased
substantially since the Second World War. Britain has a network of 15 national
parks, including the Lake District and the Yorkshire Dales in northern
England, Exmoor and Dartmoor in the south-west, Snowdonia in Wales and
the Cairngorms in Scotland. There are also 46 Areas of Outstanding Natural
Beauty, 40 National Scenic Areas in Scotland, 17 forest parks, more than
200 country parks, protected coastlines, designated areas of special scientific value and green belts around cities where building is strictly controlled.
Together, they cover more than 20 per cent of the land area of Britain. Levels
of protection vary, however, and many of these areas are protected as much
for recreation as for conservation. And unlike national parks in other parts of
the world, where permanent human habitation is not allowed, British national
parks were already settled and farmed, and continue that way, albeit with
restrictions.

Meanwhile, there is both good news and bad news on the relationship
between transport and the environment (Cahill, 2010). The good news is that
Britain's air is cleaner today than it has been since pre-industrial times. The
Victorian era saw the pollutive effects of heavy industry reach their peak,
with the Black Country of the West Midlands being particularly notorious
and inspiring this description by Charles Dickens in *The Old Curiosity Shop*
(1841):

On every side, as far as the eye could see into the heavy distance, tall chimneys, crowding on each other ... poured out their plague of smoke, obscured the light, and made foul the melancholy air. On mounds of ashes by the wayside, sheltered only by a few rough boards, or rotten pent-house roofs, strange engines spun and writhed like tortured creatures ... making the ground tremble with their agonies.

Britain finally took the first small steps to clean its air in the 1950s, but there would be many more years of it being known as 'the dirty man of Europe', and being criticized by Scandinavian governments for its major role in the production of acid pollution (the key component of which was sulphur dioxide, or SO_2), before real progress was made during the 1980s and 1990s to clean its air, and even then it was prompted mainly by the requirements of EU law (Delreux and Happaerts, 2016). The result is that Britain's air has become significantly cleaner: the average number of days with pollution levels of moderate or higher in urban areas fell from 59 in 1993 to single figures in recent years, while for rural areas the average fell from a high in 2003 of 64 to a low of 22 in 2010. There has been a particularly dramatic fall in levels of SO_2, now almost negligible as a source of air pollution in Britain. Finally, British emissions of the greenhouse gases implicated in climate change fell by an impressive 40 per cent between 1990 and 2015, a result in large part of shared EU efforts to reduce emissions.

The bad news is that road traffic is worsening, threatening the quality of the air with nitrogen oxide emissions and encroaching on the land as new roads and all their subsidiary services are built. There are 35 million vehicles on British roads, the highest volume per kilometre of any EU country except Italy and Portugal. The number of vehicle miles travelled in Britain has grown from about 30 billion in 1949 to a peak of 320 billion in 2007, since when it has fallen slightly. More traffic causes more congestion, which is worsened by the constant need to maintain roads to meet the needs of that traffic. New roads have been built – such as the M25 motorway surrounding London – but they have added to the problem by encouraging more people to travel by road. Meanwhile, the quality of public transport has declined. In 2003, London introduced a system under which drivers in central London had to pay a daily congestion charge, but while this proved successful and has been extended into western London, the broader problems of road transport in Britain only promise to become worse.

As with all other EU member states, environmental policy standards in Britain are now driven more by the requirements of European law than by those of British law (see Jordan and Adelle, 2013). The EU has been an active and productive source of new regulations and standards on environmental quality and Britain's goals are now mainly the same as those of the rest of the EU. It is unlikely that this will change for Britain outside the EU. European policy has been focused mainly on

Traffic backs up on the M25 motorway west of London. Ever larger numbers of people travel by road in Britain, which – combined with the decline in the quality of public transport – has led to increased congestion, has offset some of the gains made in improving the quality of the air, and has resulted in threats to the countryside as more new roads are built.

Illustration 2.2   Congestion

improving the quality of water and air, reducing the production of waste, improving the management of chemicals and pesticides, conserving energy and managing forests and fisheries (see Delreux and Happaerts, 2016). Sustainable development – meaning the exploitation of resources at rates that do not negatively impact the environment – has become the core goal in Britain as in the rest of the EU.

The People of Britain

Like most of its European neighbours, Britain is a crowded country. In mid-2014, the population was about 64.6 million, which was slightly less than that of France, but living on a land area half the size of France. Population density runs at 265 people per sq. km (690 people per sq. mile), although there is wider regional variation: more than 400 people per sq. km (1,040 per sq. mile) in

England and just under 70 per sq. km (180 per sq. mile) in Scotland. The most densely populated parts of the country are in and around London, the environs of Birmingham and Coventry in the midlands, a crescent in the old industrial areas from Liverpool to Manchester and Sheffield, and small clusters around Newcastle, Glasgow, Cardiff and Belfast. The most sparsely populated regions are south-west and northern England, Wales and most of Scotland.

England is the dominant partner in the United Kingdom, not just by land area (54 per cent of the total), but also by population and by demographic change. Nearly 85 per cent of the British population lives in England, which has also had the greatest population increase over the past century (64 per cent, compared to just 14 per cent in Scotland), and that population is expected to continue to grow for many years while that of Scotland has already started to decline. Most of the major cities of the UK are in England, including London, Birmingham, Manchester and Liverpool, and – like cities everywhere – it is to these that people migrate in search of jobs, wealth and opportunity.

Typically for a post-industrial society, the rate of population increase in Britain has been declining, and currently stands at just 0.6 per cent annually. But even at this modest rate, the population is projected to grow to nearly 75 million by 2040, by when it will have overtaken Germany and will be second only to France in Europe (see Figure 2.1). An increasingly important determinant in British population numbers has been the change in rates of migration. Natural change – the

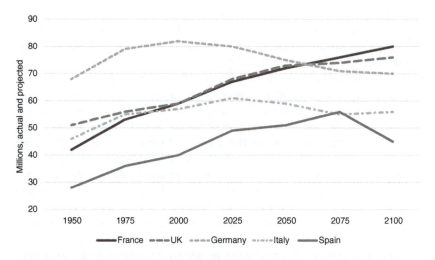

Figure 2.1   British population growth compared

Source: UN Population Division at http://esa.un.org/unpd/wpp (retrieved March 2017).

difference between births and deaths – accounted in the first half of the twentieth century for nearly all the increases in Britain's population, running in the range of 250–500,000 people annually. By the end of the century, the rate of natural change had fallen to just 60–100,000 people per year, while migration rates had changed from a net outflow of 60–100,000 (in other words, more people were leaving Britain than arriving) to a net inflow of 130–160,000 people per year, rising in recent years to about a quarter of a million people each year.

These changing patterns have had a significant impact on the diversity of Britain. Until the Second World War, Britain was racially homogeneous – most immigrants over the centuries had come from continental Europe and later came from the white dominions of the Old Commonwealth: Australia, Canada, New Zealand and South Africa. Also, the number of emigrants was much greater than the number of immigrants. But since 1945 – and particularly since the late 1980s – there have been four significant developments:

- People are leaving Britain in ever greater numbers (see Box 2.1).
- Immigration from the New Commonwealth – notably the Indian subcontinent (India, Pakistan and Bangladesh) and the Caribbean – led to growth in racial diversity, with ethnic minorities expanding from 0.2 per cent of the population in 1945 to nearly 13 per cent today.
- Immigration from the EU has grown. There was a steady growth of arrivals in the wake of efforts to complete the single European market in the 1990s, but the arrival in Britain of workers from Eastern Europe grew with EU enlargement in 2004, such that the image of the Polish plumber achieved almost mythical proportions in Britain, as in other parts of the EU. It remains to be seen how the trends will change for Britain outside the EU.
- There have been changes in the number of people seeking asylum in Britain. Thanks to some of the loosest laws on asylum in the EU, Britain since the 1990s has proved an irresistible lure to asylum seekers from a growing variety of countries. Annual applications rose from 33,000 in 1992 to more than 80,000 in 2002, placing Britain second only to Germany in the EU in terms of the number received. Since then, a tightening of regulations – including an increase in the number of removals of failed applicants – has brought numbers down to less than 30,000 annually. Most recent asylum seekers have come from the former Yugoslavia, Iraq, Iran, Afghanistan, China, Somalia and Zimbabwe, adding to the social diversity of Britain.

With all these changes, the number of people living in Britain who were born outside the country has grown to more than 7 million, or 13 per cent of the population. Of these, about 4.8 million come from outside the EU and the balance come from within it: just over 500,000 from Ireland and the balance split equally between western and eastern EU member states.

The British have also become increasingly mobile within Britain. It was once typical for people to be born, to live, to work and to die in the same city, town or village, which would likely have been where their parents and grandparents before them had lived. The pace of mobility changed with the industrial revolution, when thousands were drawn over time to mining towns and to the factories being built in the rapidly growing urban centres of Scotland, south Wales and the English midlands (for details, see Osborne, 2013). During the twentieth century, social mobility increased, prompted by improvements in transport and a revulsion against life in the city.

The most notable general trends in recent decades have been (a) the move away from the old centres of heavy industry in northern England, Scotland and Wales towards jobs in light industry and services in southern England and the midlands, and (b) the move away from the old city centres to the suburbs and to neighbouring towns, with a resulting increase in the number of people commuting to work. The biggest net movement has been out of London: prompted by congestion, worsening traffic problems, the high cost of property and rising rents, many people have moved to cheaper, quieter and cleaner towns in the areas surrounding London (although even these have seen a rising cost of living). The population of the capital has continued to grow, however, thanks mainly to the inflow of people moving to London from outside Britain, especially from other EU member states.

Another important demographic change, which has affected Britain just as it has affected all post-industrial societies, has been the ageing of the population as birth rates decline and people live longer. In 1901, just over a third of Britons were under 14, while 10 per cent were over 65; in 2011, the respective figures were 18 per cent and 16 per cent, and by 2035 they are projected to be 18 and 23 per cent. Nearly one-quarter of adults are of pensionable age (60 for women, 65 for men), which represents an increase of 18 per cent since 1971. In this respect, Britain fits with trends across the EU and in other industrialized countries outside Europe. This has important political and economic ramifications:

- Pressures on the health care system are growing as people live longer, as more must be spent on the provision of health care and as the demand for doctors and nurses continues to grow.
- The workplace is being affected as the number of retirees who opt to continue to work for financial reasons continues to grow.

Box 2.1   Britain: love it or leave it

Britain has long been a nation of emigrants, the forced or voluntary departure of millions of its people having formed the basis of white settlement in North America, Australasia and parts of southern Africa (see Richards, 2004). It remains as unsettled today as ever before, although the dynamics of emigration have become more complex; where people once moved because of economic necessity, or because of a general need to improve the quality of their lives, recent emigration flows have included work-related factors (companies moving workers to foreign offices) or 'lifestyle choices', with many Britons, for example, retiring to France, Spain or Portugal. And where emigrants once left mainly for the white dominions and the United States, the greatest numbers of those leaving Britain today (about 40 per cent) are moving to other EU member states.

There was a 140 per cent increase in the number of emigrants between 1994 and the peak year of 2008, when 427,000 people left. Although about half of these were long-term migrants returning home (mainly to Eastern Europe) after a stay of more than a year in Britain, recent polls have shown an increase in the number of Britons who have considered emigration; the numbers of departures today equate to those during the last great boom in emigration in the 1960s and 1970s, fuelled by the 'ten pound poms' who left for Australia with the enticement of subsidized travel and settlement (a not insignificant number of whom returned to Britain – see Hammerton, 2005).

The numbers are unusual for a wealthy liberal democracy. Australia has been the most popular target, followed (in order) by Spain, the United States, Canada, Ireland, New Zealand and South Africa. Studies suggest that the most common reason given for leaving is the search for a better quality of life, and while this is difficult notion to quantify (everyone has their own idea about what makes for a higher quality of life), reasons listed include declining faith in the system of government, crime rates, easy access to drugs, declining social and educational standards, the rising cost of living, overcrowding and even dislike of the British climate.

- Younger people are bearing an increased burden of the social security system as fewer working-age Britons make contributions into the system and more retired Britons make withdrawals.
- The political power of the elderly has the potential to grow. Concerns about the welfare of the elderly (or 'pensioners' as they are known in Britain) have long been a hot-button issue in Britain, but despite the existence of many organizations representing the interests of the elderly, such as the National Pensioners Convention and Age UK, they have not yet become an effective lobbying movement. This is likely to change as the population of Britain becomes older, particularly given that voter turnout in this age group is high (80–87 per cent for those aged 55 and above as compared to 50–60 per cent for those aged 35 and below).

In spite of these trends, there has been some conjecture that the ageing of the British (and European) population may not turn out to be as much of a problem as it is often thought. People may be living longer, but the quality of their lives is also improving, they are less likely to make use of health care, and thus the burden may not be as bad as is often feared. Most calculations at present define people as being old when they reach the age of 65, but this may no longer be a realistic assumption. The pensionable age for both men and women will be raised to 66 in 2020, and to 67 by 2028.

Nationalism and Regionalism

The relationship among the four partners in the United Kingdom has not always been an easy one, with memories about the way in which England subjugated the three others, concerns about the cultural, economic and political dominance of England, and efforts to protect and rebuild minority cultural identity. Despite the existence of a 'United' Kingdom, regionalism is a factor in national politics, leading even to support in Scotland for complete independence.

Wales lost its independence in 1285 and was united with England in 1536–42, as a result of which its early political institutions and processes developed along English lines, and the two countries today have the same legal and administrative systems. The story in Scotland was quite different: the Scottish and English crowns were united in 1603, but political union did not come until 1707 and even then the two countries retained many separate features, including different religions, different legal codes, separate educational systems and separate central banks. As for Ireland, the partition that came in 1922 with the creation of the Irish Free State left behind Northern Ireland, which has since been governed mainly as a semi-autonomous state, with its own civil service, its own political parties and (except when direct rule from London was imposed in 1972–99) its own Parliament (now the Northern Ireland Assembly) at Stormont.

What are the differences among the four countries?

- Each has its own flag, its own culture and its own writers and artists. Each country even has its own sports teams, so that while English, Scottish, Welsh and Northern Irish athletes at the Olympics wear the colours of Great Britain, there are separate national football and rugby teams (although the national rugby teams occasionally combine with Ireland under the colours of the British and Irish Lions).

Table 2.1   The four nations compared

| | Land area ('000 sq km) | Population | | Per capita GDP (UK = 100) |
		Million	Density per sq. km	
England	130.3 (54%)	54.3 (84%)	413	103
Scotland	78.0 (32%)	5.3 (8%)	68	97
Wales	20.7 (8%)	3.1 (5%)	149	81
Northern Ireland	14.1 (6%)	1.8 (3%)	128	77
Total	243.1	64.5	265	

Source: Office for National Statistics website, www.statistics.gov.uk (retrieved April 2017). Figures are for 2013.

- Scotland, Wales and Northern Ireland have their own regional political parties: the Scottish National Party (SNP), Plaid Cymru in Wales and a cluster of Northern Irish parties. All have representation both in the national British Parliament and in the regional assemblies.
- Class and regional differences overlap, a result of the development of industry in the eighteenth and nineteenth centuries in Scotland, Wales and the north of England. These regions saw the rise of the new industrial class of manual labourers, and have since suffered the worst effects of industrial decline and economic adjustment. So while England has a per capita GDP slightly above the average for the UK, the figures for Scotland, Wales and Northern Ireland are all lower than average (see Table 2.1).
- Scotland and Northern Ireland have legal and educational systems that are separate from those used in England and Wales, and the Church of Scotland – created in 1560 – is also separate from the Church of England (see Chapter 7).
- Wales is officially bilingual. About 20 per cent of the population of Wales (that is, about 500,000 people) speak Welsh, which has had equal status with English since 1993, and Wales also has its own Welsh language radio and TV stations. By contrast, only about 8 per cent of the people of Northern Ireland speak or write Irish Gaelic, and a bare 50,000 people in Scotland – about 1 per cent of the population – speak Scots Gaelic; forecasts have been made of its imminent extinction.

The strength of the relationship among the four countries has ebbed and flowed, some of the pressures having been reduced since the 1960s by devolution (the transfer of selected powers from the national government in London to regional governments). This is an idea that traces its origins in political discourse back to the 1880s (Deacon, 2012), but it moved up the agenda in the closing decades of the twentieth century (Moran, 2017). The Conservative Party was traditionally opposed to the idea, seeing it as the thin end of a wedge that would eventually lead to full independence, at least for Scotland. Meanwhile, the Labour Party had for many years promised constitutional reforms leading to devolution and the Blair administration held referendums in Scotland and Wales in 1997 on a proposal to create regional assemblies. Nearly 75 per cent of Scots voted in favour, while a bare majority of the Welsh (50.3 per cent) were in favour. The result was the creation in 1998 of assemblies for Scotland and Wales, followed in 1999 by the re-establishment of an assembly for Northern Ireland (see Chapter 4 for more details).

The cause of Scottish independence, meanwhile, has achieved new prominence. The 2011 Scottish parliamentary elections resulted in an outright majority for the SNP, clearing the way for the holding of a referendum on Scottish independence in September 2014. This resulted in a vote against independence (supported by only 45 per cent of Scots), but then the SNP made sweeping gains at the 2015 general election, winning all but one of the 57 UK parliamentary districts in Scotland (they had won only six districts at the 2010 election). The Brexit vote complicated matters still further: Scotland was clearly at odds with England over membership of the EU, since only 38 per cent of Scots voted to leave the EU compared to 53 per cent of English voters. With the UK seemingly headed out of the EU and most Scots wanting to remain, demands for a second independence referendum grew, leading potentially (if successful) to the end of the United Kingdom, and continued membership of the EU for Scotland.

The existence of regional assemblies has led to an interesting anomaly, known as the West Lothian question. Speaking during a 1977 House of Commons debate over devolution, Tam Dalyell – the MP for the Scottish district of West Lothian – asked how long English Members of Parliament (MPs) (and constituencies) would tolerate MPs from Scotland, Wales and Northern Ireland having a say over British political decisions when English MPs had much less say over affairs in Scotland, Wales and Northern Ireland. Since the creation of the regional assemblies, resulting in greater self-government for the regions, not only do Scottish, Welsh and Northern Irish MPs more obviously have a say over English affairs (when the reverse is not true), but they also have less say over affairs in their home regions. Some have argued that all matters discussed by the House of Commons ultimately impact the whole country, but others are not so sure.

It is also important to appreciate that regionalism is not simply about national frontiers, but that Scotland, Wales and Northern Ireland are divided within themselves. The Scots have different religions, and there are cultural rivalries between highlanders and lowlanders and between Glasgow and Edinburgh. The Welsh are divided economically between the old industrial centres and coal-mining communities of the south and the agricultural regions of the north, and between those who speak Welsh and those who do not. Meanwhile, Northern Ireland suffers a variety of religious, economic and cultural divisions, and is split between those who support continued union with Britain and those who do not.

England, too, has its own regionalism, with a recent rise in sympathy for the idea of a distinctive English national identity (Kumar, 2003; Paxman, 2007). But like Scotland and Wales, England has its own internal differences: influenced by a combination of history, economic factors and education, the values, attitudes and priorities of people who live in London (see Box 2.2) and its suburbs are different from those who live in the rural and small-town environment of the 'home counties' around London, in the farmlands and the tourist meccas of the south-west, in the old industrial areas of the midlands and the north, and in the dales of Yorkshire and the mountains and lakes of Cumbria. Most unusual of all is the enclave of Cornwall on the south-western tip of England: the Cornish are related to the Celts of Ireland, Wales and Scotland, have a distinctive culture and – although very few now speak it – have their own language.

Nationalism has had its most harmful effects in Northern Ireland. The province was created in 1922, when Ireland won its independence and was partitioned: while the 26 southern and largely Catholic counties were reconfigured as the Irish Free State, the six northern counties had Protestant majorities (tracing their roots back to the arrival in the seventeenth century of Scottish Presbyterians) and opted to remain part of the United Kingdom. Protestants discriminated against Catholics in the province, marginalizing them in schools, jobs, the police and local government. In 1968, Northern Irish Catholics held demonstrations in support of improved civil rights, to which the Protestant-dominated local police responded with force. British troops, dispatched to the province to maintain peace, were quickly accused by Catholics of taking the side of the Protestants.

Over the 30 years that followed, about 3,500 people died and many thousands more were injured in the conflict, the different communities represented both by mainstream political parties and by associated paramilitary groups that used terrorism as a means to achieving their political ends. While the Ulster Unionists and the Ulster Defence Force (UDF), among others, promoted the Protestant/unionist cause, Sinn Fein and the IRA promoted the Catholic/nationalist cause. Assassinations, bigotry and tribalism became the tragic norm, and every attempt to bring peace to Northern Ireland failed. Most Catholics identified with the nationalist cause, demanding a reunification of Ireland, while most

Box 2.2   The dominating role of London

Not all capital cities play a major role in national affairs, because power is often dissipated and shared among multiple urban areas. Washington, DC may be the capital of the United States, for example, but it is a relatively provincial city: New York has a population 15 times greater, Los Angeles a population seven times greater, and they are more nationally significant.

The situation is quite different in Britain, where London plays the foremost role in almost every aspect of British life, so much so that Britain is not only dominated by England, but in many respects is also dominated by London. This causes some resentment in other parts of the country, overlapping with resentment against the London-based political elite. Sixty per cent of Londoners voted to remain part of the EU in the 2016 referendum, indicating not just its differences with England but also promising difficulties as London – one of the world's leading financial centres – is obliged to make adjustments in the wake of Brexit. More than one-third of the British population lives in and around London, which – as well as being the seat of national government – is the national hub for the following:

- *Communications*: it is the home of almost all the major national newspapers and radio and TV stations.
- *Finance*: it is the home of the Bank of England, the London Stock Exchange and most of the major banks and financial corporations.
- *Transport*: the rail and motorway systems centre on London, which is also served by Britain's three biggest airports, Heathrow, Gatwick and Stansted.
- *Culture*: London has some of the world's finest theatre, opera, ballet and symphony orchestras, and is home to recording studios and major rock-concert venues.
- *Sports*: the national football stadium is at Wembley in north London, and the capital is also home to Wimbledon for tennis, Twickenham for rugby and Lord's and the Oval for cricket.

Inner London – including the shopping and cultural districts of the West End and the financial district of the City of London – is the wealthiest region in the EU. For statistical purposes, the EU is divided into nearly 300 regions; taking 100 as the average per capita GDP for those regions, the poorer parts of the EU have a per capita GDP of less than 50, while the figure for inner London is nearly 550 (figures for 2014 from Eurostat, the EU statistical service). Unfortunately, inner London is also one of the most expensive places to live in the world, topping comparative tables for the cost of renting and buying property, for eating out at restaurants and for going out to the theatre or the cinema.

Protestants remained loyalists or unionists, insisting that the province remain part of the UK. Successive British governments meanwhile found themselves caught between the two, pleasing neither side and occasionally making the situation worse.

A troubled peace now reigns in the province. The Blair government under-wrote negotiations between the warring factions, generating the Good Friday Agreement of April 1998, which owed much to the personal and diplomatic skills of Tony Blair (Aughey, 2001). It brought about a ceasefire between the war-ring sides, set up a regional assembly for Northern Ireland in which Protestants and Catholics shared power, and created cross-border councils that would bring members of the new assembly together with members of the British and Irish parliaments. The new Northern Ireland regional government finally met for the first time in November 1999, and – despite its suspension in October 2002 following an unwillingness by unionists to share power with Sinn Fein – the advent of a new power-sharing government in May 2007 offered some hope for the future. New questions have been raised as a consequence of Brexit: like Scotland, Northern Ireland voted by a large majority to remain part of the EU, and there are concerns about the impact on the province of the rebuilding of a hard border with the Republic of Ireland.

Immigration and Race

Racial and religious diversity is a relatively recent issue in Britain, despite many centuries of immigration. As recently as the beginning of the nineteenth cen-tury, there was virtually uncontrolled movement of people throughout Europe, and passports and immigration controls were all but unknown. However, only the wealthy could afford to travel, and since they were not an actual or poten-tial drain on national economies, neither were they seen as posing any kind of threat. This began to change with the early stirrings in the late 1800s of the era of mass emigration, prompting governments to begin restricting move-ment. The first significant immigration control imposed by Britain came with the Aliens Act of 1905, directed mainly at limiting the immigration of Jews from Eastern Europe. Even by the end of the Second World War there were still relatively few foreigners living in Britain, and most of them were white, so the issue of race barely registered on political, cultural or economic radars. It was certainly far less a source of social tensions than class.

Under a 1948 law, citizens of the Empire and Commonwealth were consid-ered British subjects with the right of entry to Britain. This elicited little con-troversy because most immigrants were still white. But labour shortages in the 1950s encouraged employers to recruit workers from the New Commonwealth (especially the Caribbean) to work in public transport, in the National Health Service and in northern factories. As increased numbers of people from racial minorities arrived in Britain, so race became an issue. The law was changed in 1962 to require that Commonwealth immigrants had work permits and was further tightened in 1968 when East African Asians holding British passports lost their automatic right to live in Britain, a move that was widely (and rightly) condemned as racial discrimination (Clarke, 2004: 333). The growth of the ethnic minority population led to an increase in racial tensions and to the infamous 'rivers of blood' warning by Conservative politician Enoch Powell in a 1968 speech of the threats posed by immigration. 'As I look ahead,' he concluded, 'I am filled with foreboding; like the Roman, I seem to see "the River Tiber foaming with much blood."' (Quoted in Heffer, 1999)

The debate continued in the late 1960s with the arrival of British citizens of Indian and Pakistani origin from Kenya, who were joined in 1971 by more Indians and Pakistanis expelled from Uganda by the military dictator, Idi Amin. The law was changed again to limit the right to enter or stay to those who had been born in Britain or whose parents or grandparents were of British origin, and as a result there were by the late 1970s only 75,000 immigrants entering the country each year, a number that was smaller than the number of emigrants leaving each year. By the early 1980s, the number had fallen to 54,000 annually, of whom just over half were from New Commonwealth countries.

Additional laws in the 1960s and 1970s made it illegal to discriminate against anyone on the basis of race, and set up a Race Relations Board (replaced in 1976 by the Commission for Racial Equality) to which anyone could appeal who felt that they had been the target of discrimination. Many minority immigrants initially had difficulty being integrated into British society and lived in economically depressed inner-city areas. Tensions peaked during the spring and summer of 1981, when violent clashes broke out between police and minorities in Manchester, in the Brixton and Southall districts of London and in the Toxteth district of Liverpool, but it is debatable whether or not these were race riots. The violence was directed against property and the police, and the rioters were both black and white. Racial prejudice was a factor, to be sure, but so were economic recession, job losses, the decline of inner cities and concerns about crime. A government inquiry into the violence (the Scarman Inquiry of 1981) was critical of policing methods, and resulted in a substantial reformation of police–community relations.

Today, just over 8 million people – or nearly 13 per cent of the population of Britain – belong to an ethnic minority (see Figure 2.2), a growing proportion of whom were born and raised in Britain and have been more fully assimilated into British society than their immigrant parents. Minority cultures have in many respects become a part of mainstream British culture, there is more social mobility for non-whites, and non-whites have become more prominent in British popular culture and professional sports; it is revealing, for example,

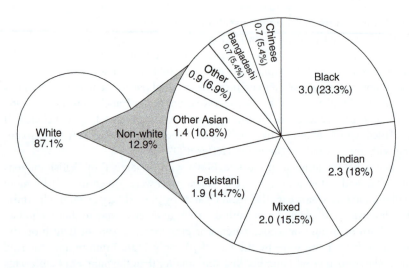

Figure 2.2   Ethnic minorities in Britain

Source: Office for National Statistics, www.statistics.gov.uk (retrieved April 2017). Figures based on 2011 census.

that the famous 1966 England World Cup football squad had not a single non-white player, whereas the 2014 squad had nine. It is also revealing that one of the five most popular names for baby boys in the UK in recent years has been Muhammad.

But racism has not gone away, as reflected in cases of racial harassment and a number of controversies in recent years involving the police and minorities in London, where 20 per cent of the population is from an ethnic minority. The issue of race was at the heart of a particularly notorious incident in April 1993, when a black teenager named Stephen Lawrence was stabbed to death by a group of white teenagers in south-east London. Failures in the police enquiry that followed led to charges of systematic corruption and institutionalized racism in the police force, and to the passage of 1998 legislation introducing new assault, harassment and public order offences, applying higher penalties in the case of those that are racially aggravated.

Immigration has become a touchstone political issue again in recent years with the arrival in Britain of new immigrants from Eastern Europe and the Middle East, drawn by the lure of Britain's strong (pre-Brexit) economy. The proportion of foreign-born residents of Britain grew from just over 4 per cent in 1951 to nearly 13 per cent in 2011, the large number of South Asians and Irish having been joined in recent years by new arrivals from other parts of Europe and those displaced by unrest in South Africa, Zimbabwe and other parts of Africa (see Figure 2.3). Britain has a smaller proportion of foreign-born residents than the United States, Germany, France or Australia, and yet opinion polls find that immigration has become a major issue of public concern, with a large majority of Britons calling for annual limits. It was clearly a motivating factor for many of those who voted against British membership of the EU in 2016, concerned as they were by the arrival of large numbers of immigrants from Eastern Europe as well as asylum seekers from the Middle East. The outcome of the Brexit vote saw a spike in the number of hate crimes and instances of public abuse, much of it directed at citizens of other EU countries such as Poland.

Political leaders approach the issue cautiously, worried about creating a backlash that would strengthen support for right-wing anti-immigration political parties such as those that have won new support in Austria, France, Germany and the Netherlands. They are also concerned about a backlash from minorities themselves, who suffer economic inequalities, have an unemployment rate that is three times that of whites and still often live in run-down suburbs. Non-whites have not yet built their own movement for political change, instead mainly preferring to work within the established Labour Party.

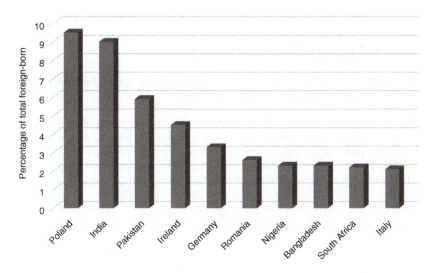

Figure 2.3   Ten biggest sources of foreign-born legal residents of the UK
Source: Office for National Statistics, www.statistics.gov.uk (retrieved March 2017).

An issue of rising concern has been the status of British Muslims, whose place in national life has taken on a new significance with the rise of international terrorism (see Ahmad, 2012). Three of the four men who carried out the July 2005 London bombings were British-born and bred, leading to concerns about a new brand of home-grown terrorism. Unfortunately the attention paid to extremists has impacted attitudes towards Muslims in general. Matters were not helped in October 2006 when former British foreign secretary Jack Straw commented that relations between communities were made more difficult when Muslim women wore veils. This sparked a debate in which troubling questions were raised about just how well Britain's brand of multiculturalism was working. In a February 2011 speech, Prime Minister David Cameron argued that 30 years of 'state multiculturalism' in Britain had failed because it encouraged different cultures to live separate lives and had weakened the collective identity of Britain. His comments echoed those made four months earlier by German Chancellor Angela Merkel, but how much the two leaders were referring to the failure of multiculturalism rather than multiracialism remains a matter of debate.

Further Reading

Crane, Nicholas (2016) *The Making of the British Landscape* (Weidenfeld and Nicolson). A history of the forces that have shaped the British landscape since the last Ice Age, creating its distinctive contemporary patterns.

Deacon, Russell (2012) *Devolution in the United Kingdom*, 2nd edn (Edinburgh University Press). An overview of the meaning and effects of devolution, with chapters on England, Scotland, Wales and Northern Ireland.

Eddo-Lodge, Reni (2017) *Why I'm No Longer Talking to White People About Race* (Bloomsbury Circus). A bestselling book critiquing the manner in which discussions about race and racism in Britain are being led by those who are not affected by it.

Pye-Smith, Charlie (2017) *Land of Plenty: A Journey through the Fields and Foods of Modern Britain* (Elliot and Thompson). A travelogue through the changed state of British agriculture, investigating the connections between land and people.

Winder, Robert (2013) *Bloody Foreigners: The Story of Immigration to Britain* (Abacus). A book taking the long view of the matter of immigration, tracing the story from the earliest invaders to the new preponderance of the idea of Fortress Britain.

3

Social System

Britain is predominantly urban, middle class, English-speaking and white. However, like most major industrialized countries, it is a variegated society. As noted in the previous chapters, its early history of invasions from the Continent combined with England's later incorporation of its neighbours and more recent waves of immigration from the Commonwealth and other European states to bring new diversity. There are economic divisions, too, which began with feudalism, were only partly addressed by the industrial revolution, and live on in a society divided today by class and opportunity; the welfare state and the expansion of educational opportunities have failed to create a level playing field. These divisions are reflected in ongoing social problems, and have in turn had an impact on the distribution of political and economic power.

British society is both fascinating and complex, Obelkevich and Catterall (1994: 1) once describing it as:

> a complicated affair, full of loose ends and bits that don't fit. This may be a good thing for the people who live in it, but it is a source of frustration for those who study it and try to understand it. Every attempt to sum it up in a simple formula – as a 'class society' or whatever – has proved to have so many exceptions and qualifications that it was more trouble than it was worth. The first thing to understand about British society is that there are no short-cuts, no master keys.

The structure of society, the ways in which people relate to one another, the kinds of opportunities available to Britons and the quality of their lives when measured by personal safety and by access to health care and education have all undergone much change since the Second World War, and particularly since the era of Margaret Thatcher (1979–90) and her programme of rolling back the frontiers of the state. But there is little agreement on what this has meant, or what kind of society it has created. There has been a redistribution of opportunity and a blurring of class distinctions, to be sure, but the predictable social divisions of the prewar era have been joined by new postwar layers of ethnic, religious and national diversity. Concerns have also been raised in public discourse about moral and societal decay, a problem that seemed to be given expression with the breakout of riots, looting, vandalism and violence in several mainly English cities in August 2011 (see Box 3.2). To a large extent, the outcome of the Brexit vote in 2016 was a reflection of what Prime Minister David Cameron once described as a 'broken society', in which many felt cut off from social and economic opportunity.

This chapter sets out to paint a social portrait of Britain. It begins with an assessment of the class system, which some feel is still strong but others argue is on its way out; either way, it still impacts the way Britons relate to each other, whether consciously or not. It then looks at the changing structure of the family and the effects of the trend towards smaller families and changing rates of marriage and divorce. It examines the welfare system, the structure of social security and the story of the National Health Service, which is both widely cherished and often criticized. It looks also at the education system, elements of which are renowned around the world, but yet which still fails to provide some Britons with even the most basic skills. Once again, however, much change has come to the system, although the jury is still out on whether these changes will be beneficial. The chapter ends with a discussion of the performance of the criminal justice system in maintaining law and order, and an examination of the public debate over incivility and anti-social behaviour.

Social Class

Not surprisingly for a society that evolved out of feudalism and still has an aristocracy, Britain has a class system. There are some who deny this, many who question its significance and others who might not use the term *class* but still make much of the social divisions that characterize Britain. Tony Blair was among the latter; several key elements of Blairite policy (notably education and welfare) were based on the argument that there are inequalities of opportunity in Britain and that the removal of the barriers to social advancement must be a priority of government. The distinctions that set one class apart from another have declined, to be sure (as they have in most other liberal democracies), with the rise of the middle class. However, enough remain for many Britons – consciously or subconsciously – to continue to relate to each other on the basis of such distinctions (see Roberts *et al.*, 2009; Mount, 2010; Savage, 2015). Whatever the arguments about class differences, the British remain fascinated with the debate and with discussing the social and economic distinctions that divide them.

During the feudal era the class system revolved around relationships with land and the monarchy: the lords managed the land, while the peasants worked the land and were obligated to the lords in almost every way. Political and economic power was focused in the hands of a landed elite. Even during the industrial revolution, which saw the rise of urban entrepreneurs who often accumulated huge fortunes, 'new money' made by hard work, initiative and personal endeavour was still seen as somehow worth less than inherited 'old money', and class distinctions continued to be driven more by heritage, occupation and social values than by relative monetary worth; thus a moneyless minor aristocrat was still seen as socially superior to a wealthy factory owner. However, the dichotomy between a landed aristocracy and a peasantry was steadily replaced by one between the urban working class and the rural peasantry.

Today's class system is more complex, with the narrowing of wealth and income differentials making it more difficult to generalize about class. There is still a pyramid of social layers recognized by the government, ranging from managerial and professional occupations to lower supervisory, semi-routine and routine workers, to the long-term unemployed (see Table 3.1). However, the balance of power and opportunity among classes has changed, the core development of the last 50 years being the rise of the middle class: about 60–65 per cent of Britons today consider themselves middle class (non-manual and managerial), up from about 20 per cent in 1914. Meanwhile, about 30 per cent consider themselves working class (skilled and unskilled manual workers), a significant drop from 1914 when the figure was closer to 80 per cent.

Class differences remain, it has been argued, in part because Britain has not experienced the kinds of revolutions, wars or periods of mass immigration that brought greater social mobility to other European states (Budge *et al.*, 2007: 37). Although most Britons will deny it, many still see each other through the lenses of economic status, family background and lifestyle. Many of the determinants of class are not easily observable or quantifiable, and are based as much as anything on what one person instinctively feels about another. But other determinants are more obvious and include education, the jobs that people do, their social habits, the communities in which people live and what Savage (2015) describes as the 'remaking' of social classes in the wake of new levels of inequality: 'Longstanding problems such as poverty appear to be getting worse even though we live in more affluent times, and have, increasingly, been juxtaposed with the burgeoning fortunes of the super-rich.'

Table 3.1   Social classes in Britain

1. Higher managerial and professional (employers and managers in large organiza-
    tions, senior bureaucrats, senior military officers and higher professionals such
    as doctors, lawyers, clergy and teachers)
2. Lower managerial and professional (nurses, journalists, actors, musicians, lower
    military and police ranks, etc.)
3. Intermediate occupations (clerks, secretaries, etc.)
4. Small employers and non-professional self-employed (farmers, taxi drivers,
    painters and decorators, etc.)
5. Lower supervisory and technical (printers, plumbers, butchers, etc.)
6. Semi-routine occupations (shop assistants, bus drivers, cooks, etc.)
7. Routine occupations (labourers, waiters, refuse collectors, etc.)
8. People who have never had paid work and long-term unemployed

The numbering system is that used by the UK government.

For many Britons, accent is the most obvious (if simplistic) determinant of
class, and there is still some truth to the sentiment expressed in 1912 by the playwright George Bernard Shaw in *Pygmalion*: 'It is impossible for an Englishman
to open his mouth without making some other Englishman hate or despise him.'
At the same time, accents are misleading, and as a badge of cultural, social and
class identity they have been on the decline (Mugglestone, 2007). The benchmark
for much of the early and middle twentieth century was Received Pronunciation
(RP), otherwise known as Oxford or BBC English, or the kind of accent with
which most members of the aristocracy (and BBC announcers) once spoke. No
more than 5 per cent of the population ever had such an accent (a proportion that
has been halved in recent years), but RP was the benchmark against which all
other accents were measured. It was widely – if undeservedly – interpreted as a
badge of education, authority and trustworthiness. Meanwhile, almost anyone
speaking with a regional accent was assumed to be working class or lower middle class. Thus the accents of Devon and Yorkshire were associated with the
rural working class, and the scouse accent of Liverpool or the cockney accent of
London were associated with the urban working class.

But where the BBC once perpetuated the distinction, the broadcasting industry has done much to undermine the dominance of RP, employing
announcers with regional accents, particularly on local radio and TV stations. Accents are still something of a social straitjacket, however, and anyone
who speaks with an accent that does not correspond with his or her social

credentials is immediately regarded as suspect. Meanwhile, there has been a spread of so-called Estuary English, an accent named for areas of south-eastern England, including suburbs and towns lying along the Thames estuary, which combines elements of working class and middle class pronunciation so that words are often shortened and key vowels are dropped (an idea first outlined by Rosewarne, 1984).

Social mobility – the ability to move from one class to another with a change of generation – has accelerated since the 1960s, reflecting new access to education, a growth in the proportion of Britons in managerial and professional jobs, a decrease in the number of people employed in manual labour, the effects of the welfare system and a weakening of the class system. But not all have benefited from such changes: the rich have become richer, the gap between the rich and the poor is substantial (see Box 3.1) and studies suggest that there is less social mobility in Britain, France, Germany and the United States than is generally supposed, or than there is in Australia, Japan or Sweden (Goldthorpe, 2005). However, the British middle class is bigger and more stable than in the past. Where children would typically follow the occupational path (and the social status) of their parents, it has become more usual for offspring to move up the occupational ladder and for those who have been able to create new wealth or status for themselves to change their class identity. This has been possible in part because welfare and improved education have helped reduce the chances of downward mobility. There has also been a decline in the value once accorded to inherited wealth – in today's more egalitarian and meritocratic Britain, 'new money' attracts more admiration.

The changing dynamics of social mobility were famously symbolized by the marriage in April 2011 of Prince William, heir to the British throne, and his fiancée Catherine Middleton. Where marriages involving the heir to the throne had long taken place within the aristocracy and rarely involved 'commoners', Catherine Middleton's credentials were squarely middle class; her paternal ancestors worked in commerce, her maternal ancestors were working class and her parents were both former flight attendants who made their fortune by setting up and running a company selling party supplies. The experience of Prince William contrasted with that of his father Prince Charles, who married relatively late (he was 33 at the time), in part because of the need to find a suitable wife with the appropriate heritage and background.

In contrast, the persistence of class differences – and an indicator of the limits on social mobility – is exemplified by the phenomenon of the 'chav'. The term (whose etymology is unclear, but has equivalents in other European countries) describes working class teenagers and young adults who engage in anti-social behaviour such as street drinking, drug use, petty thievery,

Box 3.1   Poverty and affluence

Poverty is a troubling issue in every liberal democracy, in part because of the debates over how it should be defined and understood, and in part because of the large numbers of people who are apparently still 'poor' in the midst of wealth. In Britain the quality of people's lives has improved dramatically since 1945. People have higher incomes, better job security and more access to education and health care, and more of them own homes and cars. However, not all is well:

- If the government definition is accepted (people living in households with less than 60 per cent of the median national income, after housing costs), then about 21 per cent of working-age adults, 14 per cent of retirees and 28 per cent of children were living in absolute poverty (after housing costs were deducted) in 2014–15 (Department of Works and Pensions data at www.dwp.gov.uk). Although these numbers were an improvement on the mid-1990s, when 37 per cent of adults were living in poverty, they are still among the highest rates in the EU.
- As in most wealthy societies, there is a large income gap between the rich and the poor. Despite the doubling of real household disposable income since 1971, the income gap in Britain grew rapidly in the late 1980s, fell slightly in the early 1990s, rose again in the late 1990s, fell in the early 2000s and then rose again in the wake of the rise in property prices and the global financial crisis. The median household income in the UK in 2013–14 was just over £23,500 (€27,000/$35,000), but the top 25 per cent of the population controlled 72 per cent of British wealth.
- Single-parent families and retired people are over-represented in lower income groups, as are households with children. At the bottom of the scale, as many as 250,000 people are homeless (although precise numbers are hard to calculate). Numbers have increased in recent years as many middle class Britons have lost their jobs and homes in the wake of the global financial crisis.
- The high cost of living means that incomes do not go as far as they do in other liberal democracies. There are regional variations, but London is ranked in recent studies as one of the most expensive cities in the world and the high costs of accommodation, travel, food and eating out take their toll throughout the country.

Meanwhile, affluence has become more visible in the last generation as the net worth of the upper middle class has grown. The amount of money that people had left to save or spend after taxes and other deductions (adjusted for inflation) more than doubled between 1971 and 2014 thanks to lower income and estate taxes, increases in the value of homes and profits from shares and other investments. But the visibility of the new wealth in the face of worsening poverty has contributed to social tensions and may have fed into the 2011 riots and the Brexit vote.

vandalism and other forms of delinquency. There have been many criticisms of the stereotype implied, with arguments that it is a form of elitism and snobbery, that it is a reconfiguration of the idea of an underclass (Hayward and Yar, 2006) and that its use is indicative of residual resistance to social mobility. And yet it has been sufficiently recognized in popular culture to merit portrayal in television comedy series (such as the character of Vicky Pollard in *Little Britain*) and to attract academic study (see Jones, O., 2016).

Social change has been driven above all by the emergence of the consumer society. The idea of 'going without' and of avoiding conspicuous consumption – a hangover from prewar years when most Britons were too poor to own their own homes or to furnish them with more than the basic necessities – was extended by postwar austerity and rationing. Even the boom of the 1950s reached relatively few people, and certainly the British were a pale shadow of middle class Americans when it came to acquiring material possessions or being more adventurous with their leisure time. It was only in the early 1970s that low-cost travel allowed more people to spend their holidays in Spain, Greece or Morocco rather than seaside English resorts. It was only in the 1980s that consumption began to move into high gear, and the British spent more money installing central heating and double glazing in their homes, buying new cars, TVs and other electrical appliances, and going on holiday outside Europe.

The British class system has also been impacted by several other developments:

- Changes in occupational structure. The number of jobs in labour-intensive heavy industry has fallen, to be replaced by jobs in more automated and lighter industry, and particularly by jobs in the service sector. This has altered the balance of population numbers between the working and middle classes.
- A substantial increase in private homeownership. In 1900, just 10 per cent of Britons owned their own homes, but by the end of the twentieth century it had risen to nearly 70 per cent. A breakthrough came in the 1980s with the decision by the Thatcher government to sell off council houses (state-owned housing stock) to their tenants, creating over a million new owner-occupier families almost overnight. The value of homes grew dramatically in the closing years of the century, going through booms in the mid-1980s, the early 1990s and again in 2000–03, increasing the net worth of homeowners and blurring the distinctions between different social classes. But by 2016, the mismatch between incomes and property prices had brought home ownership down to just over 60 per cent, a 30-year low, and many younger Britons were finding it hard to take their first step on the property ladder.
- The rise of the upper middle class. Increases in incomes and benefits and improvements in working conditions for managerial and professional staff

have increased the buying power, financial options and political influence of the upper middle class, resulting in what Turner (2014) describes as a system in which people are economically unequal but culturally classless.

Class distinctions, and the gap between the rich and the poor, were tragically illustrated in June 2017 with a fire that broke out at Grenfell Tower, a public housing block situated in the Royal Borough of Kensington and Chelsea, one of the wealthiest boroughs in London. A total of 71 people died in the fire and many more were seriously injured. For some (see Hastie, 2017), the fire was representative of the problem of deprivation in Britain, studies having shown that accidental residential fires were much more likely to break out in poorer areas of Britain (and, indeed, of other advanced liberal democracies), and to cause more deaths and injuries, than in wealthier parts of the country. The tragedy, argued Hastie, was representative of economic disadvantages in income, housing and health care.

The changing nature of the class system can also be seen in the changing relationship between class and political activity. While the Labour Party was for many decades the champion of the working class and the Conservative Party attracted more support from the middle class, the link between class and voting has declined. The share of the middle class vote for the Conservatives has fallen from 80 per cent to 60 per cent since the early 1970s, while the share of the working class vote for Labour has fallen from 60 per cent to 50 per cent. Labour under Tony Blair realized that economic changes meant that it could no longer rely on the working class vote, so the policies of 'New' Labour were more geared to middle class needs. In the 1950s, 10 per cent of voters in managerial and professional classes voted Labour and 85 per cent voted Conservative; by 2010, the percentages were 28 and 37, respectively (figures quoted in Leach *et al.*, 2011). Sociological factors are now less of an explanation of voting behaviour than are political factors (see Chapter 5).

The Changing Family

The British have the same worried conversations as do the citizens of most other liberal democracies about the break-up of the nuclear family, the reduced sense of community and the seeming decay of moral values in the wake of reduced parental guidance. The definition and the place of the family have certainly changed in Britain in recent years, but the process of change has been under way for more than a century. In the 1860s, the live birth rate for married women was 5.7, but by the 1920s the figure had fallen to 2.2, where it has more or less remained ever since. The nuclear family – two parents and their dependent children sharing the same living quarters – was already relatively unusual 30 years ago (accounting for just one-third of British households) and has become even more so today (just under one-quarter of households). So the idea of 'traditional' family values has been a misnomer for decades, and it is really only social pressure – and perhaps the portrayal of families in television dramas, sitcoms and commercials – that keeps the spirit of the nuclear family alive.

There are several explanations for the changing landscape:

- There has been a trend towards smaller families. There was a time when people had more babies because of higher mortality rates and because children were needed to work the land for the family. But mortality rates have fallen, children are no longer needed for their labour, there is less social pressure to have children and having a child has become an expensive proposition. To feed, clothe, house, educate and take care of the health of a child is now a major financial commitment. As a result, the average completed family size in Britain has fallen from 3.2 children in 1951 to 1.6 in 2014.
- Women are delaying having children. Many more are taking their education further, and many more are looking to establish a career before starting a family. As a result, the mean age at which British women have their first child has risen from 26.2 years in 1972 to 29.7 today. At the same time, the number of women opting not to have any children at all has increased; about one-fifth of women born after 1965 are projected to remain childless.
- There have been changes in attitudes towards marriage. The majority of British men and women still marry, but the proportion has been declining, with more people living together before getting married and more people simply living together without getting married: estimates suggest that about one-sixth of the non-married adult population of England and Wales is living together, and it is now more common to hear British adults referring to their 'partner' than to their husband or wife.
- There was almost a sevenfold increase in the divorce rate between 1961 and the peak year of 1993, since when the rate has fallen slightly but still remains high. A boost has been given by changes to the law (including the 1969 Divorce Reform Act, which introduced a single ground for divorce: the irretrievable breakdown of a marriage), but more broadly there has been a decline in the social stigma attached to divorce, couples in an unhappy marriage are more likely to break up rather than struggle on as their parents might have done, and women are earning higher wages and better qualifications and so developing more independence.
- The number of children born outside marriage has increased, the rate in Britain now being among the highest in the industrialized world: nearly

48 per cent of children were born outside marriage or civil partnerships in 2015 (up from just 9 per cent in 1976), a figure that is expected to continue to rise. Only Estonia, Slovenia, France, Sweden and Belgium have higher rates, and the rate for the EU as a whole is 40 per cent.

- The number of people living alone has grown, up from 18 per cent of households in 1971 to 28 per cent in 2016. One factor in this has been increased life expectancy, contributing to growing numbers of empty-nesters (parents whose children have grown up and left home) and of widows and widowers. Offsetting this trend has been the number of young adults (20–34 years old) who still live with their parents; the percentage grew from 21 to 25 between 1996 and 2015.

- Changes in the law have resulted in a significant increase in the number of civil partnership and same-sex married couple families; in 2016 there were nearly 50,000 households with the former and 29,000 households with the latter.

The cumulative result of all these changes has been a reduction in the size of the average household since the 1960s, from 4.6 people to 2.4 people. The 'unconventional' household has become more conventional, with important effects on the way people relate to one another, on the structure of communities, on the provision of social services and on the upbringing of children. The most alarming implications have been for the number of children living in poverty: as noted in Box 3.1, 28 per cent of all children in Britain in 2014–15 lived in households where income was below the poverty line. By no means do all of them live in lone parent households, but there is a close link between being a lone parent and being poor. Although the number of children living in poverty is nothing like it once was, the extent of the problem is still unconscionable for a wealthy industrialized society like Britain.

Social Services and Health Care

Like all liberal democracies, Britain is a welfare state, or one in which government makes provision under the law for those in need, particularly the elderly, the sick, the poor, the disabled and the indigent. There have been elements of a welfare system in place in Britain since the sixteenth century, when a Poor Law provided limited support for those in need, although churches continued to provide most of the services needed to help the poor and the unemployed. With industrialization, the population grew rapidly, as did the number of people working in cities, which became overcrowded, dirty and polluted. The expanding working class lacked basic amenities such as adequate housing, sanitation, health facilities and utilities such as a clean water supply. Working conditions were often appalling, child labour was common, the poor were exploited and typically denied the vote, and when the government finally did take action in 1834 to provide assistance for the indigent the solution was to create a network of workhouses where inmates lived in prison-like conditions, separated from their families and working long hours for little reward.

Responding to decades of pressure for social reform (see Renwick, 2017), the Liberal government that was swept into power in 1906 laid the foundations of the modern welfare state by creating state schools, providing a state pension and free school meals for children and creating unemployment benefits. However, it was not until after the Second World War – on the recommendation of the 1942 Beveridge Report (see Chapter 1) – that a comprehensive welfare system was finally developed. Entering office in 1945 on the crest of a wave of reforming zeal, the new Labour government of Clement Attlee oversaw the passage of legislation that created a social security system designed to provide help for the unemployed, widows and the retired, and a National Health Service (NHS) that would provide mainly free medical services to anyone not already covered by other programmes (Fraser, 2009).

The calculations made about welfare needs in the 1940s were quite different from the realities that have emerged since then. For example, life expectancy was only about 62 for men and 68 for women, and it was assumed that unemployment would mainly be a short-term problem and affect few people, that families would typically be supported by a male breadwinner while wives would stay at home and that the number of contributors to social insurance would greatly exceed the number of dependants (Fraser, 2009). In reality, life expectancy has grown (standing in 2012 at 79 for men and 83 for women) and Britain has witnessed long-term unemployment, changing patterns of participation in the labour market, and smaller families.

Thanks in part to such changes, the social security system has become the single biggest item on the national government budget, accounting between 1995 and 2001 for about 28 per cent of annual government spending. In 2015–16, the government spent £240 billion (€280/$360 billion) on social protection, or just under £3,700 (€4,250/$5,550) for every man, woman and child. About half of spending goes on retirement pensions, which are paid to anyone who has made a certain number of contributions into the social security system while working. The pensionable age for women is 60 and for men is 65, although changes to the law in 2010 meant a rise to 66 for anyone born after 1953, and there has been discussion of pushing the retirement age to 70. Payments are not substantial (the full state pension in 2016 was just over £6,360 annually per person (€7,300/$9,500)), but then the system is intended only to act as a safety net to avoid the kind of poverty that particularly afflicted elderly people before the advent of the welfare state. Other items in the social security budget include payments to long-term sick and disabled people (about one-quarter of spending), support to families (including maternity pay and child benefits), unemployment pay and support for widows and widowers. In all, just over a quarter of the British population receives benefits of some kind.

The second key element in the social services system is the National Health Service. Created in 1948, the NHS provides residents of Britain with a health-care system in which almost all services are free, particularly to pregnant women, new mothers, children, the elderly, full-time students and those on low incomes. The NHS is paid for out of public funds, with all taxpayers, employees and employers paying into the system, and services being provided on the basis of need rather than the ability to pay. The single biggest employer in Western Europe (with a total workforce of about 720,000 people), the NHS cost £120 billion in 2016–17 (€140/$180 billion).

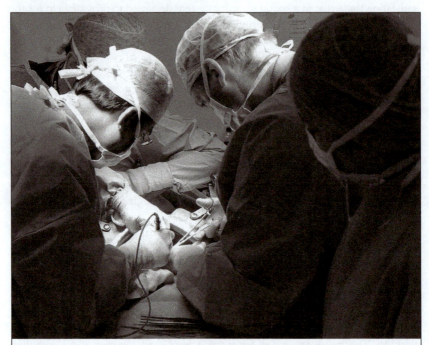

Illustration 3.1   National Health Service

Surgeons at work in an operating theatre in a National Health Service hospital. The British live longer and healthier lives than ever before, thanks in part to the availability of universal health care. Concerns about the quality of that health care have been addressed in recent years with reforms to the NHS.

Public opinion on the NHS is divided. Few in Britain question the principle of universal free medical care, and there is much pride in the concept of the NHS, but recent polls have found that only about 60–70 per cent of Britons have been satisfied with the service. (Interestingly, the public view is less positive than that of people who have actually used the service, hinting at the myths that tend to surround the NHS.) Complaints typically focus on poor standards, bureaucracy, low pay and long hours for doctors and nurses, the amount of time it sometimes takes for a patient to see a doctor, the waiting time in accident and emergency departments in hospitals, and charges that older patients are sometimes discriminated against. Most controversial of all have been the waiting lists for patients seeking operations: until recently, it could take up to 18 months for someone to receive non-urgent surgery, 9–12 months to receive hip- or knee-replacement surgery and even several months for cancer patients to start receiving treatment. The number of patients on waiting lists has fallen in recent years, although critics of government policy charge that this has happened only at the cost of patient care as resources have been diverted to meeting targets for waiting lists.

Every British government in recent decades has had to face the issue of reforms to the NHS, the only question being where to focus efforts. Most critics argue that the best response is to spend more money, one of the primary myths perpetrated by the Leave campaign for the Brexit referendum being that British payments to the EU could immediately be diverted to the NHS. Recent reforms have resulted in a fundamental redefinition of the work of the service, which has become a funder of care, the provision of that care coming from a variety of sources including the public sector (Talbot-Smith and Pollock, 2006). Other critics argue that the shortfall of staff is the real problem, citing figures which show that Britain has fewer doctors per head of population than most other OECD member states (see Figure 3.1). Some of the methods used to address this problem – such as launching overseas recruitment drives for doctors and nurses, or sending patients to other European countries for treatment – have created their own controversies. Changes to the structure and budget of the NHS that were proposed by the Cameron government in early 2011, and hailed as the biggest shake-up of the NHS since its creation, were shelved after a barrage of criticism that they amounted to privatization by stealth. While there is general agreement that the NHS could be improved, it is also clear that there are limits to how far reforms will be politically acceptable.

Alongside the NHS, Britons can take out private health insurance and attend private clinics; roughly 10 per cent of the population is covered by private medical insurance taken out with organizations such as the British

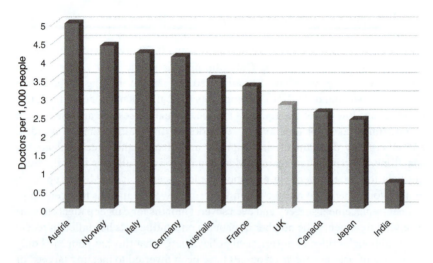

Figure 3.1   Numbers of doctors compared
Source: OECD at www.oecd.org (retrieved March 2017). Figures are for 2014.

United Provident Association (BUPA). The Conservative governments of the 1980s and 1990s encouraged the development of the private health care sector, in part to take pressure off the NHS but also to provide patients with choice and to promote the most effective use of expensive facilities and treatments. But the private sector still tends to cover only relatively minor treatments, and most long-term, expensive health care is provided by the NHS.

Despite all the debates about the NHS, the indicators typically used to measure quality of life show that the effects of health care have improved significantly in Britain. For example, life expectancy is now 81.4 years, placing Britain in the middle league of OECD countries (see Figure 3.2). Meanwhile, healthy life expectancy (defined as life expectancy in good general health) has increased by two years for men and women since 1981. Death rates from cancer and coronary heart disease – while still high – have fallen in recent years, the number of people smoking has been more than halved since the mid-1970s to less than 20 per cent, and there have been marked improvements in the British diet, with a decline in the consumption of red meat and foods containing fat, increased consumption of fruit and greatly increased public awareness about the chemical content of food (leading to new demand for organic food combined with widespread suspicion of genetically modified products).

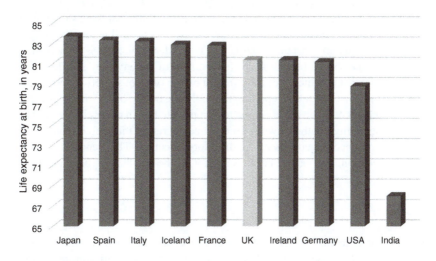

Figure 3.2   Life expectancy compared

Source: OECD at www.oecd.org (retrieved March 2017). Figures are for 2014.

While health trends are positive in some areas, in at least two others there is cause for increased concern:

- Britain has one of the most serious drug problems in Europe (see Simpson *et al.*, 2006), with drug-related deaths over the last decade holding in the range of 2–3,000 per year. Addicts are becoming younger, consumption of hard drugs such as heroin and cocaine is the highest in Europe and drugs are a central factor in crime: about two-thirds of all those arrested for mugging, burglary, robbery, shoplifting or car theft test positive for drug use. The rise in the number of drug offences is also one reason why Britain today has the biggest prison population in its history, with more than 86,000 people incarcerated.
- Britain is witnessing the emergence of a public health problem that until recently has mainly been associated with the United States: the rising incidence of obesity. In 1980, just 7 per cent of British adults were classified as obese, but by 2013 the number had increased to 24 per cent, making Britain the fattest country in Europe, and second only to the United States (where one in three adults is obese) in the OECD. The problem is not so much an increase in consumption as a combination of sedentary lifestyles, not enough exercise, genetic predisposition and the Northern European diet, which is lower in fruit, vegetables and fish than the Mediterranean one.

There has been a new consensus in Britain since the 1990s that there should be a change away from the attitude that the state must be responsible for providing a safety net, and a move instead towards a 'stakeholder' ethic; this is the idea that while everyone should benefit from membership of society they should do so only to the extent to which they have played by the rules of society (Alcock and May, 2014). This was a concept adopted enthusiastically by the Blair government, which encouraged more people to join private health care schemes and to take responsibility for their own retirement needs rather than relying on social security, and encouraged private funding for education. The trends have continued since then, but – as we have seen – not all the results have been positive.

Education

The state of education in Britain has been the subject of much debate in recent decades, as it has been in most liberal democracies. The Blair administration argued that education was a critical investment in social capital, that improved education offered people the ability to escape social exclusion and to take part in economic activity, and that it was not only good for individuals but for society at large (Alcock and May, 2014). Conscious that fewer people were being educated in Britain than in many other industrialized countries, it promised to cut class sizes, invest in building repairs, give incentives to good teachers and make education more accessible. The results have been mixed.

On the positive side of the ledger, Britain has spent more on education and more students are going on to higher education, Britain compares well in this area with other OECD states: in 2015, 49 per cent of 25–34-year olds in Britain had some tertiary education, above the figure of 42 per cent for the OECD as a whole and the figure of 30 per cent in Germany, although short of the 59 per cent in Canada and Japan (data from OECD website at www.oecd.org). But in other areas Britain is not doing quite so well:

- A government-sponsored report published in 1999 found that nearly a quarter of adults were classified in the lowest literacy level (being unable, for example, to use the index in a *Yellow Pages* phone directory) and in the lowest numeracy level (being unable, for example, to calculate the change they would receive from buying items on a simple shopping list). Matters had not improved by 2012, when an OECD study found that English and Northern Irish teenagers and young adults had some of the worst literacy rates in the developed world (Kuczera *et al.*, 2016).
- A common criticism made against British education is that its quality varies significantly, and that national statistics disguise the fact that most of

the problems have come in the more troubled state schools, while the better state schools and those in the independent sector have been doing well, with exam results improving in recent years. More school-leavers may be entering higher education, but instead of promoting social mobility and reducing differences in opportunity for the advantaged and the disadvantaged, nearly 75 per cent of university students still come from the top half of the economic and social spectrum.

The law requires that British children receive full-time education between the ages of 5 and 16 (in Northern Ireland they are required to start at the age of 4). About 70 per cent stay on in full-time education beyond 16, obtaining further schooling or going on to higher education (where women outnumber men by 11 to nine). About 20 per cent go into government training programmes and the balance enters the workplace. Schools are divided into two groups: state schools that are operated by public funds and independent schools that are privately financed. Education at state schools is free and about 93 per cent of children in England and Wales take this option. By contrast, education at independent schools is often expensive, and is usually an option only for wealthy families or for children with scholarships or financial aid.

The 1944 Education Act created a tripartite system for England and Wales in which children in the state system attended primary school until the age of 11, at which point – on the basis of a standardized exam known as the Eleven Plus – the more academically gifted were channelled into grammar schools, while those who failed the exam went to less academic secondary modern schools. (Technical schools made up the third element in the system, but few were built.) Grammar schools prepared children for national exams that qualified them to go on to higher education or for entry into the professions, while secondary moderns did not. Critics charged that the system was socially divisive, perpetuating class differences and determining life choices for children at too young an age. Beginning in the 1960s, the local education authorities that administered schools were allowed to decide whether they wanted to keep the dual system or to replace it with non-selective comprehensive schools which would provide an education for children of all ability levels and different social backgrounds. Although there are concerns that bright children suffer from being in classes with less able children, comprehensives are now attended by nearly 90 per cent of children in the state system, and there are few grammar schools and secondary moderns left.

Meanwhile, Scotland and Northern Ireland have their own education systems. Schools in Scotland have long been comprehensive, and have a different system of exams from those in England and Wales; only about 5 per cent of Scottish pupils attend private schools. In Northern Ireland, state schools are selective, with about 40 per cent of children attending grammar schools and the rest attending non-grammar schools. State schools are supposed to be open to all religions but tend to be divided into Protestant and Catholic schools, and single-sex education is more common than in England and Wales. State schools in England and Wales use a national curriculum which includes English, maths, science, history, geography, art, music and a modern foreign language. Northern Ireland has its own curriculum, but Scotland does not.

Alongside the state school system Britain has private (or independent) schools, which are both more expensive and more exclusive, and tend to give their students a better quality education overall (although there are many fine state schools in the system). Independent schools are often boarding schools, although the number of day pupils has increased, and they were once almost exclusively single-sex, although the number of coeducational schools has increased. Entry is determined by examination and is not restricted by social class or connections, although the ability to win a scholarship or else pay the often high fees is critical. Independent schools include such famous establishments as Harrow, Eton, Winchester and Marlborough, and over time have produced many of the leading figures in British political, commercial and military life. Their influence is declining, though, as Britain becomes more egalitarian and meritocratic.

Recent policy developments have brought much change to the state education system (Jones, K., 2016). The 1988 Education Reform Act allowed schools to compete with each other for pupils, the idea being that market forces would encourage schools to improve their records. A national curriculum was also introduced, standardized tests were brought in at four levels to assess the progress of students, league tables were published to show the comparative performance of schools, and schools could opt out of local government control (if enough parents agreed) and receive funding direct from national government, thus becoming grant-maintained schools. Labour added to the changes, replacing grant-maintained schools with Foundation Schools (which are run by local authorities but allowed a degree of independence), creating specialist schools that offered specialist subjects in addition to the National Curriculum and creating academies (new schools that take over from existing but failing schools and are independent but within the state system).

Higher education is provided by an extensive network of universities and of more specialized colleges offering, for example, teacher training and other vocational skills. Britain has more than 100 universities, which can be categorized into four types:

- The six ancient universities that have existed for centuries, and for a long time were the *only* universities, with admission to all of them restricted to

Illustration 3.2   Education

Pupils at a school in Farnham, Surrey, south west of London. The British education system
has gone through many changes in recent decades, aimed mainly at improving quality and
making opportunity more widely available. Questions have been asked about whether or not
the changes have helped promote social mobility.

men. These are Oxford and Cambridge (founded in the eleventh and twelfth
centuries) in England, and – in Scotland – St Andrews, Glasgow, Aberdeen
(all founded in the fifteenth century) and Edinburgh (sixteenth century).
- The civic or 'redbrick' universities founded mainly in the late nineteenth
  and twentieth centuries, including Birmingham, Swansea, Liverpool and
  Sheffield.
- The 'plate-glass' universities founded in the 1960s, often in smaller regional
  towns, and including York, Essex, Dundee, Sussex and East Anglia.
- The new universities that were once vocational polytechnics but were
  given university status after 1992, including Greenwich, Thames Valley,
  Manchester Metropolitan and West of Scotland.

British universities – and a British university education – are considered among
the best in the world, their production of high-level research reflected in the
numbers of British scientists winning Nobel prizes: 22 in the sciences and

economics between 2000 and 2016, compared to eight each for Germany and France. British universities have also long been attractive to international students, but government policy has been slow to catch up with the needs of universities, and many doubts have been cast over their future welfare by the potential effects of Brexit.

The universities receive support from the government, but they are independent institutions and have been expected to depend less on public funding and instead to raise a large percentage of their own financial support. The positive results have included more attention being paid to marketing, fundraising and academic performance. At the same time, though, there have been less happy trends:

- A reduction in staff numbers, with the student–lecturer ratio down from 9:1 in 1990 to more than 21:1 today.
- The use of a peculiar research assessment exercise in place since 1986 by which the work of every university researcher is assessed in order to decide how much government funding universities should receive. The exercise – which demands considerable time and effort – has long been opposed by many, and is criticized in particular for discriminating against good teaching and for leading to department closures, job losses and the poaching of productive researchers.
- A deterioration in the quality of buildings and other facilities.
- A bureaucratic burden on teaching staff that takes up much of their time in committees and reporting.
- A brain drain as academics have left to work overseas.

A controversial issue in recent years has been that of tuition fees. Where British university students once received a free education, a report commissioned by the Major administration in 1996 led to the introduction of means-tested tuition fees of up to £1,000 per year in 1998. Students could take out loans to cover the balance of their costs, those loans to be repaid (with interest) after graduation. Despite promises not to increase the fees, the Blair administration oversaw the passage of the 2004 Higher Education Act under which universities could charge variable fees of up to £3,000 per year (with Scottish universities charging less). They were known as top-up fees because they made up for the shortfall in the actual cost per student of offering an education. Another government review in 2009 led to the current arrangement under which universities can charge up to £9,000 per year (€10,350/$14,400). The fees are paid by the Student Loans Company, a government-owned body, and students are then to be billed after graduation and must pay back their loans with interest.

Supporters of tuition fees argued there was no other option, given the rising number of students in higher education and the rising costs of offering that education. Such fees were essential if Britain was to have a well-funded system of higher education. For their part, critics have argued that the changes will discourage poorer students from going to university out of concern for the debts they will accumulate, and that students will be diverted away from technology and science degrees because they take longer to complete and so will involve more debt. And while parents will no longer be faced with having to pay fees, the debt burden will simply be transferred to their children. Regardless of the concerns, almost all universities now charge the full fee.

In spite of the regular claims of 'failure', 'crisis' and 'decline' in British education since 1945, Ken Jones (2016) argues that levels of achievement and participation have risen, and inequalities have been reduced. Where once it was almost required that anyone wanting to advance to the highest levels of the professions or government should attend the 'best' schools and universities, a private education is no longer as much of an advantage over a state education as it once was. One of the results is that a private school education, or attendance at Oxford or Cambridge, is no longer the requirement that it once was for those aspiring to the highest levels of politics, business, academia, the media, the professions and the arts.

Law and Order

Debates about law and public safety in Britain have tended to veer back and forth between conservative concerns about the breakdown of order and allegations of an intergenerational reduction in the quality of life, and liberal arguments that the problem is one of too much control rather than too little. Reiner (2010: 175) argues that 'the British have long been regarded as peculiar in relation to order', the peculiarities shifting with time: in the eighteenth century they were regarded as ungovernable, then in the Victorian era the national image 'was one of unflappable self-discipline and orderliness ... symbolized by institutions like the queue, or the imperturbably stiff-upper-lipped gentleman', and in the last generation there have been 'a succession of law-and-order panics' ranging from football hooligans to urban and rural riots, generating agonized discussions about 'vanished virtues'. New attention was drawn to the debate in August 2011 by the outbreak of riots and vandalism in London and several other mainly English cities (see Box 3.2), leading to an anguished discussion about what they signified for the character of British society.

Box 3.2   The 2011 riots

International news headlines were dominated in early August 2011 by the remarkable sight of four days of riots in several mainly English cities (Lammy, 2012). Civil disobedience is hardly unknown in Britain, and there have several instances of mainly racially driven riots in the last few decades, but this new outbreak was notable for the difficulty of pinning down the causes and agreeing the most effective response.

The spark was provided when, during an attempt to arrest him, police shot to death a man named Mark Duggan in the north London district of Tottenham. A peaceful public demonstration against the shooting escalated into rioting, arson, violence and vandalism in several areas of London before spreading to other English cities, including Birmingham, Leicester, Manchester, Liverpool and Bristol. There were several deaths, numerous injuries and several thousand arrests. Prime Minister David Cameron and other government leaders ended their summer holiday early, Parliament was recalled and police leave was cancelled.

The debate over the causes of the riots ranged far and wide, with many arguing that race was at least one of the factors, but others offering the following explanations:

* The widening and visible gap between the rich and the poor and the social exclusion that follows in its wake.
* The decline in the family and in the kind of social support, discipline and example traditionally offered by parents.
* Austerity measures in the wake of the global economic downturn.
* A culture of entitlement and consumerism combined with a belief that if the wealthy could have their share of life's opportunities and luxuries, then so could the underclass, even to the point of helping themselves.
* Weak policing and often poor police–community relations, encouraging rioters to express their powerlessness in violence against the police.
* Technology and social networking, many noting the irony that the same methods used to mobilize democracy movements in the Arab world earlier that same year had been used to organize criminality in England.

Just as there was a debate over the causes, so there was a debate over the responses, the Right focusing on the need to punish immediately and severely, and the Left focusing on the need to address the problems of poverty, inequality and social exclusion. Many commentators argued that the circumstances were not unique to Britain, but were replicated to some degree in several other major liberal democracies such as the United States. The riots were later seen as an early warning of the kind of exclusion that fed into the decision by many to vote against British membership of the EU in 2016.

The British legal system is based on a combination of criminal and civil law, the former dealing with wrongs affecting the community and the latter with disputes involving two or more parties. No clear distinction is made between the two in England, Wales and Northern Ireland, where courts have jurisdiction in both areas. There is no common national system of law, England and Wales having its own system while Scotland and Northern Ireland each have another. National law consists of statutes passed by Parliament, common law in the form of precedents set through decisions made by courts, laws adopted by the EU and the decisions of the European Court of Justice, and international treaties of which Britain is a signatory. For example, the European Convention on Human Rights – which provides for the right to life, liberty, personal security, privacy and freedom of thought, speech, religion, assembly and association – was incorporated into British law by the 1998 Human Rights Act. (In Scotland, statutes passed by the Scottish Parliament – the old one that existed before 1707 and its modern counterpart – are an additional source of law.)

The law is enforced by professional judges and part-time unpaid magistrates (or justices of the peace), the former being qualified lawyers and the latter being given enough training to oversee a trial and apply the law. Magistrates' courts deal with about 95 per cent of all criminal cases, all of them less serious; the magistrates typically sit in benches of three members, are advised by trained law clerks and have limited powers of punishment. Indictable cases such as rape and murder are passed on to higher Crown courts for trial by jury. Parties in a case are usually represented either by barristers (advocates in Scotland) or solicitors; the former practise as individuals and tend to be trial lawyers, while the latter work in partnerships and deal also with general legal matters, such as wills, estates, taxes and the transfer of property.

Order, meanwhile, is maintained by the police, Britain having the distinction of being the birthplace of the organized police – the oldest police force in the world is London's Metropolitan Police, created in 1829 by Prime Minister Sir Robert Peel, after whom the police were long known as 'Peelers'. There is no national police force in Britain, but instead there are 52 independent forces based either around major urban centres or around counties and regions. They answer to local police authorities made up of a combination of elected officials, magistrates and independent members – the authorities in turn appoint a chief constable to run the force, taking responsibility for policy, promotion and discipline.

Statistics and trends in crime are controversial because of the difficulties of developing an accurate measure. According to the Crime Survey for

England and Wales, there were 5.3 million offences in 2010–11, rising to 6.2 million in 2015–16. Of the cases recorded by the police, fraud of various kinds was by far the most common, with burglary and violent crime a distant second and third. The British have long prided themselves on being fundamentally decent and cooperative, with a respect both for privacy and for private property. As with all such stereotypes, however, there is a hefty element of myth in this view, which is driven as much by perception as by reality. Probably as long as civilization has existed, every generation has bemoaned the decline of community, respect and public safety, and has claimed that things were better when they were young, even if this was not necessarily so: many studies have shown that incivility and anti-social behaviour have been a fact of life in Britain – as in many other countries – for generations, and most Britons seem to have misconceptions about trends in crime. Most of the indications of a decline in the quality of life are driven not so much by an increase in the volume of incivility and anti-social behaviour, but rather by a greater willingness to recognize that the problem exists and to talk about it.

Headline-grabbing events such as the 2011 riots give the impression of a decline in order and discipline, with Britons since the 1970s reminded of the often violent confrontations between management and striking workers in the 1980s, the unfortunate reputation for hooliganism that British football has won because of the behaviour of a minority of 'fans', race riots in a number of major cities, the troubles caused by 'lager louts' in bars on the Continent, the growing number of cases of road rage caused in part by frustration with traffic congestion, and everyday violence and destructive or anti-social behaviour. The impression has been created that such problems are widespread and worsening, but the popular perception may in fact be quite different from the reality, because trends in the crime rate in Britain are (at worst) not dramatically different from those in other industrialized countries, and Britain is in many ways still a paragon of orderliness and good manners.

The decline of civility has been a topic of much recent national debate in Britain, and was addressed by a new law passed in 2003 after the issue had moved up the Labour government agenda. The idea has been to give police and the government the power to punish certain kinds of behaviour, and thereby to tackle Britain's 'yob culture'. The targets include everything from littering and vandalism to dealing with noisy neighbours, reducing truancy, enforcing parental control, evicting anti-social tenants and punishing people who drink or use drugs in public. Anyone who sees anti-social behaviour can report it to their local police station or council, which can result in the issuance of an anti-social behaviour order (ASBO) that can prevent an offender from repeating the offence or from returning to a specific area for up to two years.

While the extent of the problem of crime is debatable, as is the appropriate response, there are elements of life in Britain which still support Reiner's notion of 'unflappable self-discipline and orderliness'. In their dealings with one another on a daily basis, most Britons still display courtesy, good manners and consideration (see Fox, K., 2014 for an entertaining discussion). They may appear stand-offish to Americans (famous for their willingness to strike up personal conversations with strangers), they may appear stolid to Spaniards and Greeks (with their Mediterranean expansiveness) and they may appear controlled to Italians (who often appear unable to form and maintain a queue), but they have created a society in which cooperation and order are still more common than confrontation and disorder.

Further Reading

Alcock, Pete and Margaret May (2014) *Social Policy in Britain*, 4th edn (Palgrave). A textbook review of the various influences that come to bear on social policy, including chapters on social security, health care, housing and education.

Baggott, Rob (2015) *Understanding Health Policy*, 2nd edn (Policy Press). An assessment of health policy in Britain, looking at its relationship with central government, political parties, the media and Parliament.

Jones, Ken (2016) *Education in Britain: 1944 to the Present*, 2nd edn (Polity Press). A history of the many changes in British education since the war, placing today's system within its longer-term context.

Joyce, Peter (2013) *Criminal Justice: An Introduction*, 2nd edn (Routledge). A survey of the criminal justice system in England and Wales, including chapters on the police, the judiciary and prisons.

Roberts, Ken (2011) *Class in Contemporary Britain*, 2nd edn (Palgrave). Offers a definition and discussion of class in its British context, including chapters on different classes and on social mobility.

4

Government

Britain is the birthplace of the parliamentary system, the most successful and widely adopted of the world's different governing systems. Otherwise known as the Westminster model, after the area of central London where the British Houses of Parliament are situated, the key elements of parliamentary government include the following:

- A fusion of the executive and the legislature.
- A symbolic head of state and a political head of government.
- An executive made up of a head of government and a Cabinet of ministers.
- Representative democracy, by which elected officials are held accountable to voters.
- Responsible government, by which government ministers are held collectively accountable for their decisions and for running their departments.
- A multi-party system based around strong party discipline within the legislature.

Because Britain has a long history of parliamentary government, has avoided revolutionary change and has one of the world's oldest remaining monarchies, it is often assumed that its political system is both stable and predictable. Nothing, however, could be further from the truth. Even the most cursory review of British political history shows a system that is both settled and unsettled, and in a constant process of mutation. For centuries, the changes were driven by the struggle for power between the monarchy and Parliament. More recently, they have been driven by debates over the appropriate role of government, by declining trust in government, by the fluctuating balance of power between Prime Minister and Parliament and by changes in the nature of 'government' at the European Union and local levels, which have raised questions about the very notion of 'British' politics.

The pace and the extent of change have accelerated during recent administrations. Margaret Thatcher took a more hands-on approach to leadership and more fully exploited the implied powers of her office, while Tony Blair continued to redefine the place and the character of the office of Prime Minister, and also made significant changes to the institutions of government (such as his reforms of the upper chamber of Parliament, the House of Lords) and to the balance of national and local government (notably his government's creation of regional assemblies for Wales, Scotland and Northern Ireland). David Cameron, meanwhile, became the first Prime Minister to head a peacetime coalition government since the Second World War, and organized two of the only three national referendums to be held in British history: the first (in 2011) turned down a proposal to change the British electoral system, while the second (in 2016) resulted in the tumultuous decision to leave the European Union.

This chapter examines the structure of the British system of government. It begins with a review of constitutional principles, and then looks in turn at the monarchy, the Prime Minister and Cabinet, Parliament, the judiciary, the bureaucracy and local government, explaining their relative roles in the process by which Britain is governed. It identifies the institutions with the most and least influence over the political process, discusses changes in the balance of power among (and within) those institutions, examines the centralization of power in national government and in the office of Prime Minister and critically reviews the nature of the British model of parliamentary democracy.

Principles of Government

Just as there has been much debate since the Second World War about British economic decline (see Chapter 6), so there has been much talk about the decline of the British state (for example, see Childs, 2012). Critics have accused government of failing to deliver economic growth and the kind of political stability and social cohesion demanded by citizens of a modern democratic, capitalist system. They have also raised concerns about the lack of controls on an ambitious Prime Minister, questioned the relevance of the monarchy and the House of Lords, and worried about an electoral system that misrepresents the balance of support for competing political parties (see Chapter 5) and about the lack of a codified bill of rights for citizens. So ubiquitous has the term 'decline' become in academic debates about the British political system that questions have occasionally been raised about the very legitimacy of that system.

While Britain has certainly witnessed its share of political and social upheavals, so too have many other countries. And in a world where democracy and successful free-market economic policies have taken root in perhaps only a few dozen countries, the Westminster model stands out more often for its strengths than its weaknesses. Those strengths have long stood as a model for political development around the world, and the principles of parliamentary government can be found in one form or another in all the world's most successful democracies, including almost all European states, Japan, Australia, Canada, New Zealand and the United States. Perhaps the British political system could be more responsive and transparent, but the same could be said for every other democratic political system. Perfection is impossible when you are dealing with human nature, particularly when power is at stake.

The British system has not so much declined since 1945 as it has continued to evolve. Its problems continue, but at the same time there have been adjustments to the structure of government that have made it more democratic, more relevant and more transparent. The difficulties faced by British government are most clearly reflected in the gaps between the theory and practice of the Westminster model, the British version of which is based on seven key principles:

- *Balanced government.* In theory, the powers of the executive – the Prime Minister and Cabinet – are balanced by those of Parliament, to which the executive is accountable. In practice, the balance of power has shifted away from Parliament, just as it has shifted away from legislatures more generally (Norton, 2010: 4). The marginalization of Parliament was especially clear during the first two Blair administrations; policy-making power was concentrated in Downing Street, Blair distanced himself from Parliament, and it was only in November 2005, more than eight years after he took office, that his government suffered its first defeat in the House of Commons (over a plan to extend the period for which the police could detain terrorist suspects without charge from 28 days to 90 days). The executive continues to have the upper hand.
- *Parliamentary sovereignty.* In theory, only Parliament has the right to make or unmake laws, and its powers are not limited or constrained by any other authority. In practice, while sovereignty remains, Parliament has seen its powers reduced by the expanded reach of EU law, by the work of the Scottish and Welsh assemblies, by the increased use of public referendums and by the growth of executive powers. Thus, parliamentary sovereignty has to some extent become executive sovereignty (see Goldsworthy, 2010).
- *Representative democracy.* In theory, the people rule, while the work of government is carried out by their elected representatives who stay in office only as long as they have the support of voters in their local districts. Government is directly accountable to the people in what it does. In practice, it has long

been debatable – in Britain as in other democracies – just how much elected representatives convey and champion the views of their constituents, even assuming that they can always be sure what their constituents want. Also, turnout at general elections has been falling, suggesting an increased disconnection between voters and their representatives.

- *Responsible government.* In theory, government ministers are responsible to Parliament for running their departments, and make decisions that are then implemented by a neutral bureaucracy. In practice, the actions of ministers are driven more by personality, ideology, obligations to the Prime Minister and concerns about the next election, and the bureaucracy has more influence over government policy than most people realize.

- *Collective responsibility.* In theory, the Cabinet is responsible as a group to the public and to the Prime Minister for its conduct and for its policies. Ministers may disagree over policy within the Cabinet, but if a minister cannot support the government line, he or she will either be dismissed or be expected to resign. If the government loses a crucial vote in Parliament, or if there is a vote of no confidence in the government, the Cabinet as a whole is expected to resign. In practice, Cabinet government has become less important with time, and recent Prime Ministers have often made decisions without first checking with the Cabinet, relying more on outside advisers.

- *Constitutional monarchy.* This is perhaps the only one of the Westminster principles where theory and practice still coincide. Britain has a monarch, and government is carried out in the name of the monarch (whose permission is technically needed for most key political decisions), but the monarch has little real power. Any attempt by the Queen to actually exert her theoretical powers – for example, by vetoing a new piece of legislation – would result in uproar and a constitutional crisis.

- *The centralized state.* In spite of efforts to devolve powers to all the regions except England, Britain remains a highly centralized state within which London – as the political capital – has greater dominance than is true with national capitals in almost all other European countries. The centralization is reflected in the extent to which the British state manages public spending, collects taxes and runs key public services such as the National Health Service (Gamble, 2016: 7–9).

The Westminster model has traditionally been described as a pyramid, with the Prime Minister at the top, government ministers in the middle and Parliament and the bureaucracy below. But recent analysis suggests that British government is better seen as a complex network of interdependent institutions, where power is distributed horizontally rather than vertically and is no longer concentrated in a limited number of institutions. In this 'core executive' model, the rules are often informal, institutions are less important than culture and values, roles are more important than structures and the decision-making system is less hierarchical (for more discussion, see Moran, 2011: 121–23).

The Constitution

A constitution is an instrument that outlines the rules by which a government functions. It typically lists the principles underlying the process of government, describes the structure of the major government institutions and their responsibilities, explains the process by which laws are made and spells out the rights of citizens and the limits on the powers of government. The vast majority of countries have constitutions that are codified: there is a single written document in which the powers of government and the rights of the governed are outlined and systematized. However, there is another way of looking at constitutions. Instead of simply being a set of principles and rules, the constitution might be regarded as a summary of how a society is politically constituted or how its legal and political order fits together. Rather than starting with a formal statement of norms and then looking at how they are applied, Johnson (1999: 46) argues:

> the constitution is treated as the outcome of shared experiences and practices, the result of a common history rather than a founding declaration ... It is not so much a set of instructions on how to do things as a set of precedents and notes of guidance extracted from past experience ... [It] is unlikely to have special rules for its amendment, chiefly because it is the outcome of adaptation and evolution in response to changing circumstances and needs.

This model of a 'customary constitution' applies to Britain, where – instead of a single, discrete document – government operates on the basis of many different documents and traditions (Leach *et al.*, 2018):

- *Common laws.* These are the product of custom and of judgements handed down over time by British courts. Among the most important are those dealing with freedom of speech, the power to make treaties and declare war, and the sovereignty of Parliament.
- *Statute laws.* These are Acts of Parliament which override common law and have the effect of constitutional law. Many of the details of Britain's system of government – including the relative powers of the two houses of Parliament, the expansion of the vote, British membership of the EU, and the

creation of regional assemblies – have been established (and can be changed) by the passage of new statutes. Controversially, a host of statutes have – in the wake of the rise of international terrorism – both restricted civil liberties and expanded the powers of the state.

- *European laws.* As a member state of the EU, Britain was subject to all laws adopted by the EU, which were binding on Britain and overrode British laws in those policy areas where the EU has primary responsibility (or 'competence'). These include trade, agriculture, social issues, consumer protection and the environment, but exclude tax policy, education and criminal justice (policy areas over which the EU does not have jurisdiction, or has only limited or shared jurisdiction). While the constitutional implications of EU law will change for Britain outside the EU, it will continue to remain subject to the requirements of that law through its trade with the EU.

- *Traditions and conventions.* Many of the actions of government in Britain (and in other democracies) are based on custom and tradition. For example, nothing in the British constitution says that the Prime Minister and Cabinet should come out of the majority party in the House of Commons, or that the Cabinet is bound by collective responsibility; these are simply traditions that have become an accepted part of the political process.

- *Scholarly commentaries.* Many of the principles and practices of British government have come out of commentaries written by constitutional authorities, such as Walter Bagehot (author in 1867 of *The English Constitution* and one-time editor of the news weekly *The Economist*) and Albert Venn Dicey (author in 1885 of *An Introduction to the Study of the Law of the Constitution*). Dicey was influential in confirming three of the basic features of the British system: the sovereignty of Parliament, the rule of law and the importance of conventions and customs (Thomas, 1999: 144–45).

It would be wrong to assume that government is based solely on the rules found in constitutions, even in those countries – such as the United States – where the constitution is regarded as being at the heart of government. Much of what happens in government is driven by other forces, including judicial interpretation, political feasibility, opportunism, emergencies, loopholes in the law, public opinion or simply muddling through. But constitutions provide the blueprint against which the theoretical expectations and the practical actions of government can be compared, better understood and given structure and order.

In contrast to the constitutions of France or Germany, which spell out in some detail how government should work, and whose gaps are filled in by the rulings of national constitutional courts, Britain takes a more pragmatic approach to government. As Philip Norton puts it, the rules of British government are determined 'on the basis of what has proved to work rather than on abstract first principles' (Norton, 2010: 61). This approach allows for greater flexibility and avoids the need for the government to make formal amendments to the constitution. An example of a recent change to constitutional practice is the referendum, used with increased frequency since 1997 (see Chapter 5). While referendums are intended only to be advisory, and not binding on government, political realities have effectively made them binding.

Constitutional flexibility has its advantages, but critics argue that there is too much potential for the abuse of powers and too little guidance for ordinary citizens on their rights; the effect has been a growth in support for a codified constitution, which is now favoured by about 80 per cent of Britons. But the challenge of codifying laws, legal judgements and traditions dating back several hundred years, and of agreeing both the principles and the details, is daunting; in arguing that Britain might be better off with a written constitution, the Justice Secretary at the time, Jack Straw, suggested in a speech in 2008 that it might take as long as 20 years to complete such a document. But the biggest problem is that constitutions are usually written as a result of a shift from one system of government to another (after a war, a revolution or some other crisis). To write a constitution midstream and in the absence of a crisis is almost unknown, although a departure from the EU and the possible break-up of the UK might be defined as just such a crisis.

The Monarchy

Britain is a constitutional monarchy. In contrast to an absolute monarchy (where power lies in the hands of a single ruler) or an aristocratic monarchy (where the ruler governs with the support of aristocrats) the powers of the British monarch are limited by law. The actions of government are carried out in the name of the monarch, who acts as the living embodiment of the state but does little that could be defined as exercising independent judgement over government. Indeed, so marginal has the monarchy now become that textbooks on British politics rarely give it much space. This is unfortunate, because it cannot be ignored.

Except for a brief spell between 1649 and 1660 when the Cromwellian republic was proclaimed, England has been a monarchy since the ninth-century reign of Alfred the Great (871–99). Like their continental European counterparts, English kings and queens once had a virtual monopoly on political power, but – as noted in Chapter 1 – their control began to be eroded with Magna Carta in 1215, and the 1689 Bill of Rights finally confirmed the supremacy of Parliament. Today's monarch – Queen Elizabeth II (see Box 4.1) – is little more than a ceremonial head of state. She has little in the way of a direct political role, but is instead expected to be a neutral symbol of the state, the government and the people. It is often said that the British monarch reigns but does not rule. At the same time, however, the Queen has several vestigial 'reserve powers' that are politically important:

- She can dissolve Parliament and call new elections, although in practice she does this only when asked to do so by the Prime Minister. She could theoretically deny the request, but never does.
- Before a bill can become a law, it must be signed by the Queen (that is, given the Royal Assent). Theoretically she could veto a piece of legislation, but the last time a monarch did this was in 1707 (Norton, 2010: 315).
- If no one party has an absolute majority of seats in the House of Commons after an election, the Queen can arbitrate and – on the advice of the Prime Minister – name the person she thinks most likely to be able to form a government. Queen Elizabeth has had to do this four times, most recently in 2010 when no one party won a majority of seats in the House of Commons and – after inter-party deliberations – the Queen invited Conservative Party leader David Cameron to form a coalition government with the Liberal Democrats.
- Every autumn she presides over the State Opening of Parliament, giving a speech in which she outlines the government's programme for the next year. The speech is written by the government, and the Queen simply reads it aloud, but the event still symbolizes the fact that government is carried out in the name of the monarch.
- She meets with the Prime Minister at confidential weekly meetings, during which she has – in the words of Walter Bagehot (1867) – 'the right to be consulted, the right to encourage, and the right to warn'. She is briefed on the government agenda and can share her thoughts on the decisions of government, although there is no obligation on the Prime Minister to act on her advice.
- The Queen is the Head of the Armed Forces, and it is she alone who can declare war and peace, although this again can only be done on the advice of her ministers. There was a time when monarchs raised and equipped armies, and led them into battle, but King George II in 1743 was the last to do that. The symbolic link remains, however, and all members of the Army, Royal Air Force and Royal Marines (but not the Royal Navy) must swear an oath of allegiance to the Queen.
- Above all, the Queen is the embodiment of 'the Crown', a term which in some respects is akin to 'the state'. The government works on behalf of the Crown, bureaucrats are servants of the Crown, judges dispense justice in Crown courts, and government ministers are conferred with the powers of the Crown.

Box 4.1   Queen Elizabeth II

Queen Elizabeth came to the British throne unexpectedly. Her uncle David had been heir to his father George V (1910–36) and would have been crowned King Edward VIII had he not decided to abdicate in 1936 so that he could marry the American divorcée Wallis Simpson. His younger brother Albert instead succeeded to the throne as George VI, and when he died in 1952 he was succeeded by his eldest daughter Elizabeth.

The Queen was optimistically expected to rule over a new Elizabethan age in which Britain's military, technological and cultural achievements would mirror those of the age of Queen Elizabeth I (1558–1603). But while the British economy prospered during the 1950s, and Britain led the way on the development of the jet engine, nuclear power and other new technologies, significant changes were underway that would alter Britain's place in the world and redefine the place of the monarchy. The Empire was already being dismantled, and decolonization accelerated during the 1950s. The economies of the United States, West Germany, France and later Japan all offered new competition to Britain, which slipped down the league of the world's major economic powers. Racial tensions grew as workers were invited to come from the Caribbean and the Indian subcontinent to meet Britain's labour shortages. Then came the social and cultural revolutions of the 1960s that altered social norms and expectations.

With Britain undergoing dramatic change, the reign of Queen Elizabeth took on an entirely different aspect. As anti-monarchists questioned the place of heredity in a modern democratic state, it was decided to modernize the royal family and to allow greater media and public access to its inner workings. The revelations, however, were not always edifying: the Queen's three eldest children and her own sister underwent messy divorces, and the Queen herself seemed unable always to keep up with popular demands for change in the role of the monarchy.

As an individual, Queen Elizabeth is popular, as reflected in the outpouring of support during her golden jubilee celebrations in 2002 and again for her 2012 diamond jubilee. However, opinion polls suggest that public support for the monarchy has slipped since the mid-1980s from 85–90 per cent to about 75–80 per cent today. The Queen turned 90 in 2016, and while almost no one has ever expected her to abdicate into retirement, the day approaches when Britain will face the accession of a new monarch. Her eldest son Prince Charles is heir to the throne (the longest-serving such heir in British history), but he turned 70 in 2018 and there has been speculation that he might step aside in favour of his eldest son Prince William.

The monarchy was long surrounded by an aura of mystery, and little was publicly known about the private lives and personalities of members of the royal family (although the rumour mill was always busy). This privacy was seen as an important part of the stability, success and exceptionalism of the monarchy; in the words of Walter Bagehot (1867), it was important not to 'let in daylight upon

Illustration 4.1   Queen Elizabeth II

magic'. All has changed since the 1980s, however, as the private lives of the royal family have become the focus of intense media coverage and public interest all over the world. The relevance of the monarchy to modern Britain has been the topic of intensified debate, and the monarchy has changed in response. That a divorced heir to the throne could become king – once unthinkable – has now been accepted, and attempts have been made to end the ban on the heir marrying a Catholic, to abandon primogeniture (under which a first-born daughter is over-taken in the line of succession by a younger brother: this change was finally made in 2011) and to cease expecting the monarch to be head of the Church of England. Adaptability has long been integral to the survival of the monarchy, and its recent adjustments have just been the latest in a long series of responses to new styles, expectations and political realities.

Prime Minister and Cabinet

While the monarch is Britain's head of state, the head of government is the Prime Minister, who provides policy leadership and oversees the implementation of law through a Cabinet of senior ministers. By definition, the Prime Minister is the leader of the political party or coalition with the most seats in the lower chamber of Parliament, the House of Commons. As long as he or she can keep the support of his or her party in Parliament, the Prime Minister has considerable power over deciding which laws will be passed, and which policies adopted. There are clear limits to that power, however: Margaret Thatcher's hold on office was not enough to prevent her being obliged to step down in November 1990 in the face of unpopular policies; Tony Blair – in spite of being accused of becoming more like a president than a Prime Minister – left office in 2007 after his public approval ratings had fallen to record lows; and David Cameron stepped down in 2016 immediately after his loss in the Brexit referendum.

As with all government leaders in democracies, the powers of the Prime Minister are a combination of the formal and the informal. Formally, the office-holder is head of government, appoints senior members of government, chairs the Cabinet, oversees the security services, leads his or her party, chooses the date for the general election, reports to Parliament in a weekly Question Time and represents Britain in political dealings with other countries. Informally, Prime Ministers are the driving force in setting the national political agenda, are responsible for managing crises and set the style and tone of government according to the policies they adopt, the management methods they use and the appointments they make to the Cabinet. They can also involve themselves in their favourite policy areas, sometimes overshadowing the relevant secretaries and ministers. For example, James Callaghan was interested in education policy, Margaret Thatcher in economic and foreign policy, John Major in Northern Ireland and Tony Blair in foreign policy.

The foundation of the authority of the Prime Minister lies in the power of appointment. As well as leading their party, Prime Ministers decide the size of the Cabinet, call and chair Cabinet meetings, appoint and remove members of the Cabinet and other senior government officials (about 100 people in all), can reshuffle Cabinets (bringing in new members and either removing existing members or moving them to new posts) and can reorganize government departments. The power of appointment (or patronage) allows Prime Ministers to manipulate and control the Cabinet, alter the personality and character of the government (for example, revitalizing it by bringing in new blood), reward supporters, penalize or undermine the position of opponents, marginalize those who pose a threat to their tenure and cultivate potential successors. (Prime Ministers also once had the power to decide when to call a general election, but this ended with the passage of the 2011 Fixed-term Parliaments Act – see Chapter 5.)

British Prime Ministers are normally experienced national politicians who have worked their way up through the ranks of party and Parliament. They must be members of the House of Commons, and usually serve a lengthy apprenticeship

Table 4.1   Modern British Prime Ministers

Date	Prime Minister	Governing party
July 1945	Clement Attlee	Labour
February 1950	Clement Attlee	Labour
October 1951	Winston Churchill	Conservative
May 1955	Anthony Eden	Conservative
January 1957*	Harold Macmillan	Conservative
October 1959	Harold Macmillan	Conservative
October 1963*	Alec Douglas-Home	Conservative
October 1964	Harold Wilson	Labour
March 1966	Harold Wilson	Labour
June 1970	Edward Heath	Conservative
February 1974	Harold Wilson	Labour
October 1974	Harold Wilson	Labour
April 1976*	James Callaghan	Labour
May 1979	Margaret Thatcher	Conservative
June 1983	Margaret Thatcher	Conservative
June 1987	Margaret Thatcher	Conservative
November 1990*	John Major	Conservative
April 1992	John Major	Conservative
May 1997	Tony Blair	Labour
June 2001	Tony Blair	Labour
May 2005	Tony Blair	Labour
June 2007*	Gordon Brown	Labour
May 2010	David Cameron	Conservative/Liberal Democratic coalition
May 2015	David Cameron	Conservative
July 2016*	Theresa May	Conservative
June 2017	Theresa May	Conservative

* In these years, leadership of the governing party changed – through health, resignation, or loss of political support – without a general election being held.

before winning the leadership of their parties. Margaret Thatcher served 16 years as a Member of Parliament (MP) before being elected leader of her party in 1975, and another four years as leader before being elected Prime Minister in 1979. John Major served as an MP for 11 years before becoming Prime Minister, Tony Blair for 14 years and David Cameron just nine years. Gordon Brown, by contrast, had to wait 24 years to reach the top office, and Theresa May 19 years, but both were impacted by unusual circumstances: Brown was unexpectedly beaten to the leadership of the Labour party by Tony Blair, who went on to win an unprecedented (for Labour) three general elections, while May came to the job only because of Cameron's unexpected resignation following the Brexit referendum.

Prime Ministers govern with the help of the Cabinet, a group of about two dozen men and women who head the major government departments, including the Foreign and Commonwealth Office, the Home Office, the Treasury, the Ministry of Justice and the Scottish and Welsh Offices. The Cabinet meets weekly to discuss policy, and together the Prime Minister and the Cabinet constitute Her Majesty's Government: they run their departments, plan the business of Parliament, discuss and attempt to resolve policy differences among departments, oversee and coordinate government policies and take collective responsibility for the decisions and actions of government (Leach *et al.*, 2011: Chapter 11). While a Prime Minister is technically no more than a 'first among equals' in the Cabinet, his or her powers of appointment and agenda setting mean that loyalty to the leader is a prerequisite for Cabinet members. Once the Cabinet makes a decision, all members are expected to support it in public, whatever their personal feelings may be. If they cannot, they must either resign or – more rarely – may be removed. Cabinet members are all Members of Parliament (mainly of the House of Commons), and the Cabinet is an important testing ground for anyone with ambitions to become Prime Minister.

Leadership and executive power is not limited to constitutional rules and political realities, and is as often shaped by the personalities of leaders and the problems they inherit (or create). The differing roles of Prime Ministers in the British system is illustrated by the varying experiences and abilities of recent office-holders:

- *Margaret Thatcher* (1979–90) led from the front, was noted for her forcefulness, particularly after her landslide victory at the 1983 general election, and was famous for stretching the powers of her office almost to their limit. She took key decisions outside the Cabinet, reduced the number of Cabinet meetings and removed 12 ministers in 11 years.
- *John Major* (1990–97) was in a weaker position, serving out two years of Thatcher's last term before winning his own mandate in 1992, but even then presiding over a tired and divided party, and often having to react to problems rather than leading the way. He made more use of his Cabinet, allowed a greater variety of opinion, emphasized collegiality and consensus and intervened less in the affairs of departments.
- *Tony Blair* (1997–2007) imposed strong discipline on his party and his Cabinet, helped by his large parliamentary majority. He delegated discretion to strong ministers prepared to follow the government line, relied less on the Cabinet than on a small inner circle of advisers and aides, and elevated the role of his press and communications staff.
- *Gordon Brown* (2007–10) was in the troubled position of inheriting the position through his predecessor's resignation, rather than an election, had clearly

been hoping for many years to become Prime Minister, and also took office just in time to be presented with the dire challenge of addressing the global financial crisis and the debt crisis in the eurozone. He was never fully able to make the job his own and was defeated in the 2010 election.

- *David Cameron* (2010–16) had his approach to office initially circumscribed both by the need to head a coalition that was politically unnatural (in the sense that the Conservatives and the Liberal Democrats have little in common) and by the need to impose austerity measures in the wake of the global economic downturn that preceded the 2010 general election (Seldon and Snowdon, 2015). He also quickly became embroiled in an internal party dispute over the EU, and was brought down by the very referendum that he hoped would resolve that dispute.
- *Theresa May* (2016–) inherited the fallout from the Brexit referendum, and was obliged to spend more time working through the political and legal minefield of the British departure from the EU than any other problem. Her effort to strengthen her position by calling an early general election in June 2017 failed spectacularly, but she remained in office – see Chapter 5.

There has been an ongoing debate since the 1960s about the extent to which the office of Prime Minister has become more like that of an executive president (see Crossman, 1963; Benn, 1980; Foley, 2001, for example). Analogies have been made with the presidency of the United States, reflecting the extent to which Prime Ministers have become more independent from their Cabinets and from Parliament, and to which election campaigns are dominated by personalities rather than policies. The Prime Minister's office has developed more of a life of its own, with an increasing number of advisers, aides, speechwriters and spin doctors, and the emergence of a staff that looks much like that clustered around the US president in the White House. Meanwhile, the Cabinet has played a less important role in policy making. Smith (1999, pp. 76–77) notes several reasons for this: few decisions are made in Cabinet, the bulk being made in more specialized Cabinet committees and being referred to the Cabinet only in the case of disagreement; ministers are too concerned with the work of their departments – where their reputation will rise or fall – to be involved in other areas of policy; and the Cabinet is now less a place where strategy is developed than a place where departmental interests are protected.

The result has been to place the Prime Minister in an advantageous position over his or her ministers. At the same time, however, the support of the Cabinet and Parliament is still the critical element in the ability of Prime Ministers to govern, and they forget this at their peril. Tony Blair dismissed 'all

Box 4.2   The troubling place of Europe in British politics

Britain joined what was then the European Economic Community in 1973, and while it dutifully played its part in joint European decision making thereafter, it was never with much sense of enthusiasm. Whether deriving from the EEC, or – from the early 1990s – the European Union, many policies and laws were decided collectively at the European level that had considerable impact on decisions taken in Britain, as in all EU member states. This caused much division and disagreement, and disruption for much of the work of government. In the early 1980s, it was Labour Party policy to withdraw Britain altogether from the Community, a stance that helped prompt the breakaway of the Social Democratic Party (SDP), an event which in turn contributed to Labour's long spell in opposition. By the mid-1990s Labour had reversed its policy, arguing that withdrawal would be 'disastrous' for Britain, and pushing for a more constructive role in the EU.

Meanwhile, the issue has been even more divisive for the Conservative Party, which ironically was responsible – under the leadership of Prime Minister Edward Heath – for negotiating Britain's entry to the EEC in 1973. Margaret Thatcher railed against what she saw as excessive bureaucratization and regulation by Europe, and argued that EU policies were undermining her attempts to free up the British marketplace. 'We have not successfully rolled back the frontiers of the state in Britain,' she famously declared in a speech in 1988, 'only to see them reimposed at a European level, with a European superstate exercising a new dominance from Brussels' (Thatcher, 1988). Her disagreements with pro-Europeans within her party contributed to her fall from power in 1990, and the split continued to dog the Conservatives under the leadership of John Major. David Cameron's hopes of putting an end to internal party squabbling over the EU with the 2016 Brexit referendum failed miserably, bringing an end to his political career. And Europe continued to dog the government of Theresa May, as she struggled with little success to negotiate a favourable exit from the EU.

this President Blair rubbish' (Rawnsley, 1999), arguing that similar charges had been made about his more proactive predecessors. And the fact that Blair governed in tandem with Gordon Brown, his strong and opinionated Chancellor of the Exchequer, suggested that the idea of presidentialism may be overstated (see Heffernan, 2006). It was certainly less obvious with the coalition government that was in office between 2010 and 2015.

Parliament

Parliament has long been regarded as the heart of the Westminster model, although the importance of its role in government is disputed. The conventional view, dating back many decades, holds that it is both marginal and in decline, with most real power lying in the executive and Parliament being squeezed in recent years by both its European and its regional counterparts. Because a Prime Minister with a good majority can normally count on the loyalty of party members, Parliament usually spends most of its time debating or confirming the government's programme. But Russell (2016) notes the continuation of earlier evidence of shifts towards a more assertive and important Parliament; while she also notes the possibility of future reversals, one of the core elements of the debate over Brexit was renewed sovereignty for Parliament, although whether or not this comes to pass remains to be seen.

Parliament is the British legislature, where proposals for new laws are introduced, discussed and either rejected or accepted, where existing laws are amended or abolished and where votes are taken on taxing and spending. Its main strategic advantage over the executive comes from being the link between citizens and the executive; it plays a key role in legitimizing government. It also has three other critical functions (see Leach *et al.*, 2011: 235–38, 243–44):

- It both recruits and maintains the government. Membership of Parliament is a prerequisite for membership of the government, and the support of Parliament is essential to the stability and success of the government.
- It scrutinizes the government, which must defend and explain itself in Parliament. This is particularly true of Question Time, when the Prime Minister or key government ministers must account for their policies and actions.
- It acts as a forum for national debate. Although most parliamentary debates may be narrow and uninspiring, there are times when the government needs to involve Parliament in decision making, particularly at times of crisis and war.

Strictly speaking, Parliament consists of the monarch and the two houses of Parliament, but the monarch has only a symbolic role and the upper House of Lords has only limited powers over law and policy, so the real focus of political power lies with the lower House of Commons. As noted earlier, the principle of parliamentary sovereignty means that only Parliament has the authority to make laws, but this power was reduced after 1973 by the impact of European EU law: where British and EU law conflict (in policy areas for which the EU has responsibility), British law must give way. The result has been that Parliament lost power to the law making bodies of the EU (the European Commission, the

Council of Ministers and the European Parliament) as well as to the Scottish, Welsh and Northern Irish regional assemblies.

The British Parliament has two chambers:

House of Lords

The so-called 'upper' house, the Lords, is has been undergoing a messy process of reform that has brought changes to its structure without agreement on its final form. Once a powerful part of government, the chamber is a legacy of the days when Britain was ruled by aristocrats: for most of its history, its members were hereditary male peers, including dukes, barons and earls. Since the idea of hereditary privilege was at odds with modern democratic principles, the House steadily lost its powers in tandem with the diminishing role of the monarchy. In 1958, membership was expanded to include life peers: people who had been rewarded for public service with a title by the monarch (on the recommendation of the Prime Minister), the title dying with them. One result was the arrival of the first female members of the House.

Pressures grew in the 1960s and 1970s for more change, and Labour promised during the 1980s to abolish the House when it came to power. It later abandoned that pledge, but the Blair government launched a series of reforms to the chamber. The automatic right of all but 92 hereditary peers to sit in the House ended in 1999, and a government commission was appointed to offer suggestions for where to go next. It recommended a mainly nominated chamber, limiting its members to 12–15 years of service and retaining its existing powers. More proposals have since been touted, ranging from a fully elected to a fully appointed chamber, but none has yet been agreed and the debate over the final form of the new House of Lords continues. Meanwhile, the transitional House of Lords has about 730 members, made up as follows:

- A rump of 92 hereditary peers who were elected by their colleagues and allowed to remain pending the next stage in the process of reform. By-elections are held to replace those who die or otherwise leave the House.
- About 600 life peers. In the past these have typically included former Prime Ministers and Speakers of the House of Commons, and people prominent in public life, such as actors, musicians and entrepreneurs. Political appointments continue to be made, but since 2000 an Appointments Commission has been responsible for recommending candidates for appointment as non-political peers and for vetting nominees as life peers. (Anyone who is a British, Irish or Commonwealth citizen, who is over the age of 21, and who is resident in the UK for tax purposes can nominate or self-nominate.)

- Religious leaders, or the Lords Spiritual, made up of the two archbishops and 24 bishops of the Church of England.

As well as being in a state of limbo, the Lords today has only limited power. About two to four of its members are usually appointed to the Cabinet, it has its own select and ad hoc committees (but no standing committees), and every parliamentary bill must go through the Lords, which spends most of its time revising bills sent from the House of Commons. The chamber can introduce and revise proposed legislation, but most of its decisions can be overruled by the Commons: money bills do not need the approval of the Lords, and while it can delay approval of other bills for up to a year they can be reintroduced in the Commons which can pass them without the approval of the Lords. But it does have its uses: it has more time to debate issues than the Commons, it often debates controversial topics that the Commons would prefer to avoid, it can force concessions from the Commons and it is a useful point of access for lobbyists. And given the weaknesses of the Commons, the Lords – ironically – has been more of a block on the government in recent years (Cowley, 2006; Russell, 2016).

Illustration 4.2 The Houses of Parliament

The Houses of Parliament on the bank of the River Thames in central London. Parliament is at the core of the British system of government, but it has lost powers as those of the Prime Minister have grown and as European law has superseded British law in many areas.

House of Commons

Although it is the 'lower' house, the Commons is the more powerful chamber of Parliament, and the real focus of law making. However, since the government so dominates the legislative process, it is questionable whether Parliament any longer makes law, rather than simply discussing and voting upon government bills (Leach *et al.*, 2011: 240).

The House consists of 650 MPs elected by direct universal vote from single-member districts. Debates are presided over by a Speaker, who is elected by the House from among its members, and usually comes from the majority party. The Speaker is not allowed to vote, and is expected to remain non-partisan. Party discipline in the House is tight, but discontent is not unusual; a breakdown of party cohesion – usually dubbed a 'backbench rebellion' if it is big enough – is normally interpreted as a sign of weakness, and can lead to the fall of a government, the resignation of a Prime Minister or even a general election.

The chamber of the House is small, with benches rather than seats (see Figure 4.1). The governing party or coalition sits on the left when facing the Speaker's chair, with the Prime Minister and members of the Cabinet on the front bench, while MPs without government office, or with only junior office, sit behind the front bench and are known collectively as backbenchers. The next biggest party in Parliament sits across from the governing party. Its leader sits directly opposite the Prime Minister, beside a shadow Cabinet of opposition MPs responsible for keeping up with – and challenging – their counterparts in the Cabinet. The leader of the opposition and the shadow Cabinet are formally recognized and salaried positions. If the opposition wins a majority in an election and becomes the government, its leader typically becomes Prime Minister, and many members of the shadow Cabinet become the real Cabinet. In other words, the shadow Cabinet is a government in waiting.

The process by which a bill becomes a law normally begins in government departments, which – guided by the government – identify issues that merit changes in the law, and develop proposals that are circulated to all other interested departments, and are revised by experts and affected interests. This process may take a year or more. The Cabinet then looks over the proposals and those that are accepted go to the Parliamentary Counsel, which drafts bills. (Bills introduced by the government are known as public bills; much more rarely, an individual MP may introduce what is known as a private member's bill, but few survive to become law.) The plan to introduce a bill is normally announced in the Queen's Speech at the State Opening of Parliament in October. The bill is then introduced to Parliament (either chamber), and after initial debate is sent almost immediately to the relevant standing committee, where most of the real work of Parliament is done: specialists go over the details, outside experts are invited to give testimony and changes are made to the bill. Once a bill has passed through committee, it goes back to Parliament for more debate and amendments and a final vote. Once accepted, it is sent to the Queen for her signature.

The Judiciary

Constitutional courts – such as those in the United States and Germany – typically exist to defend and interpret the constitution, and act as the final court of appeal on cases calling for judicial review: the process by which a judgement is made on the constitutionality of a law or the action of an elected official. Since Britain does not have a codified constitution, it long lacked a distinct constitutional court. Instead, judicial review was carried out in a complex system of courts topped by a Court of Appeal and the Appellate Committee of the House of Lords (or the Law Lords), which heard final appeals in five-person benches. Appointments to the higher courts were made either by the Lord Chancellor (who presided over the Lords, was a member of the Cabinet and came closest to being Britain's Minister of Justice) or by the Prime Minister after consultation with the Lord Chancellor. This arrangement long raised concerns about political interference, generating pressure for reform.

In 2003 it was announced that there would be a significant reorganization of the judicial system in the UK: the post of Lord Chancellor would be abolished, there would be a new system for appointing judges, a new Ministry of Justice would be created to take over selected aspects of criminal justice from the Home Office and the Law Lords would be replaced by a new Supreme Court of the United Kingdom. Created in 2008, the Court consists of 12 justices appointed by the monarch on the recommendation of the Prime Minister. Based in the former Middlesex Guildhall opposite the Houses of Parliament in London, it is headed by a president and a deputy president and acts as the final court of appeal for civil cases, for cases dealing with devolution and for criminal cases in England, Wales and Northern Ireland (but not Scotland, which has its own High Court of Justiciary). Its job is distinctive from that of the US Supreme Court in that it is not allowed to overturn legislation. The existing Law Lords became justices in the Supreme Court in 2008, but since 2009 all new justices have been directly appointed (on the recommendation of a selection commission) to the court.

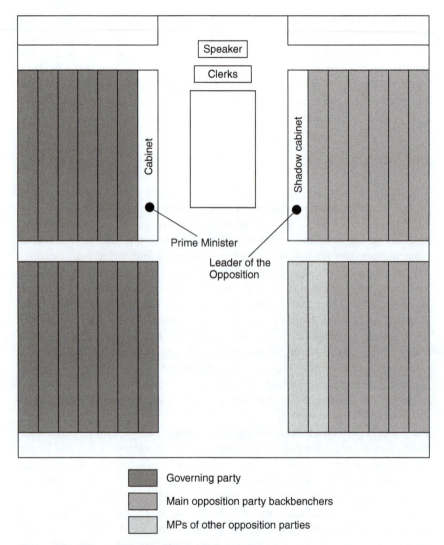

Figure 4.1   Floor plan of the House of Commons

While a member of the EU, Britain also came under the jurisdiction of the European Court of Justice, one of the key institutions of the EU. There is no codified European constitution (an attempt to agree an EU constitutional treaty collapsed in 2005 after negative votes in public referendums in France and the Netherlands), the Court instead basing its decisions on a series of treaties and a growing body of European law whose primacy over national law in many areas of policy is established. The Court also has the power to bring cases against the governments of EU member states who have not properly applied particular EU laws. How Britain will cut its ties with the Court of Justice and the body of EU law promises to be one of the most troubling aspects of the terms of departure from the EU. The influence of Europe is also felt in the field of human rights, guarded by the Strasbourg-based European Court of Human Rights (not an EU institution). Britain was one of the original signatories of the 1951 European Convention on Human Rights (see Greer, 2006), and while this was not eventually incorporated into British law until 1998 many cases were successfully brought against the British government.

The Bureaucracy

Britain has about half a million bureaucrats (or civil servants) who carry out the typical responsibilities of bureaucrats everywhere: most are responsible for collecting government revenues (mainly in the form of taxes), for making payments in the form of benefits and pensions and for running government services. Like most of its counterparts elsewhere, the British bureaucracy – sometimes known as Whitehall after the part of London where many government departments have their headquarters – is hierarchical in structure and nature and is expected to execute the laws of government and the wishes of government ministers.

The British civil service – like all other elements of government – has undergone profound change in recent years as attempts have been made to reform it by borrowing ideas from the private sector designed to make the service more efficient and responsive to consumers. The most important of these ideas have included the contracting out of jobs previously carried out by bureaucrats, the tying of pay to performance, improvements in management methods, and techniques designed to provide better service for less cost. In the view of Kavanagh *et al.* (2006), the effect has been a fundamental change to the characteristics of Whitehall:

- *Permanence.* Beginning in the early nineteenth century, bureaucrats were able to assume that their jobs were permanent. Careers in government and the civil service were treated as separate, and bureaucrats were regarded as servants of the monarch rather than of the political leadership of the day. But with the linking of performance to pay, and staff moving between the public and private sectors, the idea of jobs for life has weakened.
- *Neutrality.* As servants of the Crown, bureaucrats have been expected to be impartial and to recognize that their responsibilities are above party politics.

For this reason, they are not allowed to stand for political office or to express political opinions in public, and if they decide to enter politics they must resign from the civil service, not just take a leave of absence as their counterparts in France and Germany are allowed to do. This impartiality was easier during the period of consensus government in the 1950s, 1960s and 1970s, but became less so with the growing ideological distance between the two major parties in the 1980s and 1990s. There are also allegations that recent governments have been more aggressive in involving themselves in decisions on the appointments of senior civil servants.

- *Anonymity.* The principle of responsible government means that ministers have traditionally received confidential advice from civil servants, but have been expected to take public responsibility for the work of their departments while bureaucrats have remained largely anonymous. This principle has been eroded by public inquiries that have been more willing to name names, by greater media enquiry into the workings of the bureaucracy and by greater openness in the memoirs of former ministers and their aides.

The greatest changes to the bureaucracy were brought about by Margaret Thatcher, who cut the number of civil servants by 28 per cent, launched a programme of departmental efficiency audits, questioned senior civil servants more aggressively about policies, took a close interest in high-level promotions and more assertively imposed her views on the civil service. The most notable change in recent years has been a trend away from large government departments under the control of ministers to more than 150 small, independent agencies responsible for delivering services directly to the public. These include JobCentre Plus, the Environment Agency, the Skills Funding Agency and Natural England. Instead of being subject to ministerial control, the agencies are led by chief executives who control budgets and staffing and are held accountable by performance targets. Policy advice and the development of legislation are still the responsibility of government departments but executive and administrative duties have been handed over to these agencies, where four out of five bureaucrats now work. The old notion of a centralized Whitehall is increasingly at odds with reality.

Local Government

Britain has long been – formally, at least – a unitary state, where political power has been focused at the national level, and local government has had few significant political powers. Local government until recently has been responsible mainly for providing a variety of basic services that most people take for granted, including refuse collection and road maintenance. Most Britons show little interest in local politics, turnout at local government elections is usually low and local government officials are not as well known as national politicians. So weak is local government in Britain that it can be reformed, restructured or even abolished by the national government.

Changes made since the 1980s (the most recent in 1998) have created a complex and confusing system of local government authorities. In England and Wales, most areas come under a two-tier system of counties and districts, each with locally elected councils responsible for such issues as education, transport, housing, roads, local services, refuse disposal and the police. In selected areas, mainly larger cities, county and district functions have been combined into unitary authorities, a concept that was broadened in 2009 when the national government replaced 44 local authorities with nine unitary governments. London has its own elected city government, and six other metropolitan counties – such as Greater Manchester and Merseyside – have no county councils but are instead divided into district councils. Meanwhile, Scotland and Northern Ireland have their own unitary systems.

This arrangement was further complicated in the late 1990s by the creation of elected regional assemblies for Scotland, Wales and Northern Ireland, but not for England. Thus, Britain – while still claiming to be a unitary state in which power is focused at the national level – has actually become a quasi-federal system of government. The word *federal* has negative connotations in Britain, partly because it is widely misunderstood but mainly because of fears expressed by Eurosceptics about the possibility of a federal Europe in which many of the powers of British government would be taken over by EU institutions. Interestingly, it is rarely mentioned in academic studies of the changes that have come to local government in Britain. It has instead been more fashionable to talk of *multi-level governance*, defined as 'negotiated exchanges between systems of governance at different institutional levels' (Pierre and Stoker, 2000: 30).

The Scottish and Welsh regional assemblies were created in 1998, following public referendums, and the first elections were held in May 1999. Both are elected for fixed four-year terms, and have powers over local issues such as education, health services, housing, transport and policing. The 129-member Scottish Parliament has control over most domestic policy matters, including health, education, justice, local transport and the environment, can make primary legislation in these areas and has limited tax-raising powers. The 60-member National Assembly for Wales has control over a similar range of issues (except justice and policing), but has no taxing powers. Meanwhile, Northern Ireland – which had its own Parliament from 1921 to 1972 – has, since 1998, also had its own 108-member Assembly with powers over local issues, and also has two Ministerial Councils that address joint policy making with Ireland and with the British Parliament. (The UK government retains control over economic, monetary, employment, foreign, defence and security policy. But since the Northern Ireland Assembly has been suspended several times because of domestic political squabbles, the British government has – in practice – had greater powers.)

London – which, with its surrounding suburbs, is home to about one-third of the British population – was at one time governed by the Greater London Council, led by the left-wing Labour politician Ken Livingstone. Illustrating the powers of national government over local bodies, Margaret Thatcher abolished the Council in 1986. The Blair administration felt that a city the size of London should have its own local government, so the ceremonial office of Lord Mayor of London (whose post is specific to the City of London) was joined by a new elected office for the whole of London. The first elections were held in May 2000, and – much to the chagrin of the Blair administration, which promoted its own 'official' Labour candidate – Ken Livingstone was restored to power. He was elected to a second term in June 2004 as the Labour candidate but was beaten in 2008 by the Conservative Boris Johnson. Labour regained the office in 2016 with the election of Sadiq Khan, the first Muslim to be elected mayor of a major European city. The mayor governs with a 25-member London Assembly, elected using the additional member electoral system: 14 members are elected from individual districts, while 11 are elected on a London-wide party basis. As a global city and a leading financial centre, London stands to experience many of the more negative effects of a British departure from the European Union.

Further Reading

Dorey, Peter (2014) *Policy Making in Britain: An Introduction*, 2nd edn (Sage). An introduction to the major actors in British policy making, and the influences that come to bear on the policy process.

Jones, Bill and Philip Norton (2013) *Politics UK*, 8th edn (Pearson Longman). A survey of government and politics in Britain, including chapters on the key institutions and processes, and outcomes in a selection of areas of policy.

King, Anthony (2015) *Who Governs Britain?* (Pelican). An analysis of the transformation that has taken place in British government in recent decades, arguing that the country's leaders consistently promise more than they can deliver, overlooking the dispersal of political and economic power.

Leach, Robert, Bill Coxall and Lynton Robins (2018) *British Politics,* 3rd edn (Palgrave Macmillan). A detailed textbook on British politics, with chapters on its history, political process, and the major institutions.

Wright, Tony (2013) *British Politics: A Very Short Introduction*, 2nd edn (Oxford University Press). An interpretative essay on the ideas that drive the British political system, identifying the features that make that system distinctive.

5

Politics and Civil Society

The term *politics* usually connotes government, leaders and institutions. But the lifeblood of politics in a democracy is provided by its people, and by how they use the opportunities provided to them to influence the way their government functions. They live under the jurisdiction of the state, or the rules and institutions by which a community is governed and controlled, but they also live within a civil society, or a community of individuals capable of acting separately from the state on the basis of pluralism, tolerance, civility and mutually accepted rules, and the patterns of association they endorse and accept. Civil society consists of all the voluntary and spontaneous forms of political association that evolve within a democratic state, which are not formally part of the state system but show that citizens can operate independently of the state (see Edwards, 2014).

Vibrant democracies such as Britain have many channels through which citizens can associate and cooperate, and can mobilize their numbers, values and goals to influence government, or to create organizations that either complement the work of government or provide services where government has failed to do so. Citizens can express themselves through elections, support for political parties or interest groups, use of the mass media, and a host of other conventional and non-conventional forms of representation and participation, ranging from direct contact with elected officials to protests, boycotts, strikes and demonstrations. At the same time, and again as in other democracies, many Britons choose not to participate, or feel detached from government and society, and this has caused growing concern.

The changes that have come to the structure of government in Britain – described in Chapter 4 – are reflected in civil society. Concerns about the fairness of the electoral system have led to the introduction of proportional representation in local and European elections, and to a failed attempt in 2011 to change the national electoral system. The balance between the two major political parties has shifted as Labour has moved first to the centre and then further left and as the Conservatives have struggled to move beyond their divisions over Europe. Meanwhile, the British have turned their backs in growing numbers on two of the most traditional forms of political participation – party membership and voting in elections – and have instead become more involved in the work of interest groups and more willing to use unconventional channels to express their political views. Finally, the rise of social media has changed the sources of political information and the channels for political participation and expression, and has obliged government to be more creative in the way it relates to citizens.

This chapter begins with a survey of political culture in Britain, outlining the attitudes of Britons towards politics and civic responsibility: the views they hold regarding their role in the political system, their expectations of that system and their changing opinions about their responsibilities to the political community in which they live. It then looks at elections, explaining the electoral process in Britain and comparing the structure and implications of the single-member plurality system with those of the proportional representation systems used for elections to regional assemblies and the European Parliament. It also looks at referendums, which have played a new role in British politics as they have been used with more frequency, mainly at the regional level. The chapter then discusses the role of political parties and their changing fortunes in recent elections, which have seen declining turnout and significant change for the role of smaller parties. The chapter finishes with an assessment of the role of interest groups, traditional media and social media in politics.

Political Culture

The term *political culture* describes the collective norms, values and expectations of a society as they relate to politics and government. Political culture helps explain what leaders and citizens regard as acceptable and unacceptable about the character of government and civil society, and about the relationship between government and people. Despite this simple definition, tying down the political norms and values of a society is always a challenge, especially for a country like Britain with its multinational identity, its long and convoluted history and its constant state of change. A generation ago, most political scientists would have described the British as pragmatic, as having faith in their political system (if not necessarily in politicians), as patriotic and as politically moderate. But perceptions have changed in recent years, with new attention being paid to the decline of conventional participation and of trust and faith in government, and to questions about the definition of national identity.

Pragmatism

The British have long had a reputation for being pragmatic (realistic and practical) when it comes to their expectations of government and their aspirations for their own lives. They were conventionally seen to take an empirical approach to problem solving, eschewing theory in favour of tried-and-tested approaches and assessments of the practical reality of policies. This is not to suggest that the British do not dream, or that they fear change, or that they are opposed to innovation. On the contrary, the British political system – and people's expectations of it – has never stopped evolving, the speed and the depth of change having sparked much public concern in recent years.

Particularly among older Britons, pragmatism has spilled over into pessimism. It often seems as though the national motto should be 'mustn't grumble', or 'things could be worse', given how often some Britons utter these phrases in response to the greeting 'How are you?' The media have perpetuated the problem through their fascination with everything from lowered educational performance to rising crime and the mixed record of England's national cricket and football teams. This ties in to the widespread emphasis within the academic literature on the decline of Britain.

But the view that life was better and safer in 'the old days' is not always supported by the facts; in terms of health care, education, economic wealth, individual freedoms, gender equality, consumer protection and the state of the environment, life for most Britons has improved greatly since the 1980s. At least until the 2007–10 global financial crisis, more people were beginning to realize this, and the gloom of the 1970s and 1980s was lifting. But a new round of pessimism has been set off by the fallout from the crisis. This is reflected, for example, in the results of opinion polls showing that many Britons aspire to leave the country, and – as we saw in Chapter 2 – rates of emigration have grown in recent years. The pessimism was also reflected in the vote to leave the European Union, which was often singled out by its critics as a handy scapegoat for many of Britain's problems, even if those problems actually had sources elsewhere.

Declining Faith in the Political System

Despite this thread of pessimism, most Britons have traditionally had high levels of faith in the political system, such feelings being tied to the long history of relative political stability and evolutionary change in Britain which contrasts with the often revolutionary and violent change that has come to political systems in other European states. Faith in the political system was also long bound up in the class structure and the strong feelings of political and social deference that this promoted, as reflected in traditional views about the monarchy and the class system, and in the willingness to obey authority figures representing the state, such as the police (see discussion in Moran, 2011: 91). However, faith and deference have been on the decline, for several reasons:

- Changes in the class system have weakened the authority of political and economic elites, even if their power remains substantial.
- There is growing respect for succeeding through effort and hard work, and declining respect for privilege and old money.
- The British are becoming more self-reliant and less dependent on the state.
- The political system is seen as being less responsive than it should be, with only a small minority believing that government can be trusted to put the interests of the country ahead of the interests of parties and leaders.
- There has been less respect for elected officials and for a political class that is often accused of being out of touch with the needs of ordinary people.

A new belief in self-determination and support for alternative methods of engaging with government and expressing political opinions is reflected in declining political engagement such as membership of political parties and voter turnout at elections (Grasso, 2016). It is also reflected in the growth in the membership of interest groups and recent indications that the British are more willing to use unconventional forms of political participation than the citizens of any other democracy.

In Britain – as in many other countries – the rebellion against the political elite has been clearly on display. A series of political scandals reached a new low in 2011 with the breaking of the story surrounding the media conglomerate News International in 2011 (see Box 5.1), which raised new questions about how close political leaders and journalists had become. But the doubts are more broad-based, as reflected in the results of the annual global Trust Barometer published by the communications marketing company Edelman since 2012, which has found Britons to have low levels of trust in government, business and media. The 2017 survey found that only 36 per cent of Britons trusted the government to 'do what is right' (slightly below the average for all countries of 41 per cent, and ten points below levels of trust in non-governmental organizations). Only 18 per cent trusted political parties and only 19 per cent trusted political leaders. The British have also lost faith in the political system, along with most of their democratic peers; 60 per cent felt that the system was failing in 2017 (Edelman, 2017).

Box 5.1   The *News of the World* hacking scandal

Questions have long been asked about the ethics of journalists in Britain, particularly those working for the tabloids, but when news broke in mid-July 2011 of one of the most troubling scandals in the history of British journalism, it had implications also for politics, business, and for policing. Problems dated back to 2006 when a senior journalist on the *News of the World* was arrested and charged with hacking the phones of members of the royal family. The editor of the paper, Andy Coulson, resigned while also claiming that he had no knowledge of illegal activities, and within six months had been hired as Conservative Party director of communications.

More revelations about phone hacking emerged in 2009 and 2010, leading to several legal actions and an investigation by the London Metropolitan Police in early 2011. Coulson resigned from Cameron's staff in January 2011, and it was later revealed that nearly 4,000 people might have had their phones hacked, including celebrities and politicians. But when it was also revealed in July 2011 that the phones of relatives of British soldiers killed in Iraq and Afghanistan had been accessed, along with victims of the 2005 London bombings, and – worst of all – of Milly Dowler, a 13-year-old schoolgirl abducted and murdered in 2002, the story attracted worldwide news headlines. When News International took the decision to close the *News of the World* after 168 years in print it was widely dismissed as a cynical attempt by Rupert Murdoch, owner of parent company News Corporation, to deflect attention from the real perpetrators.

A number of high-ranking employees and executives of Murdoch companies subsequently resigned, notably News International chief executive (and former *News of the World* editor) Rebekah Brooks, as well as senior members of the Metropolitan Police who had been accused of failing to follow through with investigations of the *News of the World*. Meanwhile, Prime Minister David Cameron was obliged to publicly defend and explain the decision of his party to employ Coulson, and Rupert Murdoch, his son James, and Rebekah Brooks were summoned to appear before a House of Commons committee. The senior Murdoch expressed his deep regret but argued that he was not responsible for activities at the *News of the World*, which was only a small part of his global operations.

The scandal raised deeply troubling questions not just about journalistic ethics but also about the relationship between the media and politics, and about the internal culture of News International, a company that has long been controversial because of the methods and style of Rupert Murdoch. A parliamentary inquiry into the scandal was announced by David Cameron, and an investigation is underway by the Independent Police Complaints Commission (IPCC), which deals with complaints made against the police forces of England and Wales.

A Confused National Identity

Although they are not as patriotic as the Americans and the French, the British take pride in their history and traditions. Polls regularly find that the majority of Britons (80 per cent or more) are proud of being British, a view deriving at least in part from the history of Britain as a crucible of democracy and capitalism, and as the nucleus of the world's largest empire. However, the notion of patriotism has been muddied by the historical tendency in Britain not to wield its citizens into a united state but to allow the separate cultural identities of the English, the Scottish, the Welsh and the Irish to flourish (Gamble, 2016). The recent rise of Scottish and Welsh nationalism (see Chapter 2) has, in turn, raised questions about the definition of 'Britain' and 'British' (see Chapter 7). While the Scots, the Welsh and the Irish have long defined their identities in relation to their dominant neighbour, the English have defined themselves more in the context of the meanings of 'Britain' and 'British'. This has begun to change in recent years, however, with more residents of England defining themselves as 'English' rather than 'British' (Hazell, 2006), more overt displays of English patriotism in support of English national sports teams, calls for the recognition of St George's Day (23 April) as a national holiday in England, and support for greater recognition of what makes England different from Scotland and Wales.

Discussions of the meaning of 'Britishness' have been further complicated in recent decades by the growing racial and religious diversity of Britain. Where once there was a close association between the history and cultural symbols of Britain and the British people (national divisions notwithstanding), the impact of recent waves of immigration has forced a reassessment of national identity. Sadly, there is a perception that the British national flag – and even the English flag – may have been hijacked by racists and right-wing extremist groups bemoaning the growth of ethnic diversity. This has led some to associate both flags with intolerance, and even led one rather confused school head teacher to ban the display of English flags during the 2006 World Cup for fear that it would offend minority students. She backtracked following an outcry from her students.

A Closed Society

The British tend to be a private people, hence the old adage that an Englishman's home is his castle. Perhaps because Britain is such a crowded country where a premium is placed on personal space, the British can sometimes seem a little stand-offish to visitors. This sense of privacy was long reflected in the secrecy that surrounded the functioning of government in Britain. Issues of national security are subject to secrecy in every democracy, but critics charge that state secrets have been too broadly defined in Britain, and that this has helped increase the power and reduce the accountability of the police, weakened the power of Parliament at the expense of the executive, promoted the use of surveillance, reduced the right to personal privacy, and allowed the government to interfere with media freedom.

Illustration 5.1   Nationalism

Scottish rugby fans cheer on their team during an international match against France at Murrayfield stadium in Edinburgh. Questions of national identity have come to the fore in recent years as support for the idea of Scottish independence has grown, helping spark more overt expressions of English nationalism.

Recent years have seen a movement for greater freedom of information, governments have given new emphasis to transparency, and information has become more freely available, particularly over the internet. The Freedom of Information Act, which came into force in 2005, provides a statutory right of access to recorded information relating to the work of Parliament, government departments, local authorities, the health service, and other publicly funded organizations. Critics charge that there are too many important exceptions – including information related to policy making, and to matters where legal action may be likely or pending – and that the Information Commissioner responsible for enforcing the Act has powers only to recommend rather than compel the release of information. Nevertheless, the new law has helped make government more accessible and has helped encourage citizens to be more interested in the activities of government and in gaining access to official information. But this new openness has come at a time when civil liberties are being curbed – and the powers of government expanded – in response to terrorism, with an ongoing debate about the government having access to too much information about individuals.

Social Liberalism

In line with many of their European neighbours, the British as a whole tend to take liberal positions on social issues. The basic principles of the welfare state are unchallenged, capital punishment has been outlawed since 1964, homosexuality and abortion have both been legal since 1967, same-sex civil unions or partnerships have been allowed since 2005, same-sex marriage has been allowed since 2014, and there is little censorship on television. Where political debates in the United States are often based around the question of the extent to which government should become involved in determining the personal choices of citizens – either through regulation on such relatively trivial matters as mandating the use of seatbelts by drivers or through bigger issues such as access to legal abortion or prayer in schools – these are rarely discussed in Britain, if only because liberal social values are so ingrained in national life. Of course there is support also for conservative social positions, and attempts have been made to spark debates about the decline of 'family values' or to make access to abortion illegal, but such arguments attract little broad-ranging public support.

Elections and Referendums

Like all liberal democracies, Britain has many channels through which its citizens can take part in politics, express their opinions and try to influence government policy. These include regular elections, political parties representing different ideological and regional positions, a large community of interest groups and a diverse media establishment. The options have increased in recent years as the number of parties has grown, as new local and regional assemblies have been created, as the electoral system has diversified, as the number of sources of political news has increased and as social media have become more important channels for expression and information. And yet, ironically, most Britons are disengaging themselves from politics as usual as their faith in the political system and its leaders declines. The trends are illustrated by the figures on turnout at elections.

Elections serve the triple purpose of maintaining the legitimacy of the system of government, of offering cues for the direction of public policy, and of offering citizens a means of effecting peaceful political and constitutional change (Kavanagh *et al.*, 2006: 395). British voters are faced with three sets of elections – general, European and local – but have quite different ideas about their importance and significance.

The General Election

The general election is the contest by which members of the lower chamber of Parliament – the House of Commons – are chosen, and so by which the national government of Britain is determined. It is by far the most important event on the electoral calendar, and attracts the most political activity and the greatest media and public interest. Elections were until recently called at least once every five years on a date chosen by the Prime Minister and confirmed by the monarch. This changed in 2011 with the passage of Fixed-term Parliaments Act, under which general elections must be held on the first Thursday in May of the fifth year after the previous election. The Prime Minister is allowed to alter the date by up to two months, and early elections can be triggered either by the failure of the government to win a vote of confidence or by the vote of at least two-thirds of the members of the House of Commons, as happened in 2017 when Theresa May's government – seeking less resistance from opposition parties in negotiations on Brexit – called a 'snap' election for June that year, three years ahead of schedule.

General election campaigns are short, lasting just 18 days (excluding weekends and public holidays). The UK is divided into constituencies (electoral districts), each represented in the House of Commons by a single Member of Parliament (MP). All districts must be contested in the general election, and voters make a straight choice among the candidates from the different parties standing in their district, the winner being the candidate with the most votes. Once the results are in, the monarch asks the leader of the party with the largest number of seats to form a government. If there is no clear winner then the party leaders negotiate among themselves to form a coalition. Constituency boundaries are revised periodically to make sure that the number of voters in each is roughly the same. Until 2000, there were separate boundary commissions for England, Scotland, Wales and Northern Ireland, but they were then absorbed into an independent national Electoral Commission, which is also responsible for supervising the financial restrictions on parties and for overseeing referendums.

Britain is unique within Europe in using the single-member plurality (SMP) electoral system (otherwise known as first-past-the-post or winner-take-all), under which a winning candidate does not need a majority, but prevails simply by winning more votes than any other candidate. All other European countries use proportional representation (PR), under which parties win seats in proportion to the number of votes they win. SMP has the advantage of being quick and simple, and tends to produce stable and accountable one-party governments, but it also works in favour of parties that have large blocks of concentrated support, and against parties whose support is more thinly spread; the former tend to win seats, while the latter more often come second or third.

Illustration 5.2　Elections

Prime Minister Theresa May is greeted by the international press corps as she leaves 10 Downing Street, the official London residence of the British Prime Minister, following the indecisive 2017 general election.

The kind of skewed results this can produce were most obvious in the 1983 general election, when the ruling Conservatives won 42 per cent of the vote but 62 per cent of seats in the House of Commons. Meanwhile, Labour won 28 per cent of votes and 32 per cent of seats (a more equitable result), while the third-placed Liberal–SDP Alliance won almost as many votes as Labour (25 per cent) but just 4 per cent of seats in the House. This meant, mathematically speaking, that the votes of Alliance supporters were worth only one-tenth as much as the votes of Conservative supporters. The imbalances were also reflected in 2015, when the Scottish National Party was able to raise its share of seats in Parliament tenfold (from 6 to 56) by just tripling its share of the Scottish vote, while the UK Independence Party won nearly 13 per cent of the national vote but only one seat (Cowley and Kavanagh, 2016).

The introduction of PR to Britain was first proposed as early as 1917, but found few supporters within the Conservative and Labour parties because they benefited the most from SMP. British voters had their first taste of PR in 1998–99 with elections to the Scottish, Welsh and London assemblies and to the European Parliament (although Northern Ireland had already used PR for

European and local elections). As part of the agreement it cut to join the new coalition government in 2010, the Liberal Democrats won agreement on the holding of a national referendum in May 2011 on the question of whether or not to replace SMP with a complex new electoral system known as Alternative Vote (AV). Voters rank candidates in order of preference, and any candidate winning a majority of first-preference votes is declared the winner. In the absence of a winner, the candidate with the fewest first-preference votes is eliminated and their votes are allocated to the remaining candidates in a second round of counting, any candidate with a majority being elected. If there is still no winner, the remaining candidate with the fewest first-preference votes is eliminated and their votes reallocated until one candidate has a majority or there are no more votes to be distributed.

There was divided support among the major political parties (Conservatives were generally opposed, while Liberal Democrats were in favour and Labour was internally divided), opponents noted that few other countries used the system (Australia being one), and questions were raised about the costs involved in the switch. On referendum day, with a modest turnout of nearly 42 per cent, more than two-thirds of voters rejected the proposal. It is unlikely that changes to the system will be proposed again any time soon, leaving Britain with what – to many – is a fundamentally flawed electoral system that does not accurately reflect voter preferences.

European Elections

On a fixed five-year cycle, Britain between 1979 and 2014 elected representatives to the European Parliament (EP) in Strasbourg, France. Candidates for EP elections were fielded by the same parties that contested general elections at home, and were run on a mixture of domestic and European issues. Limited British voter interest in the EU was reflected in modest turnout at EP elections: after initially running at about 36 per cent (far below even the modest EU average of about 57 per cent), turnout fell in 1999 to an all-time low of 23 per cent (less than half the EU average of 49 per cent), before recovering to 35–39 per cent in 2004–14.

European elections are striking for the extent to which opposition parties usually do better than the governing party. The main explanation for this lies in attitudes towards first-order and second-order elections (Reiff and Schmitt, 1980). Elections that decide who runs the national government are considered first-order and always draw the most media and public interest, and the highest turnout. By contrast, second-order elections – such as European or local elections, where the stakes are lower – are usually seen as an opportunity to

Box 5.2 The changing British voter

The most fundamental quality of democracy is the right to participate. We sometimes have to remind ourselves that governments are the servants of the people, and are elected to represent the interests of the people. Elected officials may see themselves as delegates, who work to find out what their constituents want and need and act accordingly, or as trustees, who act and vote according to what they feel is in the best interests of constituents, the party and the country. Either way, government officials are there to *represent*. But to do so effectively demands that citizens participate in the democratic process, whether through voting, party activities, lobbying, joining interest groups, demonstrating, or any of the myriad ways in which they can make their decisions known. But recent evidence suggests that the British are not taking part in politics – or expressing their views on politics – as much as they once did.

For Ruth Fox (2014), this is indicative of a broader problem. Low turnout numbers among British voters:

> are a manifestation of the bigger problem of disengagement across the board, linked to a declining sense of the efficacy of politics generally and their role in it, and a sense that the parties are all the same, the politicians are all the same, they are not like us, it does not make any difference.

Part of the problem stems from the uninformed voter, a problem by no means limited to Britain, but which nevertheless raises questions about the outcome of elections and referendums. Electoral waters have been muddied by a blurring of the ideological distinctions among parties, by declining public identification with those parties, and by weakening links between class and voting (Bartle and Laycock, 2006: 77).

Voter turnout at general elections has fallen from a high of 83–84 per cent in 1950–51, to 73–79 per cent in the 1970s, to a new low of 59 per cent in 2001, since when it has climbed to about 65–70 per cent. These figures are still respectable, and indicate trends that have been found in other European countries such as Germany and France – see Figure 5.1. But they have occasionally sparked suggestions of a 'crisis' in British politics, and have been used to further illustrate talk of declining faith in the political system. The low turnout in 2001 and 2005 was probably an anomaly, explained by the particular circumstances of these two elections, in neither of which the opposition Conservatives were able to put up a real contest with Labour. But clearly there has been a reaction against party politics and a disdain for professional politicians, in Britain as in many other democracies.

A notable trend in recent years has been the growing gap between the preferences of younger and older voters. While 73 per cent of Britons aged 18–24 voted in favour of remaining within the EU in the 2016 referendum, 56 per cent of those aged 50 and older voted in favour of leaving. Meanwhile, age was clearly one of the most important determinants of the outcome of the 2017 general election, with more than 60 per cent of those in the 18–24 age group voting for Labour, while 58 per cent of those aged 60 and older supported the Conservatives.

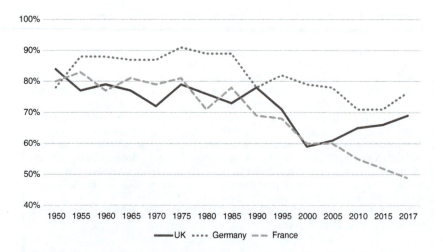

Figure 5.1   Turnout at British general elections compared

Source for Germany and France: International Institute for Democracy and Electoral Assistance at www.idea.int/data-tools (accessed November 2017).

comment on the performance of the governing party. Thus, its supporters are less inclined to vote (adding to the low turnout figures), and many other voters will cast their ballots for parties they would not normally support.

While the Conservatives and Labour at one time won the biggest shares of the vote, smaller parties made gains in later elections, explained in part by the inclination of many voters to use EP elections to cast a protest vote against the incumbent government, and in part by a Europe-wide shift to right-wing parties calling for a slowdown in European integration. It was further affected by Britain's decision to switch in 1999 to the same system of proportional representation used for EP elections in all the other EU member states. The 2004 elections saw the big gains being made by the eurosceptic United Kingdom Independence Party (UKIP), which won 12 seats mainly at the expense of the Conservatives. In the 2009 elections, UKIP beat Labour into third place, winning 13 seats, while the right-wing British National Party won 6 per cent of the vote and two seats. In 2014, UKIP beat all other parties by winning 24 of the UK's 73 seats in the European Parliament, mainly at the expense of the pro-EU Liberal Democrats. With Britain's exit from the EU, it has lost the right to participate in EP elections.

Local Government Elections

Because Britain is a unitary state (in theory, at least – see Chapter 4), and local authorities have limited power, local elections are seen as second-order contests, and have traditionally been ignored by most voters. Representatives are elected to district, county, city and town councils on a fixed four-year cycle, but the few voters who turn out usually make their choices on the basis of national issues and the performance of the national government, and turnout is rarely more than 40 per cent. Hopes that turnout might grow with the work of the new regional assemblies – which have their own powers over a variety of local policy issues – have been disappointed. Turnout at the first elections in 1998–99 was not inspiring (70 per cent in Northern Ireland, 58 per cent in Scotland and 46 per cent in Wales) and was worse in 2003 (63 per cent in Northern Ireland, 49 per cent in Scotland and 38 per cent in Wales). It fell in Northern Ireland to 54 per cent in 2011 before recovering to 65 per cent in 2017, and has settled at 50–55 per cent in Scotland and 42–46 per cent in Wales. Scottish and Welsh assembly elections are based on a combination of single-member plurality and PR, while regional and European elections in Northern Ireland use PR.

Referendums

The referendum has become an increasingly common option for British voters in recent decades, although most have been held at the regional rather than at the national level (see Table 5.1). The first ever national referendum was held in 1973, on the question of continued membership of the European Economic Community, but rather than being an exercise in democracy, it was – like the 2016 Brexit referendum – more an effort by the governing party to put to rest an internal dispute over Europe. Other than the 2011 vote on electoral reform, and the 2016 Brexit vote, all other referendums have been held at the regional level, and most have been about devolving powers from London or about setting up regional assemblies. The most significant was the 2014 vote on independence for Scotland, which resulted in a rejection of the idea by 55 per cent to 45 per cent. Following the huge gains made at the 2015 general election by the Scottish National Party, and Scotland's vote in 2016 in favour of remaining part of the EU, there was speculation that it was only a matter of time before a second vote on Scottish independence would be held.

Table 5.1   Referendums in Britain

Date	Topic	Scope	Result
1973	Northern Ireland remaining part of the UK	Regional	Yes
1975	Continued UK membership of the European Community	National	Yes
1979	Regional assembly for Scotland	Regional	No*
1979	Regional assembly for Wales	Regional	No
1997	Parliament for Scotland	Regional	Yes
1997	National Assembly for Wales	Regional	Yes
1998	Elected mayor and assembly for London	Regional	Yes
1998	Northern Irish peace agreement	Regional	Yes
2004	Regional assembly in north-east England	Regional	No
2011	Extended powers for Welsh National Assembly	Regional	Yes
2011	Change to the national electoral system	National	No
2014	Independence for Scotland	Regional	No
2016	Departure from the European Union	National	Yes

*Small majority said Yes, but not enough to cross threshold of support from at least 40 per cent of eligible voters.

Political Parties

Britain has a wide range of political parties, covering an assortment of ideological positions. However, while dozens of parties contested the 2017 general election, and ten won seats in Parliament, Britain – thanks mainly to the arithmetic of the electoral system – has long been a two-party-dominant system. During the nineteenth century, it was the Conservatives and the Liberals that took turns at governing, their dominance occasionally threatened by Irish nationalist parties. Since the end of the First World War, Labour has replaced the Liberals, and they and the Conservatives have dominated, typically winning about 65–70 per cent of the vote between them and about 85–90 per cent of the seats in Parliament (see Table 5.2). The remaining share of votes and seats has been taken up by the Liberal Party and its successors, and by regional parties; as well as Scottish and Welsh nationalists, Northern Ireland has its own parties which do not campaign on the mainland. Recent trends suggest greater fragmentation among parties and greater volatility of voter support (Webb, 2016), making the future of British party politics harder to predict.

The Conservatives

The origins of the Conservatives (also known as the Tories) date back to the late seventeenth century. Throughout the nineteenth century they alternated in office with first the Whigs and then the Liberals, their most famous Prime Ministers including the Duke of Wellington, Sir Robert Peel and Benjamin Disraeli. Since 1945 they have held power under the leadership of Winston Churchill, Anthony Eden, Harold Macmillan and Alec Douglas-Home (1951–64), Edward Heath (1970–74), Margaret Thatcher and John Major (1979–97), David Cameron (2010–16), and Theresa May (from 2016). However, despite the number of their postwar election victories, and despite their status as one of the longest-serving political parties in any democracy, they have never won more than 45–50 per cent of the national vote; their share fell to a new low of 31–32 per cent in the 1997, 2001 and 2005 elections before climbing back up to 36–37 per cent in 2010–15.

The Conservatives are a pro-business, anti-regulation party with so many shades of opinion that it is often charged that British conservatism lacks consistency or coherence. (For an assessment of the modern Conservative Party, see Bale, 2016.) Much like Labour, there have been two distinctive strands in Conservative thinking in recent years. Right-wingers in the party emphasize limited government, low taxes, self-reliance, social discipline, authority, continuity and morals, and are critical of the EU, while moderates emphasize the creation of wealth, efficient economic organization, a more active role for government in the economy and a more progressive role for Britain in Europe. Between 1945 and 1975, Conservative policies changed little, irrespective of the leader. Then Margaret Thatcher took the helm and broke with tradition, and for more than a decade the party developed policies that reflected her values. She supported monetarist economic ideas (such as controls on government spending, reducing the role of government in the marketplace, low taxation and a free market), promoted private enterprise and private ownership, believed in a strong global role for Britain and close Anglo-American relations, and was hostile to many aspects of European integration.

The party has long been divided over the issue of Europe, with some of its members arguing in favour of greater support for European integration, and some arguing that the process of integration had gone too far. After entering the 1997 general election 20 percentage points behind Labour in opinion polls, and sustaining its worst election defeat since 1832, the Conservatives spent several years in opposition, with three party leaders who were unable to make inroads into Labour's dominance. At least initially this was mainly because of the popularity and strong political standing of Labour Prime Minister Tony Blair, the internal divisions suffered by the Conservatives, Labour's co-option

Table 5.2   Recent general election results

	2005		2010		2015		2017	
	% vote	Seats	% vote	Seats	% vote	Seats	% vote	Seats
Conservative	32	198	36	306	37	330	42	317
Labour	35	355	29	258	31	232	40	262
Liberal Democrat	22	62	23	57	8	8	7	12
Regional parties	6	27	6	25	7	76*	6	57
Other	5	4	6	4	17**	4	5	2
TOTAL		646		650		650		650
Turnout	61.4%		65.1%		66.1%		68.8 %	

Source: UK Electoral Commission at www.electoralcommission.org.uk (retrieved July 2017).

* Of which the Scottish National Party won 56.

** Of which UKIP won 13 per cent.

of many of the more popular Conservative policy positions, and the inability of the Conservatives to broaden their appeal by reaching out to younger voters, women, the middle class and ethnic minorities. Just as Blair had rescued Labour in 1994 with fresh ideas and new thinking, so the Conservatives hoped that they could repeat history when – in December 2005 – they elected the 39-year-old David Cameron (b. 1966) as their new leader.

Thanks to a combination of Labour's troubles under the leadership of Gordon Brown and Cameron's ability to offer a viable alternative (even if he was often criticized for being elusive and hard to pin down), the Conservatives came out of the 2010 general election with more than 100 additional seats in the House of Commons. But this was not enough to give them a majority, leaving them no option but to form a coalition with the centrist Liberal Democrats, whose more natural partner in government would have been Labour. As a result of the compromises necessary to make the coalition work, and the strictures imposed by the need to make budget cuts, the Conservatives in power were unable to pursue many of their natural policy inclinations. One of Cameron's priorities was to end internal party bickering over Europe and to offset the rise of the eurosceptic UK Independence Party, to which end he promised a referendum on the EU should the Conservatives win the 2015 election. They duly won an outright majority, and the referendum was held against the background of lukewarm efforts by Cameron to campaign for the UK to remain in the EU. When the Leave campaign won, Cameron resigned the leadership of the Conservatives, and the prime ministership, and was replaced in both positions by Theresa May. In an effort to strengthen her Brexit negotiating position she called a snap election in June 2017, which resulted in the loss of her slim majority, forcing her into a difficult electoral alliance with the Democratic Unionist Party of Northern Ireland.

Labour

The Labour Party was founded in 1900 following debate about the need for a party to represent the interests of Britain's working class (Thorpe, 2015). It replaced the Liberals as the opposition to the Conservatives in 1922, headed its first coalition government in 1924 under Ramsay MacDonald and won outright power for the first time in 1945 under Clement Atlee, who set about building a welfare state and a managed economy, nationalizing key industries and creating a national health service, a social security system and a subsidized education system. It ran government twice in the 1960s and 1970s under Harold Wilson, but went into opposition in 1979, losing four straight general elections and undergoing a crisis of confidence before finally regaining power in 1997 under Tony Blair.

The victory of 'New Labour' symbolized a widely felt need among Britons for new ideas in government, and a concern that Conservatives had paid too little attention to social problems. Labour had also moved itself towards the centre of the political spectrum, and there was also clearly much tactical voting in the election with Labour and Liberal Democratic voters supporting each other's parties in districts where one of them was in a strong position to challenge the incumbent Conservative (Sanders, 1997). Furthermore, a new generation of young people who had known nothing but Conservative government was voting for the first time; some 52 per cent of under-25s voted Labour, up from 35 per cent in 1992.

Labour under Blair went on to adopt many of the policies usually associated with the middle ground of politics, encroaching into traditionally Conservative territory: Blair embraced the market economy, opposed traditional socialist ideas of taxing and spending, developed a closer relationship with business, reduced the influence of trade unions in the party, committed his government to developing a balanced budget, instituted a more pro-European policy (Labour was for many years hostile to the idea of European integration) and moved Labour toward foreign policy positions that were pro-globalization, pro-NATO and pro-US. Blair also claimed that improved education, reform of the national health care system, a tough position on crime, and constitutional reform were among his priorities.

Labour maintained its commanding position at the 2001 election, when its majority was reduced by just 12 seats, and its percentage share of the vote fell from 43 to 41. However, voter turnout fell to 59 per cent, suggesting that enthusiasm for Labour was waning, and that it was being returned to office partly because the Conservatives had failed to offer a strong alternative. All then changed when Blair gave his support to the US-led invasion of Iraq in 2003. Mass demonstrations against the war were held in Britain, as elsewhere in Europe, and when it became clear that the pretext for invasion – that Iraq was developing weapons of mass destruction – was false, and as questions were raised about the real motives behind the war and about the wisdom of British support for the US, Blair became increasingly unpopular.

As the 2005 general election approached, it was clear that the gloss had worn off Blair's administration. In addition to Iraq, the Labour record on public services, crime and asylum was widely criticized, as was Blair's own governing style. But he had two important advantages: a strong economy and the continued unpopularity of the Conservatives (see Bartle and Laycock, 2006: 84–88). The result was a third win for Labour, with a reduced but still impressive majority of 66. Unfortunately Blair had muddied the waters by declaring several months in advance that it would be his last election, sparking damaging debate in 2005–06 about how long he would stay in office and generating calls from his critics for him to step down, which he eventually did in 2007.

He was replaced as party leader, and as Prime Minister, by his Chancellor of the Exchequer (finance minister) Gordon Brown, whose ambitions to lead had been long delayed by Blair's success. Brown might have lasted longer had he called an earlier general election, but he prevaricated, faced widespread voter impatience for change, and then became embroiled in the early stages of the global financial crisis. He lost the May 2010 general election, when Labour lost nearly 100 seats in the House of Commons, and was replaced as party leader in late 2010 by the young and untested Ed Miliband (b. 1969), energy secretary during the Brown administration. Miliband proved uninspiring as a leader, and when Labour was soundly defeated in the 2015 election he was replaced as party leader by the more traditionally socialist Jeremy Corbyn. After failing to make much of a mark, Corbyn surprised almost everyone by running a strong campaign in 2017, denying the Conservatives their majority.

Liberal Democrats

A small centrist party, the Liberal Democrats were created in 1988 when members of the Social Democratic Party (SDP), created in 1981 by a group of moderate members of the Labour party, joined forces with the Liberal Party, one of the oldest parties in Britain and until the 1920s the major opposition to the Conservatives. The last Liberal Prime Minister (David Lloyd George) left office in 1922, and Liberal support declined as the working class shifted its allegiance to Labour. Surprise by-election victories in the 1960s and 1970s had media pundits talking of a potential Liberal breakthrough, and for a while in the mid-1980s the SDP–Liberal Alliance seemed poised to take over from Labour as the major opposition party.

The Liberal Democratic Party contested its first general election in April 1992. It won an impressive 17 per cent of the vote, but the quirks of single-member plurality meant that this converted into just 20 seats (3 per cent of the total). It won about 18 per cent of the vote in the 1997 general election but more than doubled its representation in Parliament, winning 46 seats, the best result for a third party since the 1920s. The party continued to grow between 1999 and 2006, but while it claimed to be on the verge of taking over from the Conservatives as the effective opposition to Labour, critics asked how this could be when Liberal Democratic policies were so close to those of Labour in many areas. Nick Clegg took over as party leader in 2007, and became deputy prime minister in the uncomfortable coalition government that followed the 2010 election. It proved to be an unpopular move, and – along with the rise of the Scottish National Party and new support for the UK Independence Party – contributed to the Liberal Democrats losing 49 of their 57 seats at the 2015 election, and making only a modest recovery in 2017.

Other Parties

There are many other smaller political parties in Britain, the most consistently important representing regional interests. The Scottish National Party (SNP) campaigns for Scottish devolution and has undergone dramatic growth in recent years. It won enough seats in the 1999 Scottish parliamentary elections to become the opposition to the Labour–Liberal Democratic coalition government, then swept to power at the 2011 Scottish parliamentary elections and immediately began to make preparations for the 2014 referendum on Scottish independence. It lost the referendum vote, but then won 56 of Scotland's 57 seats at the 2015 general election, making it the third largest party in the UK. Meanwhile, its much smaller Welsh counterpart Plaid Cymru has in recent years had only 3–4 seats in the UK Parliament, and only in 2007–11 had enough seats in the Welsh National Assembly to be part of a coalition regional government.

There are also nearly a dozen parties which are active only in Northern Ireland, and whose key differences revolve around their positions on the province's relationship with Britain. The biggest is the Democratic Unionist Party (DUP), a socially conservative party which represents the Protestant/unionist cause of continued union for Northern Ireland with Britain, while Sinn Fein represents the Catholic/nationalist cause and has campaigned in the past for the reunification of Ireland (a goal officially rescinded by the 1998 Northern Ireland peace agreement). The Social Democratic and Labour Party meanwhile takes a more balanced line between the two positions.

Meanwhile, the United Kingdom Independence Party (UKIP) has operated on a platform opposed to UK membership of the European Union and support for tightened controls over immigration. Founded in 1991, it long remained on the margins of British politics, never winning more than about 3 per cent of the vote in general elections, but doing better in European Parliament elections, where it won its first three seats in 1999. It won 12 EP seats in 2004, and then nearly 28 per cent of the vote and 24 of Britain's 73 EP seats in 2014. Finally in the mainstream of UK politics, it won 13 per cent of the vote in the 2015 general election, but this translated into just one seat in the House of Commons. With the Brexit referendum turning out in its favour, its primary purpose was gone and it won less than 2 per cent of the vote in 2017.

Interest Groups

As in most modern liberal democracies, interest groups play a key political role in Britain. There are thousands of such groups (also known as pressure groups or non-governmental organizations), ranging from multimillion-member pressure groups to charities with more limited objectives. Several of Britain's mass movements and interest groups have spread to other countries. For example, the movement against cruelty to animals began in Britain, long famous as a nation of animal lovers, and produced the Royal Society for the Prevention of Cruelty to Animals (RSPCA). (Ironically, it was founded in 1824, 65 years before the National Society for the Prevention of Cruelty to Children (NSPCC).) Similarly, Save the Children, Oxfam (famine relief), the World Wildlife Fund and Amnesty International were founded in Britain and have since become international.

As voters have become more disillusioned with elections and political parties, the number, variety and membership of interest groups have grown. Interest groups have also become more professional and have diversified their methods. Where they once focused their attention on ministers and bureaucrats, they have worked increasingly to mobilize media and public opinion, and have intensified their lobbying of Parliament, providing information to MPs, making presentations to parliamentary committees and trying to influence the development of legislation. The growth of interest group activity has led to more discussion about 'social capital', referring to the value of social networks including their contribution to the effectiveness and stability of democratic government (Field, 2017).

Interest-group activity in Britain has occasionally added up to broader movements aimed at bringing political, economic or social reform, and there have been three particularly important movements in Britain in recent years. First, there has been the labour movement, made up of about 300 trade unions, the biggest of which are affiliated to the Trades Union Congress (TUC). Unions long had a close relationship with the Labour Party, but the two sides began to fall out with one another in the 1970s, the 1979 general election ushering in a Thatcher government bent on reducing union power. Laws were passed requiring union leaders to ballot their members before taking strike action, and unemployment reduced union membership during the 1980s. In addition to a lengthy and divisive strike by coal miners in the mid-1980s, print and journalists' unions also went on strike – all three groups failed to meet their goals. In recent years, unions have lost much of their support and many of their members, and their political influence has declined further as their influence in the Labour Party has weakened.

Second, if the TUC represents workers, then employers are represented by the Confederation of British Industry (CBI). Financial institutions are politically important in Britain, mainly because of the influence of the financial district of the City of London (see Chapter 6). While City interests are kept separate from those of industry, and while there are no formal links between business and the Conservative Party (such as those that once existed between unions and the Labour Party), many senior managers in the City and Britain's larger companies have had significant influence within the Conservative Party. One of the effects of the global financial crisis of 2008–10 was to raise questions about the management of British business and the growing wealth gap between managers and workers.

Finally, while green political parties have not been as successful in Britain as they have in several other European countries (the British Greens won their first seat in the House of Commons in 2010), environmental concerns have been expressed through support for a large community of environmental interest groups. Much of the growth in their size and levels of activity has come since the late 1980s, and the groups with the fastest growth include those that have been most activist, such as Greenpeace and Friends of the Earth. That growth has been accompanied by a new emphasis on the role of the individual in the creation of environmental problems, leading to a new level of activism among both groups and individuals (Saunders, 2013).

The Media

Britain has one of the most diverse mass media establishments in the world, catering to almost every taste and political persuasion. Like all European countries, Britain has mainly national or regional media, so people are interested less in local affairs than in national or international affairs. Important changes have come to the British media over the past decade: they are becoming more powerful political actors, they are becoming more polarized as competition increases, their independence from political parties is growing, and – thanks mainly to changes in technology – a greater variety of sources of information has become available (see Curran and Seaton, 2009). Like all advanced democracies, Britain has experienced a rapid rise in the use and reach of social media, with the same opportunities for a wider variety of sources of more immediate news and the same concerns about the fragmentation of political communication as users increasingly focus only on those sources that fit with their interests and preferences.

Until the late 1980s, British TV viewers had a choice of just four terrestrial channels: two state-owned but independent and commercial-free channels run by the British Broadcasting Corporation (BBC), and two independent commercial channels (ITV and Channel 4). (A new commercial channel – Channel 5 – was created in 1996.) All were editorially independent, were required to give equal air-time to the major political parties and frequently became involved in political controversy. Despite being government-owned, the BBC has always had a reputation for being an impartial and dependable source of news both inside and outside Britain. In the last quarter-century, the television landscape has changed out of all recognition:

- Cable television was launched in 1984 and satellite in 1989, and the number of TV channels has leapt from four to just over 200.
- Audience share for the main BBC and ITV channels fell between 2010 and 2017 from 57 per cent to 51 per cent (they had once attracted a 90 per cent share) (Broadcasters' Audience Research Board data at www.barb.co.uk).
- Scotland has increasingly opted out of carrying national programming, and has instead aired more locally produced programmes.
- While there is more 24-hour news on offer, there is less primetime political coverage on the mainstream commercial channels.

Under the circumstances, the public-service programming that was once provided by the BBC without much competition is now viewed by a smaller proportion of the audience, which is offered more entertainment options instead. The promotion of British political issues has also declined as regional news plays a bigger role in the choices available to viewers. Finally, political parties have had to work harder – and use a greater variety of methods and outlets – to convey their message. Instead of enjoying the virtually undivided attention of viewers, they are now competing with the broadcasting fare of dozens of different channels.

The British broadcast market continues to undergo change, with the liberalization of the market, the deregulation of commercial radio, new rules allowing radio station owners to buy television stations and vice versa, the expansion of digital television (analogue broadcasting ended in Britain in 2012), the merger of independent television (currently run by two separate companies) and permission for non-European companies to buy British companies.

The print media are also experiencing change. For decades, British readers have been offered a choice of major regional daily newspapers (such as *The Scotsman* in Edinburgh or the London *Evening Standard*), and a range of London-based national morning papers:

- The five so-called 'quality' papers: *The Times*, *Telegraph*, *Independent*, *The Guardian* and *Financial Times* (all read predominantly by higher socio-economic groups).
- The five mass-circulation tabloids: the *Daily Mail* and *Daily Express* (read mainly by the middle class) and the *The Sun*, *Daily Mirror* and *Daily Star* (read mainly by the working class).

Where the 'qualities' provide a broader range of news and comment, several with a particular political or social bias, the tabloids tend to be more openly partisan and to offer an often simplified and exaggerated picture of politics (Conboy, 2005). The popularity of the tabloids has also led to concerns that they give their owners too much political influence, a problem that was particularly evident during the 2016 Brexit referendum as anti-EU newspapers such as *The Sun*, the *Daily Express* and the *Daily Mail* launched virulent and often misleading attacks on the EU and its implications for Britain.

As in other industrialized countries, newspapers in Britain have lost readers and advertising revenues to online sources of news, leading to projections that several may close down in coming years. Some have responded – like their counterparts in television – by trying to attract new readers with a shift away from hard news on politics and economics, and towards soft stories on lifestyle and entertainment. Others have invested in new business in order to help sustain the costs of not-so-profitable print editions, or have invested in the development of free editions. Yet others have expanded the options available on their online versions, which have helped them pull in readers from more countries and increase their advertising revenues.

Despite the changes, the British media still carry out the typical roles of helping form the national political agenda, providing people with information, helping determine political reputations and providing the self-appointed role of watchdog. More recently, they have also been more openly manipulated by government for political ends. Meanwhile, the availability of political information –

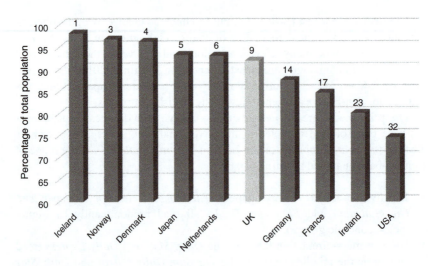

Figure 5.2   Internet use compared

Source: International Telecommunication Union at www.itu.int (retrieved April 2017). Numbers on columns indicate ranking.

and the opportunity for political participation – have been greatly affected by the rise of the internet, now the world's largest communications system. The British are among the most internet-connected people in the world, the proportion having risen from less than 10 per cent in 1998 to more than 92 per cent in 2015; see Figure 5.2). While only a small minority have used the internet for direct political purposes, it has become an important tool in political communication and in the promotion of civil society.

Social media have become an important part of the way that Britons communicate with each other, as they have in other liberal democracies, but the jury is still out on what this means for the dynamics of British society: much is broadcast but there is relatively little in the way of meaningful feedback, and we all suffer from living in a world where everyone has a view, no matter how well or badly that view is developed and constructed. As in most liberal democracies, media use in Britain has become more fragmented and more people seek out only that information that fits with their predispositions, in a phenomenon known as an echo chamber. This was on show, for example, during the Brexit campaign when it became clear that few supporters of Leave or Remain were seeking out information from the other side, and Leavers often rejected and criticized 'experts' for being part of what they regarded as the political elite whose interests were closely tied to those of the European Union. Another of the findings of the Edelman Trust Barometer (see p. 111) is that slightly more than half of people in the 28 survey countries do not regularly listen to people or organizations with whom they often disagree, and that many more people are more inclined to listen to their peers than to political leaders or the mass media.

Further Reading

Cowley, Philip and Dennis Kavanagh (2016) *The British General Election of 2015* (Palgrave Macmillan). An analysis of the 2015 general election, including chapters on the main political parties, the campaign and the outcome.

Denver, David, Christopher Carman and Robert Johns (2012) *Elections and Voters in Britain*, 3rd edn (Palgrave). A textbook assessment, including chapters on turnout, issues, parties and campaigning.

Heffernan, Richard, Colin Hay, Meg Russell and Philip Cowley (eds) (2016) *Developments in British Politics 10* (Palgrave). The most recent in the ongoing series from Palgrave, bringing together an edited collection on the current state of British government and politics.

Moran, Michael (2017) *The End of British Politics?* (Palgrave Macmillan). An analysis of the crisis of the British state, placing the Scottish independence movement and Brexit within their historical context.

Thorpe, Andrew (2015) *A History of the British Labour Party* (Palgrave), and Tim Bale (2016) *The Conservative Party: From Thatcher to Cameron*, 2nd edn (Polity Press). These offer in-depth studies of the two major British political parties and their changing fortunes.

6

The Economy

Economic matters play a primary role in the public life of every society, but in few places has this been truer since the Second World War than in Britain. From being the world's biggest economic and trading power, with its most powerful currency, Britain has seen itself first outperformed by its competitors, then hurt by the self-serving policies of labour unions and management, then confused by the contradictory inclinations of different governments to play a greater or a lesser role in the marketplace, and – after an era of relative optimism and growth in the 1990s – most recently feeling the effects of the fallout from the global financial crisis of 2007–10 and the eurozone crisis that broke in 2009. It now finds itself held hostage to the uncertainties over its redefined relationship with the European Union.

After a short-lived postwar boom, there was a relative decline in productivity, efficiency and competition, and by the late 1960s Britain's economy was in trouble. Many bemoaned the spread of a 'British disease', usually blamed on an expensive welfare system, powerful trade unions, a large public sector, falling productivity and a declining trade surplus. Conditions worsened during the 1970s, and for many the nadir came in 1978–79 with the 'winter of discontent', when it seemed that all the accumulating problems of the previous 20 years had brought the British economy to the brink of collapse.

The Thatcher government took power in 1979 determined to reverse the trends, arguing that government was too involved in market decisions, and that the entrepreneurial spirit of Britons had been dulled by high taxes and too much reliance on the state. It cut taxes, sold off key industries to the private sector and reduced the burden of regulation. New wealth was created, new businesses were launched, productivity grew, and both inflation and unemployment fell. By the 1990s, and in spite of the routine cyclical concerns that afflict all economies, Britain was wealthier and more buoyant, dynamic and productive than at any time since the 1950s. But the wealth was not evenly spread, the gap between the rich and the poor grew, and many felt threatened by globalization and immigration. Britain also became an expensive society in which to live, thanks mainly to a boom in property prices and then to the rising cost of food and household needs. New uncertainties were then injected in the wake of the global financial crisis, which necessitated painful budget cuts and a new series of debates about economic priorities.

This chapter looks at the economic system of Britain and at the causes and effects of its peaks and troughs. It begins with a survey of the structure of the economy and then examines economic trends since 1945, contrasting the boom years of the 1950s with the crises of the 1970s, assessing the content and impact of Thatcherism, and discussing the changes that have taken place over the last decade. Three in particular have had the greatest impact: large inflows of capital and investment that have strengthened the ties between Britain and the global economy, the demands and opportunities of British membership of (and departure from) the European Union (EU), and the effects of the global financial crisis and the eurozone crisis.

Until the effects of these crises play themselves out, it is hard to be sure about the long-term trends in British economic fortunes. Overall, however, today's British economy is a shadow of its former self; from a time when Britain was the world's leading economic player, it today exerts less influence regionally or globally than either Germany or France. Leaving the EU is unlikely to be the bonus that many of the supporters of Brexit hope, and Britain will have to work harder to shape economic opportunities for itself.

Structure of the Economy

Britain has all the classic features of a modern capitalist society. It is wealthy, it makes a diverse range of products (although far fewer than it once did), it offers its consumers a wide range of services, most of its economic wealth is generated by non-tangible services rather than industry, and it plays a key role in the international trading system. It is a free-market system in which prices are driven mainly by supply and demand, and in which private enterprise dominates the creation of wealth. Such enterprise was at the heart of the development of Britain's empire, but the postwar policies of an expanded public sector and greater government regulation pushed forward the frontiers of the state, which have contracted again since the 1980s as the government has withdrawn from the marketplace and placed greater emphasis on the private sector and individual enterprise.

The basic measure of national economic wealth is gross domestic product (GDP), or the total value of all goods and services produced by a country in the course of a year. Britain in 2015 had a GDP of just over $2.8 trillion, making it the fifth biggest economy in the world after the United States, China, Japan and Germany. But its economy has been unusually staid in recent years, and it ranks 13th in the world on per capita GDP, with a figure just short of $44,000 in 2015, ahead of Germany and France but behind several smaller European countries, including Norway, Ireland and Denmark (see Figure 6.1).

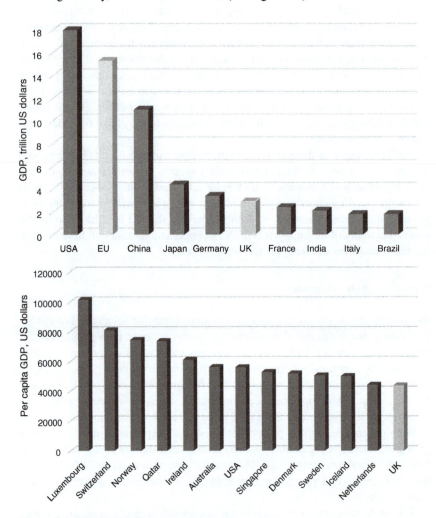

Figure 6.1   The British economy compared

Source: World Bank website at http://web.worldbank.org (retrieved March 2017). Data are for 2015.

In terms of how that GDP is generated, Britain's economic structure is typical of most other liberal democracies. Britain was once a predominantly agricultural society, but that changed with the industrial revolution, when the contribution of agriculture to economic wealth slipped as industry grew. Since the Second World War – in line with the United States, Japan and all other European countries – the contribution of services has grown as that of industry has declined. Many of Britain's factories have closed, and manufacturing jobs have been lost to cheap labour in Asia and Latin America. Where industry now accounts for just 32 per cent of Britain's GDP, and agriculture for 1 per cent of GDP, two-thirds of economic wealth is generated by services, such as retail activities, banking, insurance, financial services, tourism and entertainment.

Public spending in Britain in 2017–18 totalled £802 billion (€920/$1,040 billion). Income is derived primarily from income tax (23 per cent), value added tax (19 per cent), national insurance (17 per cent), and with the balance coming from corporation, excise and local taxes (see Figure 6.2). There are two bands of income tax: a basic rate of 20 per cent, and a higher rate of 40 per cent for those earning more than £35,000 annually. Income tax rates were significantly reduced during the Thatcher years, and the basic rate is now the lowest it has been in more than 70 years. Meanwhile, tax on the income and capital gains of companies runs at 30 per cent, the lowest rate of any of the major industrialized countries. Finally, like all European states, Britain imposes value added tax on each stage in the production and distribution of goods, the standard rate being 20 per cent.

In terms of spending, the major items in Britain – as in most advanced industrial societies – are social security, health and education, which among them account for 58 per cent of government spending. Concerns about the cost and efficiency of public services have long been at the top of the political agenda, encouraging the Blair administration, for example, to increase spending on health care, education, transport, law and order, and deprived neighbourhoods; the 2011 English urban riots suggested that there was still some way to go. It is debatable, however, whether the problem with public services is one of too little expenditure (the Labour analysis), or of too much government involvement in their management (the Conservative analysis) (Leach *et al.*, 2018).

One of the most distinctive features of the British economy is the special role of finance (Gamble, 2009: 34). When Britain was the centre of the global economy in the nineteenth century, and sterling was the dominant currency, the position of London took on new strength, and even today the financial district of London – the City – has a role in the national and international economy which gives London a dominance unmatched by the capital city of any other country. Whenever key decisions need to be taken on economic policy, the question is often 'How will it play in the City?'

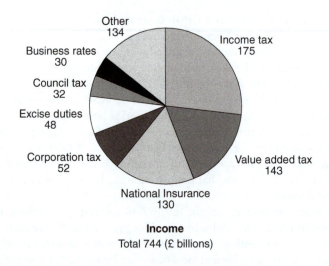

Income

Total 744 (£ billions)

Spending

Total 802 (£ billions)

Figure 6.2   The national budget

Source: HM Treasury website at www.gov.uk/government/publications/spring-budget-2017-documents/spring-budget-2017 (retrieved April 2017). Figures are in billions of pounds for 2017–18.

The key to the power of the City is that it has developed interests in a range of international commercial and banking services which do not depend for their profitability upon the state of the national economy (Roberts, 2008). London and New York, according to one report, are the only two genuinely global financial centres in the world, and – in terms of factors such as availability of skilled personnel, access to international financial markets and access to customers – have extended their competitive advantage over Frankfurt and Paris in recent years (Z/Yen Ltd, 2005). Among other things, London is the world's biggest market for gold, international insurance, international commodities and foreign exchange, it has the world's third largest stock market when measured by value, it has nearly half the global foreign equity market, and one-fifth of international bank lending is arranged in the City. But the changed relationship with the EU promises to undermine many of London's advantages.

Perhaps the most notable change that has come to the British economy in recent decades has been in the structure of business. Nationalization and the expansion of the welfare state by the postwar Labour government greatly increased both taxation and the role of the state in the marketplace, an approach that initially brought benefits to a country exhausted by war, but that over the longer term created an atmosphere in which inefficient state-owned monopolies reduced choice and stifled enterprise. The privatization undertaken by the Thatcher administration in the 1980s significantly cut back on the presence of the state in the marketplace, and helped revitalize the entrepreneurial potential of British business. There are now nearly four million businesses in the UK, and – as they once were – many of them are world-ranking. The *Financial Times* FT Global 500 survey of the world's 500 biggest companies in 2015 found that 32 were UK-based, and its Europe 500 survey of Europe's biggest companies found that 123 were UK-based. They included HSBC, BP, GlaxoSmithKline, Vodafone, SabMiller, Lloyds Banking Group, Diageo, Prudential, Barclays Bank, Rio Tinto and BT Group.

The British corporate world has seen an active programme of joint ventures, mergers and overseas acquisitions, reaching a peak in 2016 with more than $280 billion of spending, the most since records began being kept in 1969. Since the headline-making $200-billion takeover by Vodafone of the German company Mannesmann in 1999, there have been record levels of mergers and acquisitions in Britain involving foreign companies: when ranked by value, Britain is second only to the United States as a target. Prime examples in recent years have included the 2006 takeover of airports operator BAA by the Spanish company Ferrovial, the 2010 purchase of Cadbury by Kraft Foods, and the 2016 takeover by Anheuser-Busch InBev of SABMiller for £79 billion, creating the world's biggest brewing company. But doubts were cast on the future by the Brexit decision, which promised to make the UK a less attractive target for mergers and acquisitions.

Most of the key indicators suggest that the British economy had been doing well until the Brexit referendum (see Figure 6.3):

- After running at a lower rate than that of its EU partners in the 1970s and 1980s, GDP in Britain in the 1990s grew at the same rate as in the EU and the G7 group of countries, was growing faster than France and Italy in 2005–07, and – following recovery from the twin effects of the global financial crisis and the eurozone crisis – was in line with most western European countries in 2016 before falling after the referendum.
- The unemployment rate – after hovering in the range of 2–4 per cent between 1945 and 1975, then climbing to a peak of 11 per cent in 1985–86 – was back down in 2006–07 to about 5 per cent, a level it retained even after the global financial crisis.
- Inflation peaked in 1980 at 21 per cent, fell to 3–5 per cent in the mid-1980s, rose again to 10 per cent in 1991, and has since steadied in the range of 1–3 per cent. By almost any standards, and compared to the United States and all the other major EU states, Britain is an expensive place to live (see Box 6.1).
- After sitting for many years at about $1.50, the pound took a steep fall following the Brexit vote, losing about 20 per cent of its value and reaching levels not seen since the mid-1980s. This was good for exporters (whose products were thus cheaper) and for visiting tourists, but it greatly decreased the overseas purchasing power of British consumers and businesses.

Overall, and the effects of the global financial crisis aside, questions remain about Britain's productivity, there are concerns about the low rate of personal savings, and key public services are underperforming. Critics charge that too many barriers remain to the entrepreneurial spirit in Britain, made worse by the institution of austerity policies designed to pull Britain out of the problems spurred by the global financial crisis. They also argue that while the relative decline of productivity may have ended, the British marketplace is still not as free as those of the United States and Germany. It will take time to see the long-term economic effects of Brexit, but given the extent to which Britain is invested in the EU, and vice versa, business may continue without significant change.

From Hands-off to Hands-on, and Back Again

All economies are mixed, meaning that private and public enterprises coexist, often interacting and sometimes competing with one another. Economies differ relatively only to the extent to which the government intervenes in the

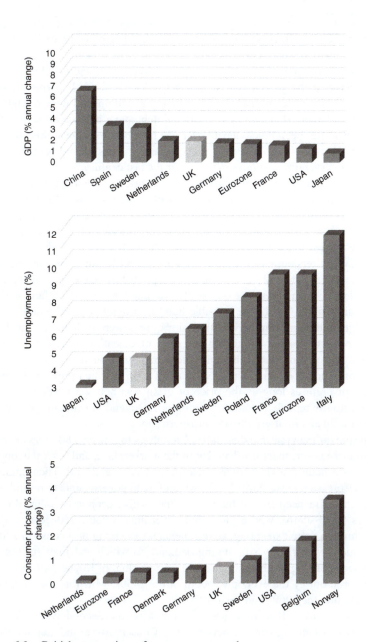

Figure 6.3   British economic performance compared

Source: *The Economist*, early 2017, various issues. Figures are for 2016.

marketplace through regulation, taxes, subsidies, borrowing, benefits and tariffs. The levels of intervention are determined mainly by the extent to which services and programmes are provided by government, and to which there is agreement that the government should help those in need. In terms of policy goals, the ideal is a combination of low inflation and unemployment, high productivity, a balanced budget, a low national debt and a balance of payments on trade. There has been much debate over just how best to achieve this combination, and Britain – like most capitalist economies – has moved back and forth between intervention and *laissez-faire* over the last century.

In 1776, the Scottish philosopher and political economist Adam Smith (1723–90) published his seminal *The Wealth of Nations*, in which he argued against the mercantilist philosophy of governments intervening to promote exports and to limit imports, instead supporting the idea of trade and competition. He argued that a market economy left to itself, while not always perfect, had a natural tendency to promote economic equilibrium (a balance between supply and demand), and – by encouraging capitalists to make and sell the goods demanded by the marketplace – it would promote the general welfare, with the individual worker 'led by an invisible hand to promote an end which was no part of his intention' (Smith, 2008). Smith's views were influential, but British governments of the late eighteenth and early nineteenth centuries were deeply conservative, and protected the domestic economy through tariffs on a variety of imports, notably grain. The Corn Law of 1816 – which prevented imports of foreign grain as long as the price of grain was below a particular level – was eventually repealed in 1846, helping bring an end to economic depression and sparking an era of growth and prosperity for Britain.

The prevailing view in industrialized countries for the next 80 years or so was to minimize government involvement in the marketplace, and to treat economic cycles as a natural and uncontrollable part of economic life. Then came the Great Depression in the early 1930s, which forced governments to rethink their approach. Influenced by the theories of the British economist John Maynard Keynes (1883–1946), who argued that governments could reduce unemployment through deficit spending, governments for the main part chose to address economic downturns by stimulating demand, to which end they cut taxes or increased spending on the public sector. The wisdom of Keynesianism seemed to be borne out by the economic boom of the 1950s, which in some countries extended into the 1960s and early 1970s.

The keyword in British economic policy after the Second World War was consensus: a tacit agreement between the Conservatives and Labour that – whichever was in power – they would work to maintain welfare, full employment and a mix of private and public ownership, and would agree on policies through compromise involving discussions between government and interest groups, particularly unions. There were in fact many disagreements over policy, so the existence of the consensus is debatable. But Britain nevertheless emerged from the brief era of austerity that followed the war, and in the 1950s enjoyed new prosperity, an era of mass consumption and a growth in productivity and exports. Over the short term, at least, government intervention seemed both wise and productive.

By the 1960s, however, Britain was in trouble, and the words 'British disease' were often on the lips of economic and political analysts. Whether the disease was a real set of economic trends, or simply the construct of the press and popular opinion, is a debatable point, but there were clearly many critical problems afflicting the British economy, including an overdependence on consultation as a method of governance, a welfare system that was proving expensive and making too many people dependent upon the state, a large public sector that had created inefficient state monopolies, a declining position in world trade, a relative decline in productivity, a declining trade surplus, little incentive for technological innovation, and – for social conservatives – a moral decline reflected in the rise of a counterculture, a conspiracy to rebel, a weakening of 'family values', an increase in the incidence of crime and the compromising of 'traditional' notions of law and order.

Many of the studies of British politics and economics between the 1960s and the 1990s bemoaned the 'decline' of Britain. On the political front, the concern was that the political system was not as responsive or efficient as it might have been, and that British influence in the world was waning. On the economic front, commentators worried about falling productivity and Britain's failure to rise to the new business challenges posed by West Germany and Japan. Their arguments seemed to be supported by the data: in 1900, Britain managed the global financial and trading system, it had the highest per capita GDP in the world and by far the largest share of the world's manufactured exports (a remarkable 35 per cent), its share of world exports equalled that of the United States, and British worker productivity was second only to that of the United States (and 150 per cent greater than the level in France) (Booth, 2001: 4). By 1973, however, Britain had dropped to fourth place on every list.

What most commentators failed to note in their analysis of its changing fortunes was that (a) Britain's global economic stature was bound to change, given the end of empire, the costs of two world wars and the accelerating growth of emerging economic powers such as the United States and Japan; (b) much of the decline could simply be attributed to other countries catching up with Britain, which had transferred resources out of agriculture much earlier than most of its competitors (Booth, 2001: 42); (c) the decline was almost entirely relative, and

Illustration 6.1   Urban decay

This abandoned terraced housing near Newcastle in the north of England is symbolic of
the economic change that has come to Britain in recent decades, with older industrial areas
declining (but recently undergoing a resurgence), and the wealth differential between north
and south becoming more obvious. These were problems that fed in to the Brexit decision.

the absolute figures showed large improvements in Britain's productivity and
its quality of life; and (d) the decline was not general, and Britain continued to
dominate and prosper in many economic sectors.

But Margaret Thatcher was one of those who – at the time – supported the
popular view of decline, and upon becoming leader of the Conservative Party
in 1975 she argued that major changes were needed if Britain's problems were
to be addressed. Her philosophy included the promotion of an enterprise culture
through a reduction in the size of the public sector, the reduction or removal
of government regulations on business, the privatization of many previously
state-owned industries and services (such as British Telecom, Jaguar, British
Petroleum, British Airways and the British Airports Authority), a freeing of the
labour market through the curbing of trade union power, and the use of monetarist economic policies aimed at reducing the increase in money supply so as
to reduce inflation and cutting government expenditure so as to reduce public
borrowing.

The reduction of taxes was designed to put more money in the pockets of British consumers, and thereby to promote savings, investment and entrepreneurial activity. At one time in the 1960s, the top rate of income tax (known as supertax) had stood at a remarkable 95 per cent, giving wealthy Britons little encouragement to start new businesses and new jobs, and creating a new class of tax exiles who left the country for parts of the world with lower tax rates. Under Thatcher, the top rate of income tax was reduced to 40 per cent and the basic rate fixed at 35 per cent. Many new businesses were started, and while many failed there was an average net increase of 500 new firms every week in Britain in the early 1980s, peaking at nearly 900 per week in 1987, and the number of self-employed grew from 7 per cent of the labour force to 11 per cent (Riddell, 1989: 53, 72, 75).

Thatcher's economic policies were typical of the trend among Western post-industrial countries since the early 1980s to reduce the level of government intervention in the marketplace. Support for Keynesianism declined, as support grew for the monetarist philosophy of Milton Friedman and the Chicago School of economists, who argued that the role of government should be to promote the supply of labour and capital in order to encourage economic growth. However, critics charged that such policies undermined key principles of the welfare state, and that they failed to take adequate note of the problems of the underclass.

Whether as a result of such policies, or for a more complex set of reasons, there is little doubt that there has been an aggregate improvement both in British economic health and in the attitudes of business towards customers. Postwar per capita GDP has grown in tandem with that of the United States, Germany, France and Japan; the distribution of wealth has broadened with the rise of the middle class; and the overall quality of life when measured by indicators such as infant mortality, life expectancy and access to education has improved dramatically. Britain has one of the freest economies in the world (when measured by such factors as personal choice, freedom to compete, and the protection of person and property), it is one of the least corrupt societies in the world, and – at least until Brexit – it was both an aggressive source of, and attractive magnet for, foreign investment. Class distinctions declined as the middle class grew, and competition helped improve the choices available to consumers and the quality of service provided by retailers.

Writing at the end of the last century, Middleton (2000: 25) concluded that almost all the key indicators suggested that Britain's economy, despite its many problems in the 1960s and 1970s, had kept pace over the long term with its competitors, and had 'delivered unparalleled and sustained improvements in living standards and personal economic security for the majority of its people over the past half-century'. Booth (2001: 6, 88ff.) argued that Britons were far better off at the end of the twentieth century than at the beginning, that judgements on the performance of British manufacturing trade were too harsh, that many historians were now prepared to argue that the economic weaknesses of the later twentieth century were exaggerated, and that many of the problems that caused so much concern in Britain were evident in other developed economies as well. And yet many questions remain about the economic problems that Britain continues to face, the global financial crisis notwithstanding. There are clearly remaining structural problems at work, at least one of which has been the mixed views of Britons about the place of business in public life.

This is ironic for a country where the creativity of industrialists and inventors had first driven the industrial revolution of the eighteenth and nineteenth centuries, then underpinned the commercial revolution of the twentieth century. Attitudes in Britain stand in stark contrast to those in the United States, where some of the best-known names in public life have been entrepreneurs, ranging from the Rockefellers, DuPonts, Disneys and Waltons of the past to the more recent likes of Bill Gates, Steve Jobs, Mark Zuckerberg and Jeff Bezos. And yet the history of British business is peppered with names of comparable stature, including Cecil Rhodes (founder of the De Beers diamond corporation), William Lever (whose company became the foundation of Unilever), the Cadbury and Rowntree families of chocolate fame, Charles Rolls and Henry Royce, Jesse Boot (whose name lives on in Boots, the national chain of chemists), W.H. Smith (founder of the chain of news and stationery stores of the same name), Michael Marks and Tom Spencer (founders of the chain of clothing and food stores) and William Morris, later Lord Nuffield (one of the founders of the British automobile industry).

Americans admire those prepared to work hard to build new enterprises and create opportunities, despite recent scandals in the United States that have tainted the reputation of corporate leaders and reduced admissions to post-graduate business schools. For their part, most Britons still do not particularly admire the business profession, and despite the economic freedom they enjoy the British are still less likely to start up a new business than their counterparts in most other industrialized countries. There are signs, however, that attitudes may be changing, and the owners and operators of large businesses are becoming increasingly prominent in public life, if not necessarily admired.

A prime example of the rise of the modern British business celebrity is offered by Sir Richard Branson, whose Virgin business empire has grown to include many different interests. Virgin began in the late 1960s as a cut-price record store in London. Branson then moved into the recording industry, becoming known more widely for the launch of the low-cost airline Virgin Atlantic, and expanding to areas as diverse as fashion, soft drinks, publishing, property, hotels, cinemas and even railway services. Virgin Atlantic has been in a struggle

---

Box 6.1   The rising cost of living

By almost any measure, and by comparison to other wealthy liberal democracies, Britain has become an expensive place in which to live. Making generalizations is always dangerous, to be sure, because the cost of living varies from one part of any given country to another (capital cities and their surrounding regions usually being the most expensive, in part because they are also often the most popular tourist destinations), and from one commodity to another. But comparative studies typically place Britain at the top of the league tables, thanks mainly to a combination of declining household incomes and increases in the cost of housing, energy, transport and food. The problem prompted Labour leader Ed Miliband in February 2011 to warn of a 'quiet crisis' unfolding in British households, with long-term changes in the British economy meaning that people were often 'working harder for less', leading to the prospect of a crisis as the rising cost of living outstripped wage rises for people on low and middle incomes.

London is particularly notorious for being one of the most expensive cities in the world in which to live and work, or simply to visit as an outsider. The international human resources and financial company Mercer publishes a regular annual survey of the cost of living in major cities. This found that London ranked 18th in the world in 2011, rising to 8th in the world by 2016, and topped in Europe only by Zurich, Geneva, and Reykjavik (see Mercer website at www.imercer.com). It should also be noted that the Mercer rankings look only at costs for expatriate residents, when the costs for local residents and tourists are often quite different.

More revealing as an indicator of relative costs are the concerns among younger Britons about how difficult it is to take their first step on the property ladder because of the inflated costs of houses and apartments, and the concerns among British consumers about the rising costs of food and of transport. Your author can also attest to the problem in an entirely unscientific manner; while the dollar–pound exchange rate in the lead-up to the Brexit vote was about $1.50 to £1, the effective exchange rate was more like $1 to £1 in the sense that – as a general rule – the cost of commodities or services were approximately the same in numbers on both sides of the Atlantic; in other words, something that cost $50 in the US would cost £50 in the UK, meaning that it was in effect 50 per cent more expensive in Britain than in the United States. Meanwhile, salaries in the United States were generally higher for similar jobs than they were in Britain. Median household income in Britain compares favourably with its larger European neighbours (see Figure 6.4), but this does not account for the differences in the cost of living, and thus while median income in France and Germany may be lower, that income generally goes further.

---

against British Airways in its attempt to capture a greater share of the transatlantic air-travel market through an alliance with American Airlines. Branson's ventures have not always been successful, but a flair for publicity has made him a well-known figure, contributing to a reassessment of public attitudes towards business and of business as a career option.

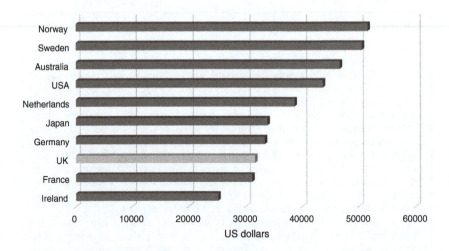

Figure 6.4   Median household income compared

Source: Gallup data quoted by Phelps and Crabtree (2013). Aggregated figures for 2006–12.

Despite criticism that the Thatcher administration failed to take care of the needs of the underclass, and despite continued problems with poverty, a growing income gap between rich and poor, and homelessness (see Box 3.1 in Chapter 3), the free-market philosophy had become so popular and institutionalized by the time Thatcher left office that when Tony Blair became leader of the Labour Party in 1994 he set about 'modernizing' the party and committing it to the maintenance of some of the more popular aspects of Thatcherism, most notably privatization. Indeed, many of the elements of the Labour manifesto as it went into the 1997 general election sounded more conservative than socialist. They included a balanced budget, greater independence for the Bank of England, efforts to reduce welfare dependency, promotion of the work ethic, close ties to business and a rejection of special deals for unions. In spite of the improvements in the quality of British life, debates continue about the areas in which Britain still lags behind its European counterparts.

Of particular concern in recent years has been the declining quality of public services. The British once took great pride in the merits of their transport network (notably the railway system), the National Health Service (NHS), the education system and the police force, but recent decades have seen growing problems in almost all these areas. The quality of the transport system has

Illustration 6.2   Public transport

High-speed trains await their passengers at St Pancras International station, London. Britain was the pioneer of railways, and yet it has fallen behind its European neighbours in the provision of both regular and high-speed services, a failing that exemplifies broader problems with the state of its public services.

declined as railways have become more inefficient, with public faith undermined by frequent delays and cancellations of service, and by a worrying number of fatal accidents. Faith in the NHS has been shaken by how long patients often have to wait for non-essential surgery. Concerns have been raised about the education system as comparative studies have found British pupils lagging behind their counterparts in several other industrialized countries. Respect for the police has been undermined by charges of racism in several police forces, notably the London force.

The Blair administration increased spending on public services in response to the concerns, but critics continued to argue that the problem was not so much a lack of spending as too much government control and inefficient management. Critics argued that there was too much resistance in Britain to choice in both health care and education, and that the idea of running health care on a private or semi-private basis – or of filtering children into different educational streams according to their ability or desires – did not have enough political or public support to prompt the kinds of changes needed to make the provision of services more efficient. In this respect, Britain was clearly on a different path from that of most of its European neighbours.

It is not just over the question of choice in public services that Britons differ, but also over the question of personal wealth and financial independence. Conspicuous consumption is an idea that has come quite late to the British, to some extent because of the residual effects of 'going without' during and after the Second World War, but also because of a preference since then for allowing the state to provide many basic services rather than opting for private alternatives. Most Britons prefer public health care to private health care, look to the state to provide social security rather than building their own retirement plans, and depend on state education for their children rather than private education. Among the effects of these attitudes is that Britons save little (typically less than 5 per cent of household disposable income, half the rate in Germany and one-third of the rate in France), and also invest relatively little.

The global financial crisis that broke in 2007 brought a shift both in the direction of British economic fortunes and in the debates about where the future should lead. The crisis had its origins in the United States, where banks and financial companies – encouraged by weak financial regulations and growing home prices – lent to low-income homebuyers, and later turned the loans into securities that could be sold off, earning large profits while also passing on the risk. Many British banks and financial institutions participated in the sales, so that many of the risks ended up being imported into Britain. When the US housing bubble burst, the value of assets held by banks and financial institutions fell, and many either went bankrupt or turned to the government for help. Meanwhile, stock prices fell, many people lost their jobs, and shrinking consumer demand led to financial woes for business. The British government could not respond in isolation, given the multinational nature of the problem, and faced many of the same problems as its neighbours. The key effect was a need to impose significant cuts in spending, but while these guided Britain through the immediate crisis, they also created social pressures that fed in to criticism of globalization, which in turn helped drive many in 2016 to vote against continued membership of the EU.

Britain in the Global Economy

As an island state whose leaders and entrepreneurs have long understood the need for trade and the opportunities it offers, Britain has traditionally been an outward-looking society. It continues to be a major actor in world trade today: it has less than 1 per cent of the world's population but accounts for 3 per cent of world exports of merchandise and more than 7 per cent of world exports of services (it is the second largest such exporter after the United States). The value of its exports is equivalent to nearly 30 per cent of GDP, and it has the highest ratio of inward and outward investment of any major economy (all figures for 2015 from the World Trade Organization website, www.wto.org). It is also a leading member of all the main international trading and economic organizations, including the G7 group of countries, the World Trade Organization (WTO) and the Organisation for Economic Co-operation and Development (OECD).

British exports and imports have grown in tandem in recent years (although usually with an annual deficit), nearly tripling from a combined value of about $560 billion in 1994 to about $1.63 trillion in 2015. Finished manufactured goods such as machinery, equipment, road vehicles and consumer goods make up nearly half of all exports, services account for about a quarter, intermediate goods such as chemicals, pharmaceuticals and metals account for about 20 per cent, and the balance is made up of food, drink, tobacco and raw materials, notably oil – Britain was once a major exporter of oil, although its reserves are rapidly running out. The EU is by far its biggest trading partner, accounting for about 44 per cent of exports and 53 per cent of imports. Asia, the Middle East and Australasia account for about 20 per cent of British trade, and the United States for about 12 per cent (see Tables 6.1 and 6.2).

One of the most notable features of the British economy is the volume of inward and outward foreign investment. In recent years it has been the second largest target for foreign investment after the United States (briefly, in 2005, becoming the largest target in the world and attracting more than the United States and Germany combined), although investments have fallen off in the wake of the global financial crisis and the rise of interest in China; by 2010 Britain had fallen to seventh place, behind even Belgium and Australia, and by 2015 it had fallen two more places. As the effects of the global financial crisis made themselves felt, Britain fell in the rankings of sources of external investment, from second to the United States in 2007 (when it invested more than $270 billion overseas) to 49th in the world in 2015 (figures from the UN Conference on Trade and Development (UNCTAD) website at www.unctad. org). Its attractions as a target of investment can be explained in parts by its low levels of corporation tax, but American and Japanese companies are also attracted to Britain because of the convenience of using English, which has become the international language of commerce. It will lose many of those attractions outside the EU, but how exactly the post-EU flows of investment will change remain to be seen.

Table 6.1   Britain's major imports and exports

Imports	%	Exports	%
Machinery	12.7	Machinery	14.7
Road vehicles	11.7	Road vehicles	12.6
Gems, precious metals	11.1	Pharmaceuticals	8.0
Electrical machinery	9.2	Gems, precious metals	6.7
Mineral fuels and oil	6.2	Electrical machinery	6.6
Pharmaceuticals	5.2	Mineral fuels and oil	6.4
Aircraft, spacecraft	2.8	Aircraft, spacecraft	5.1
Technical, medical apparatus	4.2	Technical, medical apparatus	4.2
Plastics	2.7	Plastics	2.7
Furniture, bedding, lighting	1.7	Organic chemicals	2.6

Source: International Monetary Fund World Economic Outlook Database at www.inf.org.
Ranked by value. Figures are for 2016.

Britain traded with other parts of Europe centuries ago, and trade was at the heart of the development of the British Empire in the seventeenth century when the first settlements were made in North America and the Caribbean, and the first trading stations opened in India. By 1700, Britain was already a dominating force in world manufactured trade, and in the commercial and financial services – and the non-financial services such as merchanting and brokering – that supported that trade. It imported primarily food and raw materials, and exported a select range of so-called export staples: machinery and transport equipment, cotton and wool textiles, iron and steel, and coal (Booth, 2001: 53). By 1900, Britain was the manager of the international financial and trading system, its corporations and manufactures dominated that system, and it had invested heavily in emerging overseas markets.

However, the early signs of Britain's eclipse had already begun to emerge. The heavy reliance on food imports meant that insufficient investment was made in the industrial sector, US industry expanded rapidly during the late nineteenth century and German manufacturing power was on the rise. British industrial competitiveness fell dramatically during the First World War and never fully recovered, while demand for export staples grew only slowly, undermined by growing competitiveness from Japan and the United States and then hit by the market crash of 1929 and the depression that followed. Furthermore, Britain had entered the war as a creditor nation but emerged as a debtor (Booth, 2001: 59). From the early 1930s to the late 1950s, British trade was heavily orientated towards the Empire, and the use of sterling for international transactions within this group created an informal sterling area.

The economic recovery of the later 1930s, which allowed Britain once again to become a major creditor nation, was dealt another heavy blow by the

Table 6.2 Britain's major trading partners

Imports		Exports	
EU	£291 billion (53%)	EU	£230 billion (44%)
Germany	70	Germany	48
Netherlands	37	France	33
France	36	Netherlands	32
Spain	25	Ireland	26
Belgium	23	Italy	18
Non-EU	£256 billion (47%)	Non-EU	£287 billion (56%)
USA	59	USA	96
China	38	Switzerland	21
Norway	14	China	17
Switzerland	13	Gulf Arabian	16
Japan	10	Japan	11

Source: Office for National Statistics at http://visual.ons.gov.uk/uk-trade-partners. Data for 2015.

Second World War. The wartime economy was good for manufacturing and agriculture, but Britain's overseas assets were quickly used up, exports fell, and Britain had to borrow so much to conduct the war that it came out almost bankrupt. (It finally finished paying off its wartime debt to the United States in December 2006.) In 1944, the United States and Britain led an international conference at Bretton Woods at which plans were made for the postwar international economy. Agreement was reached on the goals of stable monetary relations, freely convertible currencies, expanded trade and economic growth, and the establishment of the dollar as the new international reserve currency.

At first the system seemed to work and Britain benefited from rapidly growing world trade, although its exports grew more slowly than those of other industrialized countries. Many different theories have been offered to explain this, including an excessive commitment to the sterling area, where markets were growing only slowly, and disproportionately high spending on defence in order to prove British independence and its continuing status as a world power (Booth, 2001: 74–75). Whatever the reasons, the British share of global exports was cut by two-thirds between 1950 and 1973, and there was a similar fall in the British share of world trade in services.

Britain today is heavily invested in the fortunes of the global economy, as was made all-too clear by the effects of the global financial crisis. It depends heavily for its economic wellbeing on inward investment, many of its biggest industries are foreign-owned, and it is heavily dependent on imports (Leach *et al.*, 2018). As a result, one of the key pressures on the British economy is globalization: the growing interdependence of states, organizations, processes and people, with a resulting reduction in the freedom of national governments to make economic policy choices. At the same time, Britain has also been subject to the forces of Europeanization: the alignment of laws and policies throughout the EU.

The Economic Implications of Europe

Britain's decision to leave the EU has considerable economic implications, although just how events will evolve over the next few years (assuming Britain actually leaves the EU) is hard to predict. The British economy is intimately connected to the broader EU economy through trade, investments and the EU laws that impact the economies of the member states, and the cases of Switzerland and Norway show that even those European countries that have remained outside the EU have had to shape their economic policies around the influences of being connected to one of the two wealthiest marketplaces in the world. If it leaves the EU, Britain will have to make many economic changes, and market forces will mean an additional set of changes whose consequences remain to be seen (for a survey of the EU, see McCormick, 2017).

When six European countries launched an experiment in international integration in 1952 by merging their coal and steel industries, and then in 1958 by reaching agreement on the creation of a common market, Britain still saw its economic interests as lying primarily outside Europe; it attempted to rebuild its economy by concentrating on the sterling area, and trying to retain its status as a world power. By the end of the 1950s, however, the government of Harold Macmillan had begun to realize that it would be in British interests to join the European Economic Community (EEC); the Community was enjoying fast growth and improved living standards, and its industrial strength was underpinned by growth in trade among its members. After two false starts (when its application was vetoed by Charles de Gaulle), Britain finally joined the EEC in 1973, just 18 months after the United States took the dollar off the gold standard, signalling the end of the Bretton Woods system and tolling the death knell for the sterling area. Although the hope for a new boost for British trade did not at first materialize, membership of the Community (now the EU) soon became the major influence on Britain's place in the global trading system.

The EU may have more than two dozen national members, but instead of a group of independent national economies (to the extent that any economy can really be independent), there is now a federalized economy in Europe, or one where the national and the EU economies have separate and independent powers but neither level operates without the other. The most significant effect of European integration on economic activity has been the creation of a single European market in which there is all but uncontrolled movement of people, money, goods and services, and where many of the barriers that once existed among EU member states have gone. Those barriers took three main forms.

First, there were physical barriers such as customs and border checks, which allowed member states to control the movement of people, collect sales and excise taxes, enforce different health standards, control banned products, and prevent the spread of animal and plant diseases. Member states particularly wanted to control illegal immigration and the movement of terrorists and other undesirables. Under the Schengen Agreement, opened for signature in 1985, a computerized database of undesirables was developed, which helped address many political concerns. With effect from March 1995, virtually all border controls were finally eliminated by the signatories to Schengen, and the European Police Office (Europol) was created to help collect information and improve cooperation. Britain, citing its special concerns as an island state, opted only into selected elements of Schengen, so its borders have not been as open as those of other EU member states.

Second, there were fiscal barriers, the most important of which were different levels of indirect taxation (such as VAT, or value added tax), which caused distortion of competition and artificial price differences, posing a handicap to trade. There were also different levels of excise duties, driven mostly by varying levels of concern about human health. In the 1980s, for example, Spanish smokers paid half as much tax on cigarettes as those in France, a quarter of the rate in Ireland, and one-sixth of the rate in Denmark. Agreement was reached in the 1990s on a minimum rate of 15 per cent VAT, and on working towards a single rate of VAT, or at least variations within a very narrow band. Much more controversial has been the suggestion that the EU harmonize tax rates in other areas, notably corporation tax or the setting of withholding tax on savings. Tax harmonization is seen by many as the first step towards the development of EU authority over the setting of income tax, and while Britain led the resistance to this, giving more control over fiscal policy to the European Central Bank has been an essential element of efforts to rescue the euro.

Finally, there were technical barriers, including different regulations and standards based on personal safety, food safety, public health and environmental protection. Many of these regulations were in the interests of consumer safety, and so were welcomed, but others amounted to protectionism. The European Commission tried to develop EU standards and encouraged member states to conform, but this was a time-consuming and tedious task, and did little to discourage the common image of interfering Eurocrats. Several breakthroughs helped clear the political hurdles, notably a 1979 decision by the European Court of Justice establishing that a member state could not block imports from another member state on the basis of local health regulations. Member states have since had to accept products from other states that meet domestic technical standards. Progress has been made on removing technical barriers to the single market in a wide variety of areas, from safety and operating standards for road vehicles to the content of processed food.

By reducing or eliminating these barriers, the Single European Act remains one of the most radical of all the steps taken in the process of European integration since it made its first halting steps in the 1950s. Completion of the single market not only accelerated the process of economic integration, but it has also changed the lives of every European, making economic integration more real even to the most diehard British Eurosceptics. The changes it has brought include the following:

- With a few exceptions, residents of Britain could live and work in any other EU member state, open a bank account, take out a mortgage, transfer unlimited amounts of capital, and even vote in local and European elections. At the same time, the single market led to a growth of immigration into Britain from other EU member states, notably those in Eastern Europe.
- The single market helped remove many of the barriers that British corporations once faced, and increased the number of consumers they could reach. Combined with privatization programmes in many countries and the general trend towards globalization, it increased the number of opportunities for acquisitions, joint ventures and corporate mergers, both within the EU and between European and non-European corporations. The EU mergers and acquisitions market is now bigger than that of the United States, and – as noted earlier – Britain had the biggest such market in the EU.
- Because integrated infrastructure – such as transport, energy and communications networks – is an important element in the successful operation of markets, the EU has promoted the development of so-called Trans-European Networks (TENs). Helped by the enormous growth in European tourism (which has been particularly important to Britain, one of Europe's biggest tourist destinations), and by the revitalization of rail transport as a cost-efficient and environmentally friendly alternative to road and air transport, the EU has been developing a high-speed train network connecting Europe's major cities. Key elements in this have been the opening of the Channel Tunnel, and investment in British railway tracks to bring them up to the quality of those in France and Germany.

A critical change spearheaded by Britain was the loosening of regulations on air transport. Most European countries once had state-owned national carriers that had a national monopoly over most of the international routes they flew, so air transport was highly regulated and expensive to consumers. When the Thatcher administration launched a liberalization programme in the mid-1980s that led to the privatization of British Airways in 1987, and negotiated bilateral agreements with other EU member states, the lid was taken off the air-transport market. Big carriers took over smaller ones, national carriers created international alliances, new cut-price operators such as Ryanair and easyJet were founded, and consumers were given greater choice and could fly more cheaply than before.

Box 6.2   The economic implications of Brexit

The biggest question mark hanging over the British economy as this book went to press concerned the impact of Brexit. Given the ties that bind Britain to the EU, the effects of leaving are likely to be substantial, but whether they will free the British economy to seek new opportunities globally (as supporters of Brexit hope) or push Britain to the margins of the enormous EU marketplace (as opponents of Brexit worry) remains to be seen.

Several core realities need to be taken into account:

- Britain does most of its trade (53 per cent in 2015) with the rest of the EU.
- Britain has been tied for decades into the EU single market, with rights to free movement of people, money, goods and services, all of which will be reduced once Britain leaves the EU.
- Many of the regulations that govern the behaviour of British industry come out of European Union law rather than domestic law. Unravelling these ties will not be quick or easy.
- Britain is part of the free trade area of the EU, meaning not only that it will have to negotiate a new trade agreement with the EU prior to leaving, but also that it will no longer be part of the trading behemoth that is the EU, and will have to negotiate new and separate agreements with all its trading partners.
- The EU is the dominating source of foreign investment in the UK, and the dominating target of foreign investment from the UK.
- Outside the EU, the attractions of Britain as a staging post for foreign corporations will be reduced, as will the attractions of London as a financial centre.

For its critics in Britain, the EU is too inward-looking, too protectionist, too bureaucratic and too regulated (Gamble, 2016), and the advantages of leaving include a removal of such handicaps. Outside the EU, runs the logic, Britain will have renewed access to the biggest and fastest-growing global markets, including those of Asia and Latin America. But as a member of the EU, Britain was not only part of an enormous regional marketplace, but it was also part of a global actor that increasingly made the rules for those with whom it traded, and was part of the biggest trading power in the world. It remains to be seen how Britain will fare without those advantages. It may have had the world's fifth biggest economy in 2017, but will that be enough of a base to allow it to work out its own deals, and make its own opportunities, with the USA, China, India, Japan and Brazil?

While the single market brought generally positive change to the British economy, the British showed their resistance to European integration by failing to adopt the euro. Britain had initially opted to remain out of the exchange rate mechanism (ERM) that was set up in 1979 as a prelude to the creation of the single currency and required that member governments take the action necessary to keep their currencies stable relative to each other. It then joined in October 1990 against a backdrop of economic recession in Western Europe, and found that the high interest rates needed to keep the pound within the agreed range of exchange rates hurt exports and contributed to unemployment. On 16 September 1992 – otherwise known as Black Wednesday – Britain was forced out of the ERM and the pound was devalued (for details, see Leach *et al.*, 2018). The economy began an almost immediate recovery, a fact which played into the hands of opponents of British membership of the single currency.

Upon winning office in 1997 the Blair administration argued that it would not take Britain into the single currency without a positive vote in a national referendum, which would be held after the next election, should Labour win. Labour did indeed win the 2001 election, but it quickly became clear that Blair was reluctant to move too quickly, instead launching a campaign to convince British voters of the virtues of joining the euro. The euro itself was introduced in January 2002, and – after a brief transitional phase – fully replaced the national currencies of 12 of the 15 EU member states in March 2002. Britain did not join, but Gordon Brown, then Chancellor of the Exchequer (Finance Minister), instead set several 'economic tests' for British membership of the euro, focused on the likely effects of joining on conditions for business, the financial services industry and jobs.

Those who thought that British public opinion might turn more in favour of the euro once it was adopted by other EU states, and once British travellers had become accustomed to using it, were disappointed by polls that showed a hardening of opposition. Their arguments were undermined as the pound gained strength, as it became clear that the British economy was performing well outside the eurozone, and as a number of countries that had adopted the euro continued to experience poor numbers on inflation, unemployment and growth. The credibility of the euro was also undermined by the 'growth and stability pact' agreed by European leaders prior to the launch of the euro, and designed to ensure investor confidence. Under the pact, member states agreed to control their budget deficits, limiting them to less than 3 per cent of GDP. However, several countries – including France, Germany and Portugal – experienced difficulties meeting these targets.

The breaking of the eurozone crisis in October 2009 put all talk of Britain even thinking about adopting the euro on the back burner. The crisis began in Greece, which had been allowed to join the eurozone in 2001 in spite of being unable to meet all the terms of membership, and where economic mismanagement and corruption had ensured a subsequent imbalance between spending and revenues. When the global financial crisis took hold, the Greek economy was weak and exposed, and the government was obliged to implement drastic and politically unpopular spending cuts and to raise taxes on fuel, tobacco and alcohol. But the problem was not limited to Greece; fears grew that the crisis might be contagious, leading to problems in other eurozone countries facing budgetary pressures, such as Ireland, Italy, Portugal and Spain. The crisis was a wake-up call for the entire eurozone, which had allowed movement on the single currency to go ahead in spite of the failure to give the European Central Bank many of the tools needed to manage the euro, including greater influence of the fiscal policies of the eurozone member states.

A combination of the global financial crisis, the eurozone crisis, the perceived inequality of the effects first of the economic downturn and then of the economic recovery (the south-east of England fared the changes more easily than much of the rest of the country) and the perceived costs of globalization on the British worker all ultimately combined to help the cause of those who supported an exit from the EU at the 2016 referendum. The EU, however, has learned much from the eurozone crisis, and stands to learn even more from Brexit. Reform is at the top of the EU agenda, and with the advantage of hindsight it is likely to be found that the economic costs of Britain leaving the EU outweigh the hoped-for but mainly imaginary benefits.

Further Reading

Bailey, David, Keith Cowling and Philip Tomlinson (eds) (2015) *New Perspectives on Industrial Policy for a Modern Britain* (Oxford University Press). An edited collection looking at recent changes in industrial and employment policy in Britain.

Baker, David and Pauline Schnapper (2015) *Britain and the Crisis of the European Union* (Palgrave Macmillan). A critical review of the links between recent crises in the EU and Britain, including chapters on the economic dimensions of these events.

Giudice, Gabriele, Robert Kuenzel and Tom Springbett (eds) (2012) *UK Economy: The Crisis in Perspective* (Routledge). An edited collection focusing on the impact of the global financial crisis on British economic policy.

Morphet, Janice (2013) *How Europe Shapes British Public Policy* (Policy Press). An assessment of the impact of the EU on British policy generally, including several chapters on its economic and trade influence.

Whyman, Philip and Alina Petrescu (2017) *The Economics of Brexit: A Cost-Benefit Analysis of the UK's Economic Relationship with the EU* (Palgrave Macmillan). A study of the economic impact of Brexit, including chapters on trade, investment, migration and productivity.

7

Culture and Lifestyle

Western popular culture may have a strong American accent, but – as the birthplace of the English language, and a once aggressive colonizer – Britain has played a primary role in the evolution of the culture and lifestyle that we associate with 'the West'. Its impact has been greatest in the fields of literature, popular music, film and drama, no reference to which is possible without consideration of the impact of writers such as Chaucer, Shakespeare, Shelley, Austen, Wordsworth, Tennyson, the Brontë sisters, Dickens, Hardy, Kipling, Golding and Greene, or of musicians such as the Beatles, the Rolling Stones, the Who, David Bowie, Eric Clapton, the Sex Pistols, Queen and Adele. The impact of the former has been greater thanks to the spread of the English language, and of the latter thanks to the universal following for rock music. British cinema also plays an important supporting role to the popularity of American cinema, although just how the two are different any more is difficult to say.

Britain is less well known for the visual arts and classical music, but has nonetheless had significant influence:

- It has produced artists such as Thomas Gainsborough, Joshua Reynolds, John Constable, J.M.W. Turner, William Hogarth, Francis Bacon, Lucien Freud and David Hockney, and sculptors such as Henry Moore and Barbara Hepworth, but its reputation is overwhelmed by the work of continental painters and sculptors.
- It has produced architects such as Christopher Wren, Inigo Jones, Richard Rogers and Norman Foster, and great buildings are to be found in abundance in Britain. After many years during which the wealth of prewar architecture was sullied by the frequent eyesores produced by bad postwar town planning, recent developments have begun to right some of the wrongs, and London in particular has become an architectural trendsetter.

- It has produced classical composers and musicians such as Henry Purcell, Edward Elgar, Frederick Delius, Gustav Holst, Ralph Vaughan Williams and Benjamin Britten, although few have achieved the same stature as their continental counterparts.

This chapter sets out to examine the features, personality and global impact of British culture, beginning with an overview of the definition of culture and of the dimensions and impact of the British version. It then goes into more depth on the meaning of 'Britishness', building on earlier references and discussing its impact on understanding national identity and its links with culture. It argues that the multifaceted nature of English, Scottish, Welsh and Irish culture has been further diversified by the postwar arrival of ethnic minorities, with the result that Britain today is more multicultural and multiracial than ever before, and diversity has become essential to an understanding of what makes Britain distinctive. Not all in Britain are entirely content with this, as reflected in the recent rebirth of nationalism that fed into the Brexit decision.

The chapter then examines the state of the arts in Britain, with an emphasis on the contrasting role of theatre, film, television and popular music in culture. This is followed by a discussion of the ways in which the British spend their spare time, including an examination of the undeservedly amorphous reputation of British cuisine. It ends with an examination of the role of sports and religion in national life, the former often a source of frustration because of the failure of British national teams and sporting figures so often to live up to expectations, and the latter a matter of declining influence and relevance.

Culture

For its size, Britain has had a remarkable influence on world culture, helped by the twin influences of imperialism and the role of English as the dominating global language (see Box 7.1). To be sure, the spread of English – particularly since the Second World War, and mainly as a second language – has come largely out of the popularity of American culture and the reach of American business (Crystal, 2003: 59), and more recently out of the impact of the internet, the bulk of the sites on which are in English. But it was generations of British writers who nurtured the language and made it so portable and attractive in the first place. This has made it easier for the reputations of British writers to be carried on the back of the spread of their language; there have been creative minds of equal or greater stature in many other European countries, but – unlike painters, sculptors, photographers and musicians – their impact has been greatest where they have communicated in English.

Box 7.1   English: the global language

No one knows precisely how many people in the world speak English, but it is generally recognized as the dominant global language (see Crystal, 2003), its stature based not so much on how many speak it as on who speaks it, and on how widely it is spoken as a second language. There are many more people in the world who speak Mandarin (probably 800–900 million), but most of them live in China and are relatively poor. Most estimates of the number of people who speak English range from 400 to 500 million, but they can be found in many different countries, notably the United States, Britain, Canada, the Philippines, India, Australia, New Zealand, South Africa and Nigeria. English has also become the language of political and business elites around the world, the language of international communications, technology, diplomacy, science and education, and the language most commonly used by employees of all major international organizations, and of the EU.

English is not only an official language in nearly 60 countries containing about one-third of the world's population, but English words and phrases have entered many other languages, even prompting government-sponsored attempts in France to develop French equivalents of English words and phrases that have entered daily conversation. In non-white former British colonies, the use of English has been criticized as a symbol of the colonial past, but despite attempts to restrict its use and champion local languages, it has prevailed, adopting – along the way – many new words and phrases from those subjugated by Britain, including *guru, jungle, nirvana, bungalow, jackal, karma* and *juggernaut.* Furthermore, many English words have now become virtually universal, and are recognized all over the world; they include *airport, cigarette, hotel, OK, passport, stop, police, telephone* and *weekend*.

The status of English has been good for the British economy, notably in the sale of English-language training programmes: the British Council (which promotes British culture and educational opportunities around the world) estimates that the teaching of English is one of Britain's largest sources of invisible earnings. It has also helped attract foreign students to British universities, seeking not just a British education but also the opportunity to learn or improve upon their English.

Why has English done so well? Part of the explanation lies in its longstanding role as the preferred language of international politics, diplomacy and business. It is also remarkably rich: estimates of the number of words in English range from 500,000 to 1 million, compared to about 100,000 in French. Furthermore, simple English words and phrases convey often complex meanings, in a way that no other European language can match; this has prompted German corporations to encourage their executives to learn English, which is often better for communicating technical concepts than German. Interestingly, though, there are signs that the British are starting to make more of an effort to learn other European languages, probably inspired by a combination of the increased movement of Europeans around the EU and of growing business and holiday travel by Britons to the continent. Even with Britain outside the EU, and English no longer formally an official language of the EU, it is likely to continue its growth as the lingua franca of Europe.

Despite the global significance of British culture – and of icons such as the royal family, James Bond, the Beatles, Monty Python and Harry Potter – it is, like all cultures, ultimately the product of home-grown values and experiences, not all of which can be understood by foreigners. Seen from the broad view, British culture is the result of a long and complex history in which politics, economics, religion, nationalism and the arts are all intertwined. The Second World War stands as a watershed, such that the idea of Britain can be broadly divided into two eras: the imperial glories of the prewar years (even though these 'glories' were often anything but, and their retelling has been tangled in myth and misconception), and the redefinition that has come with the postwar years, including the rise of the welfare state, the changing place of Britain in the world, the watering-down of the class system, and the increasingly multifaceted nature of British society.

During the opening decades of the twentieth century, Britain's national leaders were often individuals of global stature, its corporations reached around the world, its products could be bought almost anywhere, and its music, literature and films were at the core of what was already being seen as an emerging Western culture. Then came the Second World War, and while Winston Churchill may have summed up the feelings of a generation when he proclaimed that the struggle against Nazism was Britain's 'finest hour', the war was to fundamentally alter Britain's place in the world and the view that Britons held of themselves.

The debacle at Suez in 1956, combined with the early successes of European integration to compel the British to think less from a global perspective and more from a European one, and even ultimately to open a debate about the very identity of Britain itself: was it still a united kingdom, or was it a rusty amalgam of England, Scotland, Wales and Northern Ireland? A post-imperial melancholy set in, characterized by inward contemplation, nostalgia, conformism and arguments over everything from Britain's place in the world to relations between management and workers, economic decline, the class system, race, the monarchy, and relations with America and Europe. The tensions came to be reflected in literature, theatre and films, which moved from a celebration of British exceptionalism to a self-conscious examination of everything that seemed to be going wrong with the country.

The contrast is reflected in British films. In the late 1940s and early 1950s the Ealing comedies (named for the Ealing Studios in London) celebrated many of the stereotypical hallmarks of being British, including simplicity, community, basic decency and the ability not to take life too seriously. They were followed in the early 1960s by the bleak realism (or pessimism) of the

British New Wave, and films such as *Saturday Night and Sunday Morning* and *The Loneliness of the Long Distance Runner* emphasized isolation and social dysfunction. Since the 1990s, British cinema has stopped being so self-conscious, and filmmakers have mined the rich seam of eighteenth- and nineteenth-century domestic literature, have celebrated the experience of being middle class during a time of economic revival, have commented on the new problems and inequalities brought by the free market, or have thrown social comment to the winds and have simply set out to entertain their audiences and to make money.

At the heart of the cultural changes taking place in the 1960s and 1970s was the evolving class structure, and the greater willingness by Britons to question the assumptions made about their appropriate 'place' in the social hierarchy. Nowhere was this process more obvious than in the use of satire, which gave rise to a string of shows on radio, television and the stage in which poking fun at the class system was a central theme. A line can be drawn linking *The Goon Show* on BBC radio throughout the 1950s, to the stage show *Beyond the Fringe* in the early 1960s, to the cult television series *Monty Python's Flying Circus* (late 1960s and early 1970s), and more recent series such as *The Young Ones* (1982–83) and *Have I Got News For You* (1990–). These were examples of an emerging countercultural trend which helped the British deconstruct and poke fun at many of the stereotypes that had until then coloured the class-driven values of much popular culture.

Further changes grew out of the new ethnic diversity of Britain. As the non-white population grew from the 1950s, black and Asian culture became an increasingly important part of the national culture. White Britons had to redefine themselves according to their response to the issue of race, which made its mark through the growth of minority neighbourhoods in the bigger cities, the spreading popularity of Asian cuisine, the entrance of minority themes into literature and the cinema, and the new religious diversity of Britain. Symbolically, fish and chips may still be seen as the quintessential representative of British cuisine around the world, but chicken tikka masala is probably more popular. It traces its origins to Indian tandoori chicken, but it was developed in Britain to meet British tastes, and has become so much a part of national life that it was acclaimed in 2001 by then British Foreign Secretary Robin Cook as 'a true British national dish' and 'a perfect illustration of the way Britain absorbs and adapts external influences' (quoted in *The Guardian*, 19 April 2001).

Today, it is only older and/or more conservative Britons who recall the war, the Empire, the class system at its height, pre-European Britain, and the political, economic and social troubles of the 1960s and 1970s. The last decade has seen the emergence of newly confident and reformed cultural trends in Britain, less focused on the problems of the past than the opportunities and realities of the present. Younger Britons know and care little about the war or the Empire, Britain has been a multiracial society and a member of the EU as long as they have been alive, and (at least until recently) most enjoyed the benefits of an economy that was growing rapidly. It is telling that support for Brexit was much higher among older Britons than younger Britons; those aged 65 and older supported leaving the EU by 60 per cent to 40 per cent, while those in the 18–24 age group supported remaining by 73 per cent to 27 per cent.

The change in attitude was summed up neatly in two comments made by Americans. In 1962, former US Secretary of State Dean Acheson famously observed that Britain had lost an empire and not yet found a role. In 1999, a journalist for the *New York Times* commented that the British had 'finally stopped seeking a role and started getting a life' (quoted in *The Economist*, 6 November 1999). Unfortunately, a combination of the global financial crisis, questions about the meaning of Britain in a multiracial era, resistance to immigration, ongoing class distinctions and questions about the implications of Brexit have cast something of a pall over debates about British culture.

The Changing Identity of Britain

The task of understanding British culture is complicated by debates over the meaning of 'Britishness' (see Storry and Childs, 2017). Culture is closely tied to national identity, but as noted in Chapter 2 one of the characteristics of life in Britain is the strength of regionalism and nationalism. National identity in Britain is diluted by the superimposition of separate English, Scottish, Welsh and Northern Irish identities, a phenomenon symbolized by the national flag (the 'Union Jack'), which combines the cross of St George (for England) with those of St Andrew (for Scotland) and St Patrick (for Ireland) (Figure 7.1). The concept of 'Britishness', which was always questionable, has come under increased scrutiny in recent years.

A 'nation' is usually defined as consisting of three components: a distinctive group of people with a common language and history; a specific territory occupied by those people; and a strong bond between the people and the territory (see discussion in Anderson, 2016). There is no British nation as such, because the people who make up the United Kingdom have separate (albeit overlapping) histories and cultures, and they lack a common bond to a shared piece of territory (see Weight, 2003; Bryant, 2005). A number of developments in Britain

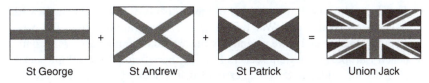

| St George | St Andrew | St Patrick | Union Jack |

Figure 7.1   The Union Jack

The British Union Flag, otherwise known as the Union Jack, dates from 1606, shortly after the Scottish King James VI succeeded to the English throne as James I and the flags bearing the crosses of St George and St Andrew were combined. The cross of St Patrick was added in 1801 following the Act of Union with Ireland. Wales is not represented in the flag because it had been united with England in 1282. No law has ever been passed to confirm the status of the flag; it has simply become the national flag through common usage. What effect the possible independence of Scotland would have on the design of the flag is unclear.

Incidentally, the old flag of Northern Ireland – a red hand inside a white star on a red cross – has strong connections with the Protestant community, and is no longer official but is still occasionally flown. The official flag of Northern Ireland is the Union Flag of the United Kingdom.

since the Second World War have emphasized the contradictions in the concept of national identity and national culture, and have challenged the meanings of the symbols of Britishness, of which four in particular stand out:

- The Empire no longer exists, but it was once one of the forces that brought Britain together, and encouraged the four nations of the United Kingdom to think of themselves as British.
- The monarchy may have lost much of its allure and some of its credibility, and is today regarded with less respect and reverence than perhaps at any time in its history, but it remains a representative of Britishness. There is significance in the fact that the present royal family traces its ancestors to both Scotland and England, and that the male heir to the throne is invested as the Prince of Wales. However, there is still much about the royal family that is more English than British.
- Britain's long-time resistance to the forces of extremism, nationalism or fascism on the continent has been diluted by the effects of European integration. British Eurosceptics fought against integration by arguing that Britain is separate from Europe, and that British distinctiveness – as symbolized, for example, by imperial weights and measures, and the pound sterling – should be preserved as a means of protecting the identity of Britain. In spite of a generational shift that has encouraged younger Britons to take a more European view than older Britons, the resistance to Europe was sufficient to ensure the vote to leave the EU.

- The shared history of the residents of the British Isles has been complicated since the Second World War by the arrival of immigrants from the New Commonwealth, and more recently by the arrival of immigrants from continental Europe, and asylum seekers from further afield. The resulting social diversity has added to the complexity of British identity. The political Right has often overtly or covertly identified 'Britishness' with 'whiteness', and the far Right has aggressively adopted (and thereby demeaned) the symbol of the British flag in its protests against multiracialism.

Even if the British themselves may have some doubts about how to define their culture and identity, it is apparently not a problem for foreigners: the tourist trade is one of the biggest long-term economic growth sectors in Britain, attracting increasing numbers of people from continental Europe, North America and Asia, most of whom come in search of the history and culture that sometimes seems so hard for the natives to tie down. Travel and tourism have been hurt by terrorism, and will be made more complicated by the

Illustration 7.1   Broadway, Worcestershire

The charm of Britain's small towns and villages is exemplified by this view of Broadway, at the heart of the Cotswolds in west-central England. Tourism – both internal and from abroad – is a major source of income for Britain, although it is also a major source of traffic and people congestion in the more popular attractions.

changed relationship with the EU, but Britain continues to hold its position among the top ten tourist destinations, bringing in nearly 35 million overseas tourists in 2015 (see Figure 7.2).

The major countries of origin of overseas visitors to Britain (in order) are the USA, Germany, France, Australia, Spain and Italy (International Passenger Survey 2013, Office for National Statistics). The majority come through London, where they often spend much or all of their time, attracted by its historical sights (such as the Tower of London, Westminster Abbey and Buckingham Palace), its museums and galleries (such as the British Museum, Madame Tussaud's, the National Gallery and the Natural History Museum), and its theatres and restaurants. Outside London, tourist attractions include cathedral towns such as Canterbury, York and Chester, historic cities such as Bath and Edinburgh and royal castles and palaces such as Windsor Castle and Hampton Court. Unfortunately, Britain is suffering the same effects from mass tourism as other European countries: overcrowding, the rise of a tourist culture at the expense of the native way of life, and rising prices. With so many tourists taking their holidays at the same time of the year, and congregating in the same places, cities like London, Canterbury, Oxford, Cambridge and Bath become nightmares of congestion during the summer season.

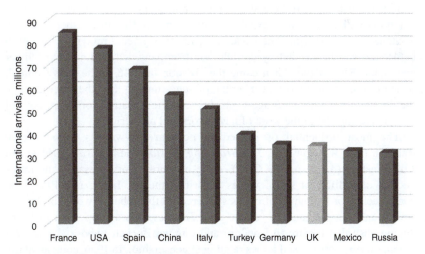

Figure 7.2   World's top ten tourist destinations

Source: UN World Tourism Organization, *World Tourism Barometer*, at www2.unwto.org (retrieved March 2017). Figures are for 2015.

The Arts

Britain's artistic heritage is both broad and deep, based on the work of countless men and women who have become well known far beyond their national borders, and have contributed centrally to the development of the Western cultural tradition. Their impact has been strongest in literature, film, popular music, theatre, poetry, painting and classical architecture, and perhaps weakest (but still considerable) in classical music and modern architecture.

Britain has a particularly rich history of theatre, dating back hundreds of years. The Elizabethan era saw the first great flowering of British theatre, with the work of playwrights such as Christopher Marlowe and Ben Jonson, but it was dominated by William Shakespeare (1564–1616), unquestionably the most influential playwright in the history of the English language. He was so creative that he is credited with having coined more than 2,000 words, and many phrases that are still in daily use today (such as 'vanish into thin air', 'foul play', 'play fast and loose', and 'a tower of strength'). His plays are still routinely performed around the world in many languages, and continue to inspire new interpretations in contemporary settings.

The work of postwar British dramatists has often been compared to the golden age of the Elizabethan theatre. Their plays have fed off the complex social and political changes that have come to Britain since 1945, ranging from the initial optimism and the prospects of the welfare state to the dismay at continued austerity and the end of empire, and eventually running on through emerging nationalism, the sexual revolution, the conflict in Northern Ireland, Thatcherism and racism. The London theatre was given a reviving boost even before the war had ended by the Old Vic Company, led by Laurence Olivier and Ralph Richardson. Then came the creation in 1946 of the Arts Council, which provided an important injection of state funding, and the emergence in the 1950s of the English Stage Company and the Theatre Workshop, both of which give support to the work of new actors and playwrights.

The most influential of immediate postwar playwrights were Terence Rattigan (*The Winslow Boy*, *The Browning Version* and *Separate Tables*) and J.B. Priestley (*An Inspector Calls*), some of whose work presaged the introduction of a different set of values to British theatre. In the mid-1950s, the complacency of British theatre was shattered by the debut of works by Bertolt Brecht and Eugène Ionesco (whose play *The Lesson* was important in introducing absurdist theatre to London) and Samuel Beckett (whose *Waiting for Godot* raised controversial issues relating to censorship). In 1956, coincidentally the year of the Suez crisis, *Look Back in Anger* by John Osborne introduced a more radical tone into British theatre, representing a break with the past and a suggestion that the old world order was over (Billington, 2007). The middle-class virtues of theatre were replaced by a new strain of drama that was more issue-based, and rooted more in the realities of daily life for most Britons. This period saw the birth of the Angry Young Men, a group of writers who were deeply critical of the conformity they saw around them.

In the early 1960s, two theatrical companies were created that were to have a lasting impact: the Royal Shakespeare Company in 1960, and the National Theatre (now the Royal National Theatre) in 1963. These inspired the development of new companies and the opening of new theatres in most of the major regional cities of Britain. The decade also saw the staging of such groundbreaking plays as *The Birthday Party* by Harold Pinter, *A Day in the Death of Joe Egg* by Peter Nichols, *In Celebration* by David Storey, and *Entertaining Mr Sloane* by Joe Orton. It also saw the development of the reputations of a string of new playwrights, including Peter Shaffer, Tom Stoppard, Alan Ayckbourn and David Hare, and a growing crossover between stage and television drama, notably by writers such as Trevor Griffiths and Dennis Potter.

An important change came in the late 1960s with the end of censorship. One of the frustrations faced by the theatre world until then had been the role of the Lord Chamberlain, whose tasks included licensing new plays and thus acting as a censor by deciding what was permissible and what was not. Strong language, nudity and themes such as homosexuality, abortion, and satire involving the royal family were all limited by his decisions. Social changes brought growing support for revisions to the law, which eventually came with the Theatres Act of 1968 which revoked the Lord Chamberlain's authority over new plays. The rock musical *Hair* and the erotic review *Oh! Calcutta!* followed in short order, but the flood of permissiveness that supporters of censorship most feared never happened. Instead, a new spontaneity and sense of freedom was introduced to British theatre, which was followed by a new prominence for political and avant-garde themes, and more plays being written by women and ethnic minorities.

Meanwhile, Britain continued to be well represented in stage musicals, building on the tradition begun in the Victorian era by W.S. Gilbert and Sir Arthur Sullivan, whose most popular creations – including *The Mikado, The Pirates of Penzance* and *The Gondoliers* – had lasting cultural impact. Many of the most commercially successful stage musicals of the last generation have been written or co-written by Andrew Lloyd Webber and/or Tim Rice; they include *Jesus Christ Superstar, Cats, Evita* and *Phantom of the Opera*. Some have achieved critical success, and have been credited with helping bring badly needed tourist income into London, but questions have been raised about the extent to which they detract from the more 'serious' goals of theatre.

Although it faced cuts in government subsidies during the Thatcher years, the theatre continued to prosper, and the West End of London continues to be one of the pre-eminent concentrations of drama in the world, with locals and tourists attending shows in increasing numbers, whether at the Adelphi, Aldwych, New Ambassadors, Royal Court, Young Vic or Theatre Royal. Nearly £250 million (€375/$480 million) was invested in the building of new theatres and the restoration of old theatres in the period 1995–2002, and the Blair government approved a substantial increase in the subsidy provided to theatre. Even regional theatres are mainly doing well, offering a variety of performances and attracting many of the leading actors of the day. There are more than 300 professional theatres in Britain, fed by a steady stream of world class material ranging from Shakespeare through to the work of modern playwrights such as Michael Frayn, Steven Berkoff and Caryl Churchill. Britain's many actors and actresses are among the best-known names on either the stage or the screen, counting among their number Judi Dench, Tom Hardy, Kate Winslet, Benedict Cumberbatch, Idris Elba, Helen Mirren and Emma Thompson.

There has been much crossover between theatre and film, and although the latter is another of the linchpins of British culture there is much less agreement about the health of British cinema (see Sargeant, 2005). It has been suggested by some that but for the intervention of the First World War, Britain – not the United States – might have become the dominating force in world cinema. Before the war, when cinema was in its infancy, British and other European directors were among the most innovative in the world, but after the war they lost their impetus, and the Americans not only better appreciated the commercial possibilities of cinema but their technology was more advanced, and they quickly founded the conventions and genres that established Hollywood as the 'global home' of cinema (Davies, 2000). The United States also attracted many of the most talented British directors and actors, including Charlie Chaplin, Stan Laurel, Alfred Hitchcock and Cary Grant. This drain of talent handicapped the British film industry before it had the chance to flower. British cinema never fully recovered, and while Britons today have a presence in Western cinema that is second only to that of Americans, they have achieved this not through a home-grown industry but rather by hitching a ride on – and contributing to – the dominance of American cinema. Street argues (2008: 197) that 'it is more or less impossible to think of British cinema without reference to its relationship to Hollywood'.

The British film industry was moderately successful between the 1930s and the 1950s, helped by healthy cinema attendance figures, government subsidies and a reduction in the number of films coming out of the United States during the war. Production companies such as Gaumont-British, London Films (founded by Hungarian émigré Alexander Korda) and the Rank Organisation had many commercial successes, and the work of British directors such as Michael Powell, David Lean and Emeric Pressburger, and of actors such as Alec Guinness, Noel Coward, James Mason, Leslie Howard and Peter Sellers, had a large domestic following. During the Second World War there were successful films with appropriate themes, such as *In Which We Serve* (1942, an ode to the Royal Navy), *The Way to the Stars* (1943, an ode to the Royal Air Force) and *Brief Encounter* (1945, about how the war impacted the relationship between characters played by Trevor Howard and Celia Johnson). After the war there were comedies and films with social comment, many of them produced by Michael Balcon and coming out of Ealing Studios in London, including *Passport to Pimlico* (1949), *Kind Hearts and Coronets* (1949), *The Lavender Hill Mob* (1951) and *The Ladykillers* (1955).

The government tried to sustain the industry after the war, but British cinema was still too class-ridden, while American cinema provided the escapism that cinemagoers in an austere postwar Britain sought. Then the advent of television led to a sharp drop in cinema attendance, which fell in the period 1955–63 alone by a remarkable two-thirds (Richards, 1997: 149). British production companies became unwilling to invest in making films, and only the big American producers, such as Paramount, Twentieth Century Fox and Universal, could afford to take the risks and sustain the losses.

Perhaps the last truly home-grown genre in British cinema was the British New Wave of the early 1960s, a series of films which reflected the realities of postwar life in gritty detail, particularly for the working class; they included *Room At The Top* (1959), *Saturday Night and Sunday Morning* (1960), *A Kind of Loving* (1962) and *This Sporting Life* (1963) (Hutchings, 2009). They were all in black and white, and stood in contrast to the product then coming out of the United States, all of it in colour and some using new technology such as Cinemascope. The only commercially successful films being made in Britain were catering to the mass market, and included horror films produced by Hammer Studios, and the *Carry On* series based on a particular brand of risqué British humour that had little prospect of being exported.

There was a brief change of direction in the early 1980s, headed by the work of the producer David Puttnam and the production company Goldcrest. They came together to make *Chariots of Fire*, which in 1981 unexpectedly won the Academy Awards for best picture and best screenplay. Another Goldcrest film, *Gandhi*, won the best picture Academy Award in 1983, but in spite of its work, and that of Handmade Films, Channel 4 and Merchant Ivory Productions, and the revival of the English costume drama (see Higson, 2003), British films were unable to break into the American market in a sustained fashion. Nonetheless, the list of British films that have had either commercial and/or critical success on both sides of the Atlantic in recent decades has been impressive, and includes *The Killing Fields* (1984), *A Fish Called Wanda* (1988), *Howards End* (1992), *The Remains of the Day* (1993), *Four Weddings and a Funeral* (1994), *The English Patient* (1996), *Shakespeare in Love* (1999), *Love Actually* (2003), *The Queen* (2006), *Slumdog Millionaire* (2008) and *The King's Speech* (2010).

Ultimately, though, it is difficult to be sure any longer what distinguishes a *British* film from a film using a story based in Britain and featuring British actors but financed and produced by Americans. Walker (2005) notes the irony in the long list of impressive actors and directors generated by Britain, contrasting with its inability to sustain a native film industry. The British film industry has been almost entirely absorbed by Hollywood, as evidenced by the fact that the Academy Awards make no distinctions between American and British nominees and winners, but treat almost everyone else, except Canadians, Australians and New Zealanders, as foreigners. There are still independent British films, it is true, but the definition of that independence is debatable. As in many other countries, the bulk of films released in Britain are American, and even the most well-known 'British' films of recent decades, such as the James Bond series, any of the costume dramas based on Victorian novels, the Harry Potter series and the *Lord of the Rings* trilogy, have been produced and financed by American film companies.

A related medium is television, where British directors, writers and actors have developed a long and productive history, and popular programmes have become part of the shared culture of the country (Moran, 2013). The Scotsman John Logie Baird was one of the inventors of television, and in November 1936 the BBC launched the world's first television service, yet until the 1950s it was subordinated to radio, and until relatively recently British television viewers had few choices available to them. British television has been a creative home for documentaries (such as *Civilisation*, *The Ascent of Man* and countless natural history programmes), for drama (notably historical series such as *Upstairs Downstairs*, *Brideshead Revisited* and *Downton Abbey*), for soap operas (such as *Coronation Street* and *EastEnders*) and sitcoms (such as *Are You Being Served?*, *Fawlty Towers*, *Only Fools and Horses* and *Absolutely Fabulous*). Few have broken into foreign markets, however, except as local versions of British series. In the United States, for example, there have been American versions of the sitcom *The Office* and quiz shows such as *Who Wants to be a Millionaire?* and *Weakest Link* – but series such as *Downton Abbey* have built large followings on non-commercial public television.

While pre-eminent in theatre and film, Britain's most visible role in modern popular culture has been staked by rock music, one of the few art forms in which foreigners have really made any impact on American domestic culture. Until the late 1950s, Western popular music was dominated by Americans, whether through the big bands of the 1930s and 1940s or through the pioneers of rock and roll, such as Elvis Presley and Buddy Holly. British singers of the 1950s – like Cliff Richard – either tried to ape their American counterparts, or developed their own home-grown form of music called skiffle. This all changed in 1962 when the Beatles developed a new and distinctive variation on rock which helped take Britain out of its postwar and post-imperial melancholy. Representing an emphatic response to what was widely seen as the decline of British popular culture in the face of overwhelming American competition, the Beatles first took their home city of Liverpool by storm, then the country, then – in 1963–64 – the United States (see Stark, 2006). The Beatles became the advance force of what was to become known in the United States as the British Invasion, opening the floodgates for a string of singers and bands from Britain to dominate popular music around the world, tracing a line through the punk-rock years of the late 1970s and early 1980s to the Britpop years of the mid-1990s (see Harris, 2004).

Rock music has not only been a mainstay of British culture but has also been an important part of the British economy: in 2014, according to IFPI (an international organization representing the recording industry), the UK was the fourth largest music market in the world, accounting for more than $1.3 trillion in sales. There are signs, though, that British popular music may not be having as powerful an effect on global culture as it once did, certainly if its popularity in the United States is any indicator. Between the rise of the Beatles and the end of the 1980s, not a year went by without British artists featuring prominently in the American charts. There followed a spell of about 10–15 years during which British artists mainly failed to make the charts in the United States, but there has been something of a comeback since, headed by artists and bands such as Adele, Ed Sheeran, Sam Smith, One Direction, Coldplay and Leona Lewis.

Sports and Leisure

The British are good at relaxing, although perhaps too good if recent studies are any indication. Where they would once leave the house regularly to attend sporting events, have a drink at the local pub, visit the theatre or an exhibition, or go for a walk in the country or a nearby park, they are becoming increasingly sedentary and staying at home. They have been discouraged by the increased expense of going out to restaurants, sporting events or the theatre, by worsening traffic problems and by the declining quality of public transport, and encouraged by the greater ease of finding entertainment at home, whether on a growing number of television channels or the internet, and by a desire to invest

in their homes by making improvements; among the most popular recent programmes on television have been home improvement and gardening shows.
Ironically, though, the amount of free time that the British have available has
grown, and they are spending twice as much of their income on leisure as they
did 50 years ago.

The increased focus on leisure is nowhere more evident than in the matter
of where people go on holiday. The economic and social changes that followed
the war allowed the British to become more mobile, by giving them more disposable income and more leisure time. Until the late 1960s, the typical holiday was spent at a seaside resort town such as Blackpool, Torquay or Brighton,
the average family staying in a hotel and not doing much more than exploiting
the modest resources associated with resorts: sitting on the beach, swimming,
walking and perhaps going to a show. The advent of cheap, mass tourism in
the late 1960s and early 1970s changed all this, and the British started becoming more adventurous, often holidaying on the mainland of Spain, the Balearic
Islands, the Canary Islands or the Greek islands. These still remain the destinations of choice for the majority of British package holidaymakers, but long-haul
vacations to the United States (particularly Florida), the Caribbean, Australasia,
South East Asia and southern and eastern Africa have become more popular,
as has greater independence on the part of vacationers. According to UN World
Tourism Organization data, Britain in 2015 was the fourth biggest source of
international tourists (by expenditure) after China, Germany and the United
States, spending more than $60 billion.

One of the country's most popular leisure activities is sport: about two-
thirds of adults claim to take part in some kind of activity, the most popular
being walking, cycling, swimming and football. The British are also dedicated
followers of professional and amateur sports, and Britain has been either the
birthplace or the nursery of most of the world's most popular sports, including
football (the world's most popular sport), cricket, rugby, hockey, badminton,
squash, golf, snooker and the modern version of tennis. Other sports with a
large following in Britain include boxing, equestrianism (particularly show
jumping), horse racing, greyhound racing and sailing. Unique to Britain are
the Highland Games pursued in Scotland (with events such as caber tossing
and hammer throwing) and the Gaelic Games pursued in Northern Ireland.

If diversity is one of the hallmarks of sport in Britain, then the others are
regionalism and the class basis of many sports (Holt and Mason, 2000: 168–72),
two concepts which to some extent overlap. Cricket, for example, has always
been primarily an English sport rather than a British one, and at least until
the 1960s was closely associated with the upper class and the idea that playing the game was more important than winning, hence the famous put-down

of ungentlemanly behaviour: 'It's just not cricket.' Equestrianism is associated with the landed gentry and the upper middle class, mainly because of its expense, which also explains why polo is often described as the sport of kings. The two different brands of rugby – rugby union and rugby league – are divided both by class and region. The more popular rugby union, which originated in the nineteenth century at Rugby School, an English private school, has its greatest support within the middle class, while rugby league, a breakaway version, is concentrated in northern England and has long been seen as a working man's sport. Horse racing straddles class divisions, with some of the premier events – including the annual Derby at Epsom, and the Royal Ascot meeting every June – attracting aristocratic and upper middle class interest, while routine weekly horse races will more often be supported by the lower middle and working class.

One of the great ironies about Britain is that despite the centrality of sport to British culture (see Table 7.1), the country has a less than stellar record in almost all the sports it invented or nurtured (international rugby being one of the exceptions). Consider its record in football: Britain is home to the Premier League, the most famous and wealthiest football league in the world, which attracts numerous major foreign players, and yet England (there is no British team) has only won the football World Cup once (in 1966), and every four years

Table 7.1 Britain's main sporting events

Event	Sport	Venue
All England Lawn Tennis Championships	tennis	Wimbledon
Football Association Cup Final	football	Wembley
Open Championship	golf	various
The Derby	horse racing	Epsom
The Grand National	horse racing	Aintree
Henley Regatta	rowing	Henley
Cowes Week	sailing	Isle of Wight
Formula One Grand Prix	motor racing	Silverstone
Isle of Man TT Races	motorcycling	Isle of Man
Six Nations Championship	rugby	Twickenham
		Murrayfield
		Cardiff Arms Park
International test matches	cricket	Lord's
		The Oval
		Edgbaston
Badminton Horse Trials	equestrianism	Badminton

the names of the heroes of the winning team – including Bobby Moore, Geoff Hurst and Bobby Charlton – are revived as if to remind the British what none of their teams has been able to do since (Hughson, 2016). England typically qualifies for the World Cup, but then is knocked out after a lacklustre performance. Its 2014 record was illustrative; it came bottom of its group after being beaten by Uruguay and drawing with Costa Rica. Meanwhile, none of the British national teams – England, Scotland, Wales or Northern Ireland – has won the quadrennial European Football Championship since its inception in 1960.

England's record in international cricket is better, but still patchy. The sport was exported with success to many former colonies, including India, Pakistan, Sri Lanka, Australia, New Zealand, South Africa and Zimbabwe, but the English national team is repeatedly defeated in international competition. One of the most famous rivalries in cricket is that between England and Australia. Following England's defeat by Australia in 1882, a joking obituary was written for the game of cricket, and a year later a cricket bail was burnt and its ashes placed in an urn. The two countries have since competed against each other for the Ashes. Despite the national pride that rides on an English victory, Australia won twice as many matches as England in the period 1980–2002. When England won the Ashes in an exciting five-match competition in 2005, the depth of national rejoicing was a reflection of how acute had become the desire for victory. Then in 2006–07, Australia beat England 5–0 for the first time in 85 years, leading to more soul-searching, relieved somewhat by England's defeat of Australia at home in 2010–11 for the first time in nearly a quarter of a century.

Britain is home to some of the most hallowed golf courses in the world, such as St Andrews, Muirfield, Turnberry and Royal St George's. But while British players have performed much better over the last 30 years, with Luke Donald and Lee Westwood, for example, holding the top two places in the world rankings in mid-2011, it is difficult not to conclude that Britain has often played below its potential. Northern Irish golfers won five majors in 2010–14, but only two mainland British players have recently won a major: Justin Rose and Danny Willett.

Formula One racing is very much coloured by British influences: many of its teams are based in Britain, and many of its cars are built with British technology and by British designers and engineers. Yet while British champions have not been uncommon (Jim Clark, Graham Hill, Jackie Stewart and James Hunt, to name a few), British drivers in recent years have often been outwitted by their Brazilian, German and Scandinavian counterparts. After a drought in the 1980s, there have been four British world champions: Nigel Mansell in 1992, Damon

Illustration 7.2   Sports

Briton Lewis Hamilton celebrates winning his fourth Formula One Drivers' World
Championship, in October 2017. Driving for Mercedes, he became the first British driver –
and one of only five drivers in the history of the sport – to win four titles.

Hill in 1996, Jenson Button in 2009, and Lewis Hamilton in 2008, 2014, 2015
and 2017.

Wimbledon is one of the four events in the international Grand Slam of tennis, but – again – Britain has not done well; its last women's champion was
Virginia Wade in 1977, and it went decades without a men's champion, the last
one being Fred Perry in 1936. Several men came close, doing well in the early
stages before being knocked out in defeats that were agonizing to watch for
those hoping for an end to the long dry spell. Andy Murray finally won in 2013
and again in 2016, but how far his wins will translate into Britain becoming
more competitive in international tennis remains to be seen.

The United Kingdom Sports Council, a government body which coordi-
nates support to sports in which Britain competes internationally, claims that
Britain is one of the five most successful sporting countries in the world. To be
sure, there are plenty of examples to add to the occasional triumphs in rugby,
golf and Formula One, notably Britain's presence in track and field sports,
where world records and titles are often held by Britons and where Britain's

dismal record at the 1996 Atlanta Olympics (15 medals, including just one gold) has been steadily improved upon:

- Sydney, 2000: 28 medals, including 11 gold.
- Athens, 2004: 30 medals, including 9 gold.
- Beijing, 2008: 47 medals, including 19 gold.
- London, 2012: 65 medals, including 29 gold.
- Rio, 2016: 67 medals, including 27 gold, and third place in total medals won after the United States and China.

What are we to make of this variable sporting record? There are probably two major factors at work. First, the government in Britain has been notorious over the years for its unwillingness to provide much funding for sports, or to support the kinds of training and scholarship programmes that are available in many

---

Box 7.2   The revival of British cuisine

In much the same way as Britain has been a creative inventor of new sports, but has not done well at them, so it has a rich and diverse cuisine for which it receives little recognition. If the cuisines of France, Italy and Germany have deservedly strong reputations and identities, that of Britain is usually associated with stodge, a lack of variety or imaginative flair, and with the ubiquitous 'meat and two veg': an unimaginative dish of cooked meat and vegetables, with condiments added to provide flavour. So low has Britain's reputation fallen in the eyes of many that President Jacques Chirac of France infamously quipped in 2005 that only Finland produced worse food than Britain. Clearly he had never tried any of Britain's famous meat and game dishes, its many different meat pies, its wealth of cakes and desserts (from trifle to bread and butter pudding, spotted dick and rhubarb crumble), or its variety of cheeses, ranging from Double Gloucester to Stilton, Caerphilly, Red Leicester, Sage Derby and Cheddar (the world's bestselling and most widely emulated cheese).

In fact, Britain has a long and inventive culinary tradition (see Spencer, 2011), which suffered greatly from the effects of the Second World War, when rationing meant that preparing meals was driven more by practical necessity than by imagination and inventiveness. Fortunately this has all begun to change in recent decades as Britain has rediscovered its native cuisine and has adopted influences from abroad. Britain has produced a long line of famous and influential cooks, from Eliza Acton in the nineteenth century to Fanny Cradock and Elizabeth David in the mid-twentieth century, to today's cookery authors and television celebrity chefs, including Nigella Lawson, Jamie Oliver and Gordon Ramsay, several of whom have picked up a following in other parts of Europe and in the United States. These writers have helped Britain rediscover its traditional dishes, and have also contributed to a new culture of creativity in restaurants and domestic kitchens. Britain's changing fortunes are reflected in the fact that in 2016 nearly 160 restaurants in the UK had been recognized with stars by the Michelin Guide, the highest number ever.

continental European countries. Second, British sportsmen and sportswomen often seem to lack the 'killer instinct' that makes them go the extra mile in competition. For generations, the notion of good sportsmanship has meant that greater emphasis has been placed on taking part than on winning, and amateurism has been more admired than professionalism.

Perhaps the greatest change that has come to British sport in the last two decades has been commercialism. Where once it was considered almost indecent to have a link between sports and corporate interests, the outfits of team members in cricket, football and rugby now carry the names of their sponsors, mainly electronics companies, banks, brewers, and – until they were barred from advertising – tobacco companies. The injections of cash from sponsors have been joined by increased government spending, by greater sums being paid to the governing bodies of key sports for television rights, and by income from the National Lottery. Started in 1994, the lottery was set up on the condition that 28 per cent of its income should go to 'good causes', including sports. Swimming, football, cricket and tennis have since benefited from the injection of millions of pounds from lottery income.

Religion

Religion plays only a marginal role in British national life, as it does in most of Western Europe. Only about one-third of Britons believe in God, a proportion that is significantly below the 51 per cent for the EU as a whole (see Figure 7.3).

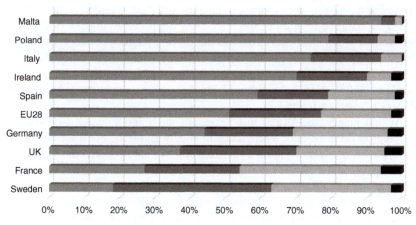

■ Believe there is a God ■ Believe in spirit or life force ■ No God, spirit or life force ■ Declined to answer

Figure 7.3   Belief in God compared

Source: Special Eurobarometer poll on biotechnology, undertaken January–February 2010, at http://ec.europa.eu/public_opinion/archives/ebs/ebs_341_en.pdf

For most people, religious activity typically involves no more than occasional attendance at church; most Britons are still baptised and married in a church, and most funerals are held in a church, but regular weekly attendance at church is low. Davie (1994) argues that the British have developed a habit of 'believing without belonging'; in other words, it is not belief in God that is challenged, but rather participation in organized religion. So while about 26 million Britons (nearly half the population) identify themselves with the Church of England, less than 2 million are active on a regular basis. Overall, fewer than one in five Britons participate in religious activity in any kind of sustained manner. The exception to the general rule can be found among Britain's newer religions, such as Islam, Hinduism and Sikhism; not only is support for these religions growing quickly, but their followers generally have a stronger sense of identity with the faith.

This restricted role for religion has not always been the case. Once Roman Catholicism had been accepted as the state religion in 664, all English kings maintained a close spiritual relationship with the Pope, and the hierarchy of the church was an important part of government, administration and law. However, the relationship changed forever in 1534 when King Henry VIII broke with the Roman Catholic Church. The break was partly a result of a dispute over his attempt to divorce his wife Catherine of Aragon, but it was also an attempt to restrict the power of the church. The ploy succeeded, and to this day the role of religion in public life is limited to the monarchy: the British monarch remains the head of the Church of England (and Defender of the Faith, as he or she is formally known), which is regarded as the 'established' or national religion of England. (It is important to make a distinction between an established church and a state church; Anglicanism is regarded as the national religion, but the Church of England is not a state church, because it receives no financial aid from the government.) Meanwhile, the Church of Scotland is the national church there, but there are no established churches in Wales or Northern Ireland.

At first glance, the formal link between church and monarch would seem to compromise the idea of a separation of church and state, but it actually does the opposite, drawing attention away from any overlap between church and the elected government. The religious views of elected members of government, for example, are not usually a matter of public discussion, and it is almost unheard of – in recent times at least – for the religion of a Prime Minister to be an issue of public debate; this was true even of Tony Blair, who – unusually – was quite open about his Christian beliefs. There are many reminders in the traditions of government about the links with religion, such as prayers in the House of Commons, but these are little more than symbolic gestures, or traditions that most members of government accept without much thought. In policy areas where religion might play a role – such as abortion, the teaching of religion in schools, or euthanasia (allowing a doctor to end a patient's life) – there is almost no overlap between religious values and government policy.

The Church of England is part of the international Communion of Anglican churches, which has 38 national members and claims to have a following of some 70 million people. It is divided into two provinces, one headed by the Archbishop of Canterbury and the other by the Archbishop of York. The former is regarded as the senior of the two, and has the title Primate of All England. The provinces are divided into dioceses overseen by 24 bishops, and these are subdivided into more than 13,000 parishes, each centred on a parish church overseen by a priest and (in larger parishes) assistants known as curates. The monarch appoints the leaders of the church on the advice of the Prime Minister, and those leaders have the right to sit in the House of Lords. Every ten years, the Lambeth Conference brings together Anglican bishops from the different countries where Anglicanism is practised, and decisions are made on doctrine and important policy questions.

The Church has about 13,000 ordained ministers, about 2,100 of whom are women. The ordination of women priests has only been allowed since 1994, and their advent has been symptomatic of a broader division within the Church of England (*The Economist*, 12 January 2002: 53). On the one hand there are Anglo-Catholic traditionalists (otherwise known as high-church Anglicans) who are opposed to the idea of female and gay priests, and many of whom left the church after 1994, leading to talk of a possible split. On the other hand, there are evangelicals who describe themselves as more progressive and more willing to accept change in the character and structure of the church. There has been an unspoken understanding over the years that the post of Archbishop of Canterbury should alternate between representatives of the two groups. However, when the evangelical George Carey retired in 2002 after 13 years in the post, he was replaced by another evangelical – Rowan Williams – who became the 104th Archbishop of Canterbury, and the first Welshman to hold the job in at least 1,000 years. Regarded as a liberal, Williams supported the idea that the Church of England should lose its established status and have a standing equal with the Catholic Church and other Christian churches in Britain. For many, his appointment represented the triumph of the progressive over the traditionalist element in the church. He was succeeded in 2013 by Justin Welby, another progressive.

While it has fewer overall members than the Church of England, the Catholic Church now has the largest active adult membership of any religion in Britain, with an average weekly attendance at mass of more than 1.2 million people. Where active participation among adults in the Church of England has fallen by nearly 45 per cent since 1970, participation in the Catholic Church has fallen more slowly, such that it is now the biggest church in the country. Organizationally, it is divided into eight provinces overseen by Bishops' Conferences for England and Wales, and for Scotland. It is subdivided into 30 dioceses, each with a bishop appointed by the Pope.

One of the most notable trends in British religion in recent years has been its growing diversity. For centuries, the British have been predominantly Christian, the only notable divisions being between the Churches of England and Scotland, and between Protestants and Catholics. But the arrival since the 1950s of immigrants from the Indian subcontinent has brought more Muslims, Sikhs and Hindus to Britain. While active adult participation in Christian religions has fallen by more than one-third since 1970, the number of Hindus has doubled, the number of Sikhs has quadrupled and the number of Muslims has quintupled. There are now more than 1,000 Muslim mosques in Britain, more than 200 Sikh temples, and more than 140 Hindu temples. Unfortunately, the diversity has brought social tensions, in part because these new religions are identified with ethnic minorities (and thus are an element in the racism that has become a feature of society in Britain), and in part because of the broader conflict between Muslims and the West. The impact of terrorism on Britain is discussed in the next chapter.

Further Reading

Davie, Grace (2015) *Religion in Britain: A Persistent Paradox* (Blackwell). Reviews the state of religion in Britain today, contrasting the increasing secularity of the country with the growing presence of religion in public debate.

Fox, Kate (2014) *Watching the English* (Hodder and Stoughton), and Chris Parish (2016) *Being British: Our Once and Future Selves* (Chronos). A bestselling anthropological study of the quirks of the English people, and a discussion of the often contested meaning of British identity.

Gibbins, Justin (2014) *Britain, Europe and National Identity: Self and Other in International Relations* (Palgrave Macmillan). An analysis of recent changes in British national identity in the wake of developments in Europe and within the UK.

Houlihan, Barrie, and Iain Lindsey (2013) *Sport Policy in Britain* (Routledge). An assessment of the effects of the unprecedented levels of public investment in (and political support for) sports in Britain since 1990.

Storry, Mike and Peter Childs (eds) (2017) *British Cultural Identities*, 5th edn (Routledge). An edited collection that looks at the ways in being British relates to the identities of the country's multiple cultures, including the fallout from Brexit.

8

Britain and the World

In a speech to the Conservative Party in 1948, Winston Churchill argued that Britain was located at the intersection of three circles of influence: the British Empire/Commonwealth, the United States and Europe. This notion was to have a lasting impact on British foreign policy, promoting the rather fanciful idea that Britain could act as a bridge connecting the three circles. But the balance among them has changed since 1948, and so has Britain's international position; the Empire is gone, the ties within the Atlantic Alliance have changed, and Britain's place in Europe – always questionable – has been fundamentally altered by its decision to leave the EU. Britain today is faced with a Commonwealth that is marginal, a United States whose foreign and economic policies are not as credible as they once were, a China whose global role Churchill could not have imagined, and a changing Europe to which it remains reluctantly but closely tied. It may be able to continue to offer its services as a bridge, but the international system is not what it once was, and Britain is less important than it once was.

Its diminished status is all the more ironic given that Britain has long been an outward-looking society, interested and involved in events beyond its shores. As an island state, it might have followed the example of medieval Japan and cut itself off from the outside world. But migrations from the Continent made it impossible to ignore events on the other side of the English Channel, the North Sea and the Irish Sea. The rule of monarchs with estates in France perpetuated the links, as did the need both to intervene in, and protect itself from, military and political events on the Continent. Then came the industrial revolution, and the need for new sources of raw materials and new markets, along with the need to outwit its European competitors, encouraged Britain to expand its political and economic interests all over the world.

The growth of its empire gave Britain a vital historical role in global affairs, given substance by the spread of the parliamentary model of government, by the permeation of global culture by British literature, drama and music, and by the spread of English to become the most widely spoken language in the world and the standard for international commerce and communications. Britain's economy is among the five biggest in the world, Britain plays a key role in most international organizations (retaining the power of veto on the UN Security Council, for example), it is a nuclear power, and its military – while relatively small – is efficient and well-respected. But Britain is no longer the dominating international power that it once was, and since the end of the Second World War has found itself trying to adjust to changing circumstances. Its equivocation over Europe has brought the biggest problems, but there has also been a rising chorus of criticism of its willingness to fall in step behind US foreign policy. The Anglo-American 'special' (or 'essential') relationship has some residual nostalgic attractions, but critics charge that Britain receives little in return for its support of US policy.

This chapter looks at Britain's changing international position. It looks in turn at Churchill's three circles of influence and at the competing influences of the Commonwealth, the Atlantic Alliance and Europe. It assesses the significance of Britain's political and military role in the world, and analyses the effects of European versus Atlanticist pressures on British foreign policy. It concludes that Britain's place at the confluence of Churchill's three circles has changed profoundly over the past two generations, and will continue to evolve as the importance of the Atlantic Alliance declines, as China's global reach expands and as Britain works to redefine its relationship with its EU neighbours.

The Changing British Global Role

In spite of its record as an imperial power, and its more recent euroscepticism, Britain over the last millennium has been as much a part of the political and military history of Europe as any of those neighbours. Its territory was several times ruled by monarchs with interests in parts of France, it often had to fight off threatened invasions by its competitors (notably the French and the Spanish), and it was one of the dominating actors in the struggles that determined the continental balance of power. This drew it frequently into European conflicts, from the Hundred Years' War (1337–1453) to the War of the Spanish Succession (1701–14), the Seven Years' War (1756–63), the Napoleonic Wars (1799–1815), the Crimean War (1853–56) and the two world wars.

Britain first began to look beyond Europe to pursue its economic and political interests during the reign of Elizabeth I (1558–1603), and eventually built an empire that would stretch around the world. To maintain this empire demanded the construction and protection of trade routes, and the commitment of soldiers and bureaucrats whose activities contributed in turn to the expansion of British political and military influence. By the nineteenth century, Britain was the dominating economic and military power in the world. Its factories were the engines of the global economic system, it traded with almost every part of the world, its troops were stationed on almost every continent, it took an active role in military operations in Europe, Asia and Africa and it had a navy that dominated the world's oceans. The British Empire was the biggest the world had ever known, on which it was claimed that the sun never set. The world lived under the *Pax Britannica*, the expectation being that Britain would take a leading role in maintaining global peace (see Roberts *et al.*, 2009: Chapter 25).

But all has changed since 1945. Britain emerged from the Second World War with its economic resources stretched beyond their limit, with nationalist movements in many of its colonies agitating for independence, and without the financial ability or political agreement to support a large and widespread military. It took the shock of Suez to wake diehard supporters of British global power from their dreams of past greatness, but – when it came – the dismantling of the empire was carried out in a relatively orderly fashion, the military was soon withdrawn from many of its former fields of activity, and Britain was reduced to a supporting actor in the cold war. Dean Acheson's 1962 comment (see Chapter 7) that Britain had lost an empire but not yet found a role seemed to sum it all up, as did his argument that its attempt to play a role separate from Europe, as head of the Commonwealth, and based on a special relationship with the United States, was 'about to be played out'.

Britain has retained its strong internationalist credentials, as illustrated by its contribution to the work of six key international organizations:

- It was a founder member in 1945 of the United Nations (UN), is one of the five permanent members of the Security Council with veto power (along with the United States, France, Russia and China), is the sixth largest contributor to the UN regular budget, and is a leading contributor to UN peacekeeping operations (Britain's biggest troop contributions in recent years have been in Cyprus and Kosovo). Its veto power in the Security Council is, however, more a legacy of its past global role than a reflection of its current international status.
- It was a founder member in 1949 of the North Atlantic Treaty Organization (NATO), and is second only to the United States in the extent of its influence over NATO policy and its contribution of military resources to the organization. Most Royal Navy ships are committed to NATO operations, and 55,000 British troops are committed to NATO's Allied Rapid Reaction Corps. But

its military is a shadow of its former self, and is rarely any longer committed in much more than a supporting role to the United States or as part of an international coalition.

- It is a member of the Group of Seven industrialized countries (G7), whose leaders meet at well-publicized and well-guarded annual summits, and where it plays a central role in the development of G7 policies.
- It is a member of the Organization for Security and Cooperation in Europe (OSCE), a regional security organization founded in 1994 that brings together 56 states to promote security, prevent conflicts developing, observe elections and provide post-conflict rehabilitation.
- It is the leading actor in the Commonwealth, an association of mainly former British colonies and dominions that includes nearly one-third of the world's population.
- Even as its relationship with the EU changes, it remains the third largest economy in Europe after Germany and France, is deeply connected to the European marketplace, and plays a key role in multiple pan-European organizations, including the Council of Europe.

But despite Britain's interest and role in international affairs, it is not the power it once was, and most of its contemporary influence is exerted not unilaterally but in concert with other groups of states. This hard reality seems to be lost on many Britons, however, for whom there is something of a subconscious hankering for past glories. It has been more than 70 years since the end of Britain's 'finest hour' of the Second World War, and yet – notes Gamble (2016) – 'British culture at all levels is still saturated with references to [the war, and] ... the British political elite from right to left is still deeply preoccupied with geo-politics and Britain's international status and international influence'. British political culture, Gamble also notes, remains 'noticeably more willing to celebrate its military and favour military action than has been the case in most other European states'. While they may not openly admit it, older Britons in particular are likely to yearn nostalgically for a largely mythical idea of the era of Britain as a great power, and of standing alone against impossible odds.

It is partly for these reasons that Britain has stubbornly continued to place its relationships outside Europe ahead of those within Europe, and by doing so has missed the opportunity to work alongside Germany and France in shaping the regional and global role of the European Union. History will surely show that Britain outside the EU will not be able to exert itself in a rapidly changing world as effectively as it would have been able to within the EU, one of the two wealthiest marketplaces in the world. How its exit from the EU will impact its relationships with the rest of the world – and with Churchill's two other circles of influence – remains to be seen.

The Commonwealth

Although it is more important for nostalgic cultural reasons than for hard political or economic reasons, the Commonwealth nonetheless helps mould the way Britain defines its position in the world. A legacy of empire, it is a loosely structured and voluntary organization that consists of 52 countries, most of which were once British colonies or dominions (see Table 8.1). It is described by Weiss (in Shaw, 2007) as 'a slightly anachronistic, somewhat hidden, but nevertheless important actor in global governance'. Members include Australia, Canada, New Zealand, India, many Caribbean states, former British African colonies, two EU states (Cyprus and Malta) and three countries that were never colonized by Britain: Mozambique, Namibia and Rwanda. Based originally around the older white dominions of Australia, Canada and New Zealand, the Commonwealth grew and became increasingly diverse in the 1950s and 1960s as Britain's African, Caribbean, Asian and Pacific colonies won their independence. It now has a collective population of 2.2 billion people (about 30 per cent of the world total).

The Commonwealth Secretariat is based in London, its staff coordinating policy and operating many educational, economic assistance and cultural-exchange programmes. It promotes sustainable economic development, and manages regional investment funds designed to encourage trade within the Commonwealth. Its economic interests are heavily influenced by the perspective of the relatively poor African and Asian states that make up the bulk of its membership; thus, its priorities tend to be driven by issues such as poverty, economic development, trade, and aid to underdeveloped countries.

The Queen is head of the Commonwealth, and *de jure* head of state in 15 member states, including Australia, Canada and several Caribbean states such as Grenada and Jamaica, where she is represented by a governor-general. There are biennial summits of the Commonwealth heads of government of the member states, and every four years the Commonwealth Games brings together athletes from the member states in a mini-Olympics (the most recent on the Gold Coast, Australia, in 2018). The Commonwealth also has an important cultural role in world affairs, thanks in part to its use of English as the sole official language, and in part to the contribution it makes to the promotion of diplomatic ties among its member states.

Table 8.1   Members of the Commonwealth

Antigua and Barbuda	Kenya	Samoa
Australia	Kiribati	Seychelles
Bahamas	Lesotho	Sierra Leone
Bangladesh	Malawi	Singapore
Barbados	Malaysia	Solomon Islands
Belize	Malta	South Africa
Botswana	Mauritius	Sri Lanka
Brunei	Mozambique	Swaziland
Cameroon	Namibia	Tanzania
Canada	Nauru	Tonga
Cyprus	New Zealand	Trinidad and Tobago
Dominica	Nigeria	Tuvalu
Fiji	Pakistan	Uganda
Ghana	Papua New Guinea	United Kingdom
Grenada	Rwanda	Vanuatu
Guyana	St Kitts and Nevis	Zambia
India	St Lucia	
Jamaica	St Vincent and the Grenadines	

However, the Commonwealth is by no means a convincing power bloc in the world, and still less a vehicle for significant British influence (Jones and Norton, 2013); it has little to do with the imperial heritage from which it derives, and is based instead on the principle of sovereign equality (Shaw, 2007). While it has a record for holding its members to the obligations of upholding democracy and human rights, and sanctions them if needed, it has sometimes been defined more by what divides it than what unites it, with the competing interests of its wealthier white members and its poorer non-white members occasionally causing strains. For example, while it may have expelled South Africa in 1961 because of the latter's policies of apartheid (it re-joined in 1994), the Thatcher government was unwilling to agree in the 1980s with Commonwealth arguments in favour of imposing sanctions on South Africa.

More recently, its claims to being a champion of democracy, human rights and the rule of law have not always been convincing, in part because it has long sought to avoid controversy. It suspended Nigeria in 1995–99 because of the authoritarian policies of its military government, and has twice suspended Pakistan and Fiji following military coups in those countries, but it prevaricated on the issue of Zimbabwe. During 2001–02, Britain spearheaded attempts to punish the authoritarian regime of President Robert Mugabe for its seizures of white-owned farmland, its intimidation of the judiciary and opposition political parties and journalists, and its manipulation of the 2002 presidential election. Although agreement was eventually reached in March 2002 to suspend Zimbabwe from the Commonwealth for one year – a move which was more symbolic than practical, and had little impact on the policies of the Mugabe regime – it came only after months of disagreement that saw African members falling out with non-African members. While some felt that the decision over Zimbabwe would restore some credibility to the Commonwealth, others argued that the damage had already been done. Zimbabwe took matters into its own hands in December 2003 by withdrawing from the Commonwealth.

The significance of the Commonwealth for British interests also declined once Britain strengthened its ties with Europe. Prior to joining what was then the European Economic Community (EEC) in 1973, Britain had preferential trading agreements with several Commonwealth states that were either abandoned or significantly rewritten when Britain joined the Community (Clarke, 2004: 285, 349). Furthermore, as Canadian interests continue to focus on North America, and Australian interests switch to South East Asia and the Pacific Rim, the old cultural ties that defined the relationship between Britain and key members of the Commonwealth continue to weaken.

As for Britain's colonial interests, few remain. From a time when the British Empire included a quarter of the world's population, it has shrunk to a pale shadow of its former self (see Fogle, 2004). Since the return of Hong Kong and its 7 million residents to Chinese control in 1997, there have been just 15 Overseas Territories left, containing a total of 180,000 people: Anguilla, the British Virgin Islands, the Cayman Islands, Montserrat, and the Turks and Caicos Islands (all in the Caribbean), Bermuda, the Falkland Islands, St Helena, Ascension Island, Tristan da Cunha, South Georgia and the South Sandwich Islands (all in the Atlantic), Gibraltar on the south coast of Spain, British Antarctic Territory, British Indian Ocean Territory, and four small islands in the Pacific, including Pitcairn.

Most have a high degree of self-government, with locally elected legislatures responsible for domestic affairs, and governors or commissioners who are appointed by the Queen and are responsible for foreign affairs and security. None of the Territories has asked for independence, although the future of Gibraltar (a British possession since 1713) has been the subject of debate for many years. Under the 1969 constitution, Britain is committed to the principle that it will never pass the sovereignty of Gibraltar to another state (that is, Spain) without the support of Gibraltar's people. But the Spanish have long made clear their desire to see Gibraltar returned to their control.

Meanwhile, the thorny issue of the Falklands (Malvinas) refuses to go away. Sovereignty has been disputed between Argentina and Britain ever since the latter asserted its claim to the islands in 1833. The two countries fought a war over them in 1982, since when they have maintained their competing claims to possession while trying to cooperate – not always with success – on practical issues such as fishing rights and commercial flights between Argentina and the Falklands. The problem has been complicated by studies suggesting the presence of rich oil reserves in surrounding waters.

The Atlantic Alliance

Throughout the cold war (roughly 1945 to 1990), Britain was a partner with its Western European allies, the United States and Canada in the ideological, military and political engagement with communism: the Atlantic Alliance. But despite the common belief of its members in the value of democracy and capitalism, the alliance was always a marriage of convenience: the United States needed Western Europe as a market and as the first line of defence against the Soviets and their allies, while the Western Europeans needed American economic investment and security guarantees. The two sides often disagreed – for example, over Suez, Vietnam, the Middle East and nuclear weapons – but the Alliance survived and the disputes were rarely made public (see Lundestad, 2003, 2008).

Much has changed since the end of the cold war. Europeans have become more politically assertive, more economically competitive, and less dependent upon American investment and security. They have also become increasingly aware of the many ways in which they differ from the United States on political priorities, policy positions and even cultural norms. The result has been to raise many questions about the current health and future direction of the Alliance, posing fundamental challenges to Britain's foreign policy options and casting doubt (once again) on the nature of its relationship with the United States (see Box 8.1).

For much of its life, security issues were at the heart of the Alliance. Along with Canada, the United States and most other Western European countries, Britain has been committed to the common defence policies of NATO, created in 1949 against a backdrop of threatening behaviour by the Soviet Union, notably its refusal to work with the Western powers on the administration of postwar Germany and its institution of the Berlin blockade of 1948–49. Under the terms of

---

Box 8.1   The Anglo-American relationship: special, essential or neither?

In his famous 1946 speech in which he warned of an iron curtain descending on Europe, Winston Churchill also spoke of the importance of the 'special relationship' between Britain and the United States. The term has since been used regularly (see McKercher, 2017), but rarely without being contained in quotation marks, reflecting doubts about just how 'special' the relationship really is. While the two countries might have a common history and cultural heritage, and have been allies in many wars, there have also been times when they have been at odds.

Shortly before finally stepping down as Prime Minister in 1955, Churchill warned his Cabinet colleagues: 'Never allow yourselves to be separated from the Americans.' Many British leaders have taken that advice to heart, often supporting US foreign policy even in the face of public opposition at home, and at the expense of good relations with Britain's EU partners. The French in particular have often charged that Britain is being used by the United States as a conduit for its ties with the rest of Europe, and their wariness of US influence in European foreign and security policy has stood in contrast to Britain's Atlanticism.

At no time was the relationship more controversial than during the Bush–Blair years. How could George W. Bush, a neoconservative unilateralist, find common ground with Tony Blair, a reformed socialist and champion of multilateralism? Blair remained close to the United States (Wallace and Oliver, 2005) and made much of the 'pivotal' role that Britain could play in world affairs, with its twin loyalty to the United States and to the EU. But his support for the 2003 invasion of Iraq was unpopular at home and hurt British relations with France and Germany (which both opposed the war). Blair might have reasoned that having the ear of the Bush administration was better than being given the cold shoulder, but this would have been true only if Britain had earned some advantage in return, and there was little evidence of this; Bush clearly planned to pursue his own definition of policy priorities with or without British backing. Support for the war in Iraq, charged Blair's critics, had done little more than associate Britain with a bankrupt policy, and had drawn the ire of Islamic militants.

West German Chancellor Helmut Schmidt once quipped that the Anglo-American relationship was so special that only one side knew it existed (quoted in Garton Ash, 2004: 183). At the time of Iraq, Chancellor Gerhard Schroeder suggested that the transatlantic bridge only seemed to run in one direction (quoted in Cox and Oliver, 2006: 178). During a visit to the United States in July 2010, David Cameron preferred to speak of the 'essential relationship', a term repeated by Barack Obama during his May 2011 visit to Britain. There has always been reason to question the nature of the relationship, and for the British to ask hard questions about its real content. This will be even truer with Britain outside the European Union.

---

the treaty, an armed attack on one member state was to be considered an attack on them all, and each member promised to take 'such action as it deems necessary … to restore and maintain the security of the North Atlantic area'. The treaty was signed by the United States, Canada and ten Western European countries (excluding West Germany, which did not join until 1955) (see Sloan, 2010).

Britain played a leading role in committing troops to NATO interests in Europe throughout the cold war, but always followed the military lead of the United States. With the end of the cold war, and the collapse in December 1991 of the Soviet Union, the underlying rationale of NATO – to neutralize the threat posed by the Soviet Union and its allies – disappeared and the character of the Atlantic Alliance became more fluid. Britain joined in supporting the US-led coalition against Iraq following its invasion of Kuwait on 2 August 1990, placing its assets under US operational command and committing 35,000 troops, 60 warplanes and 15 naval vessels. It was also alone among European states in participating in – and supporting – US efforts to enforce the no-fly zones over southern and northern Iraq, took part in the UN regime imposed in 1991–99 to inspect sites within Iraq where weapons of mass destruction were thought to have been under development, and played the leading role in providing political and military support for US pressure on Iraq to remove obstacles to UN arms inspectors during 1998.

Elsewhere, Britain was a fully fledged member of Operation Allied Force, the NATO attack on Serbia in March–April 1999 that came in response to the ethnic cleansing visited on the predominantly Albanian province of Kosovo by the regime of Slobodan Milošević. European leaders were quick to condemn what was happening, and there was general support in the EU for the bombing war that took place in March–May, although levels of support varied. In the absence of American resolve, Tony Blair won a reputation as the leader most in favour of the attack, committed British forces to the operation, and went so far as to suggest the use of ground troops before the bombing had ended. With the end of hostilities, the British military played a central role in reconstruction, making up one-third of the peacekeeping force sent in to Kosovo.

Britain later made major military and political commitments to the wars in Iraq and Afghanistan, but the cold war has long been over and numerous questions have been asked about the purpose of NATO, its continued existence being in large part a reflection of the failure of the Europeans to develop their own independent military capability. The Atlantic Alliance has been strained by disagreements on two critical fronts:

- There is the new economic might of the EU: compared with the United States, and including the UK, its combined GDP is greater, its population is 60 per cent bigger and its share of world trade is about three times bigger. The new European confidence can be seen most clearly on the trade front, where the Europeans have faced off with the Americans with growing frequency since the creation of the World Trade Organization (WTO) in 1995 over issues such as the US embargo on Cuba, the US imposition of tariffs on steel and the question of subsidies to farmers and aircraft manufacturers.

- There have been many disagreements on policy between the United States and the EU. In addition to the dispute over Iraq starting in 2003, which saw France and Germany being openly critical of US policy, and strong majority public opinion throughout Europe opposing the American venture, the Europeans have also been at odds with the Americans on a wide range of more limited issues, including the problems of Israel and Palestine, the most effective response to international terrorism, dealing with rogue regimes such as Libya, Iran and North Korea, and international agreements on issues as varied as climate change, land mines and the work of the International Criminal Court. Such differences promised to continue to deepen during the unpredictable administration of Donald Trump.

In light of such disagreements, it seems logical to many that the Europeans should follow up their more independent and assertive role in international economic matters with greater independence on security and defence issues. European integrationists in particular want to see the EU developing a common foreign and security policy as a means of providing a counterbalance to US influence in the world. The challenge, however, has been to encourage EU member states to build agreement on foreign policy as effectively as they have on international trade policy. Doubters point to the many instances where EU states have been unable to rise to important challenges (such as in the Balkans in the 1990s) or have disagreed over policy (as with the issue of Iraq). But optimists note that there has been much progress since the 1990s in moving the EU towards common positions. Supporters of Britain's exit from the EU hope that Britain will be able to pursue foreign and economic relations with the United States that are less dependent on an EU consensus, but this is unlikely: the US has long been in favour of UK membership of the EU, and the value of the UK as an American ally was always much greater so long as Britain was a member of the EU. Outside the EU, Britain is likely to find itself torn between the United States and the EU, having more in common – and more immediate and abundant economic and security interests – with the EU.

Britain and Europe

While the importance of the Commonwealth has waned, and the health of the Atlantic Alliance has been under new scrutiny, Europe has long loomed large in British calculations (Geddes, 2013). It may still be regarded as 'foreign' by many Britons and their leaders, and the British relationship with the EU may be undergoing fundamental change, but Europe (broadly defined) has long had critical implications for domestic politics and policy in Britain. History reveals numerous political, economic and social interactions between the British Isles and the continent that have redefined the meaning of Britain.

More recently, membership of the EU has changed the structure and character of the British political system, meant the introduction of a new tier of law that demanded changes at the national level, and introduced a new level of governance with influence over domestic matters. Like all EU member states, Britain came to be defined less in national terms and more in the context of its membership of the world's biggest capitalist marketplace and its biggest trading power. However its post-Brexit relationship with the EU evolves, Britain will still find itself affected by the enormous gravitational pull of the EU marketplace. And it is also important to remember that 'Europe' is not just the EU, but the broader community of cooperative European institutions and the political and financial ties that bind all European states to one another.

When Europeans began building those ties in the 1950s and 1960s, they concentrated on reducing the barriers to trade and on building a single European market, with common external tariffs on goods coming into that market, and free movement of money, people, goods and services within its borders. European integration has since broadened and deepened significantly. There are few remaining barriers to internal trade (even between EU members and non-members), EU citizens can live and work in any of the member states, intra-European investment and corporate takeovers and mergers have grown, internal transport networks are expanding, and the member states have brought domestic laws into line with EU law in many different policy areas, including agriculture, transport, trade, competition, immigration and consumer policy.

Britain joined what was then the European Economic Community in January 1973, but soon earned a reputation as an 'awkward partner' (George, 1998). Not only was it late to join the Community (although this was not entirely its fault), but it was also late joining the exchange rate mechanism that predated the euro, eschewed the Social Charter on workers' rights, and never joined the Schengen Agreement designed to accelerate the removal of internal border controls. Along the way, Britons have had a less than stellar turnout at quinquennial European Parliament elections, have long shown low levels of enthusiasm for EU membership, and have failed always to understand how it works, often prodded by a domestic tabloid press that has persisted in misleading and jingoistic attacks on the EU.

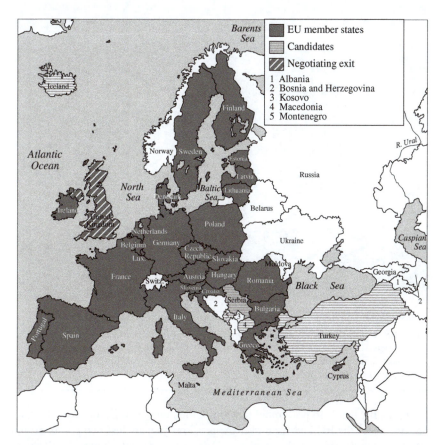

Map 8.1   The European Union

The extent to which British public opinion has been out of step with that in much (but not all) of the rest of the EU is reflected in the regular polls carried out by Eurobarometer, the EU polling service. These have revealed a relatively low level of psychological attachment to the EU by most Britons: a 2006 poll found that only 28 per cent had a positive view of the EU (significantly fewer than the 46 per cent of EU citizens as a whole) (Eurobarometer 66, Autumn 2006), but a survey taken just after the Brexit referendum in August 2016 found that the number with a positive view had grown to 34 per cent, while the EU number had fallen to 35 per cent. By then, more Britons had a more positive view of the EU than was the case in France, Spain, and – not surprisingly – Greece (see Figure 8.1).

Illustration 8.1   European Parliament

The European Parliament building in Strasbourg, France. British voters have had a less than
stellar record in turnout for EP elections, as often as not using them as an opportunity to
comment on the government in power in Britain rather than to vote on European issues, or to
support the true party of their choice.

Ironically, the 2016 poll found that while the number of Europeans who felt
positive about the EU had risen over the previous year by just two points, from
49 per cent to 51 per cent, the number of Britons who felt attached to the EU had
grown by six points, from 40 per cent to 46 per cent. There was also a clear age
and educational differential: while 59 per cent of those Britons in the 25–34 year
age group felt positive about the EU, only 30 per cent of those older than 65 could
say the same. Meanwhile, 67 per cent of those with the highest levels of education felt positive about the EU, while only 26 per cent of those who had left school
aged 15 or less could say the same.

At the same time, many Britons also admit to a poor understanding of how
the EU works, although their knowledge improved with the debate surrounding
Brexit. The 2006 poll – for example – found that when asked to rank themselves
on a scale of 1 to 10 in terms of their knowledge of the EU, Britons gave themselves a score of 3.5, lower than any other EU member state, for which the average score was 4.2 and the highest (in Luxembourg) was 5.4. By August 2016, the

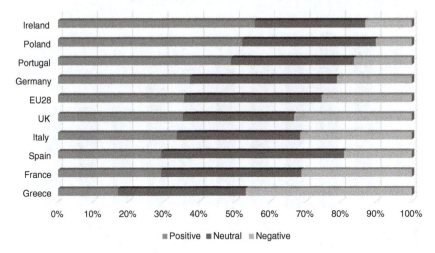

Figure 8.1   Public image of the European Union compared
Source: Eurobarometer poll 86, Autumn 2016.

question on the poll had been changed, asking people to what extent they agreed with the statement 'I understand the EU': 60 per cent of Britons felt they could agree, slightly higher than the EU average of 56 per cent (see Figure 8.2), and not far short of the figure for Germany. However, the more important question – to which there was no objective answer – was how many *actually* understood the EU, as opposed to how many *thought* they understood the EU.

There are several possible explanations for the lukewarm British outlook:

- At the time that continental European leaders were planning the first steps in the process of integration, Britain still had many interests outside Europe: it had an empire, it had strong cultural links with its dominions and colonies (many of which still saw Britain as the mother country), and it had a strong relationship with the United States (in contrast to the distrust with which the French viewed – and continue to view – that country). None of this is any longer true, but old habits and attitudes sometimes die hard.
- Where European states concluded that only cooperation and integration could prevent future wars, it was its independence which – in the minds of many Britons – helped Britain avoid becoming caught up in the kinds of conflicts which brought so many changes to the borders of continental European states.

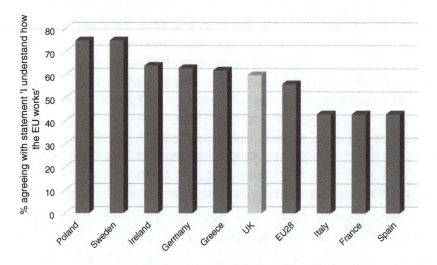

Figure 8.2   Public knowledge of the European Union compared
Source: Eurobarometer poll 86, Autumn 2016.

- Britain's physical separation from the Continent has helped make the British feel that they are somehow different from other Europeans, and that they are not really European at all. Even today, many Britons still talk about Europe as something quite distinct from Britain (see Box 8.2).
- Many Britons understand neither the EU nor its implications. They are not helped by mass media, which often promote myths and misunderstandings about the EU, for example misrepresenting the powers of the EU institutions, the financial costs of British membership, and the number of British laws that are a consequence of EU law.

Having said all this, the British reputation for euroscepticism has not always been entirely deserved, and there have sometimes been reasons for questioning the conventional wisdom:

- Because Britain has been so widely branded as a Eurosceptic, it has tended to attract more attention than other member states with similar leanings. It is often forgotten, for example, that Britain has never voted against a European treaty (as have Denmark, Ireland (twice), France and the Netherlands), and that British doubts about joining the euro were reflected in Germany, Denmark and Sweden. Similarly, indeed, Denmark has developed a strong record of euroscepticism, but has been less visible in its actions.

Box 8.2   Is Britain European?

We saw in Chapter 1 the semantic problems that arise from the differences between the names *England*, *Britain* and the *United Kingdom*. But while it is clearly wrong – in geographical, political and legal terms – to use the term *England* to describe Britain or the UK, the question of whether or not the UK is part of Europe is more difficult to resolve. It is notable how many Britons refer to the continent of Europe as something quite distinct from Britain; they will often talk about going on holiday to 'Europe', and political leaders will often refer to 'Europe' as shorthand for the EU but with the unspoken effect of making a distinction between Britain and Europe.

In geographical terms, Britain – in spite of being an island state – is just as much a part of Europe as other islands such as Crete, Corsica, Sardinia, Sicily, Ireland and Iceland. In political and social terms, Britain has been very much a part of the European experience and of the political changes and conflicts that have formed the idea of Europe. There is a tendency in much British thinking to regard their country as somehow exceptional, but exceptionalism has been a factor in the thinking of almost all other European states. Garton Ash (2001) notes that the residents of several of these states – including Spain, Portugal, Poland and Greece – also speak of Europe as being somewhere else, but goes on to argue:

> the difference is that for them, Europe may be somewhere else, but it's somewhere else they would like to be. There are … only two countries in Europe which not only talk about Europe as somewhere else but are still not at all sure if they want to be there. These are Britain and Russia.

One element of the exceptionalism of Britain that stands out is the length and depth of its connections with the rest of the English-speaking world. Other European states had empires and engaged in bouts of overseas settlement, but none came close to matching Britain in the geographical spread and the permanence of those settlements, nor in how much their effects continue to be felt today. The British continue to have a strong cultural attachment to the rest of the English-speaking world, if only because they share a language with that world and find it more familiar than continental Europe, with its significant linguistic and cultural barriers. But as to the question of whether Britain is European, there is no definitive answer and many different opinions.

- France has done more to seriously disrupt the work of the EU. It was France (or at least Charles de Gaulle) that twice vetoed the membership applications of Britain, and that set off the Community's most serious crisis in 1965 when it refused to take part in joint decision making for six months. France was also the principal architect and most dogged defender of the controversial and expensive Common Agricultural Policy, has been out of step with most of its

EU partners over policy on NATO, and refuses to allow the chamber of the European Parliament to be moved to Brussels (with the farcical and expensive result that Parliament must move for one week per month to Strasbourg).

- Britain was often criticized for negotiating hard on the development of new EU laws and policies, but it was driven less by stubbornness than by a philosophy that it should not make agreements that it could not honour. Other member states, by contrast, may say 'yes' and then find themselves unable to deliver on their promises (Italy being the prime example). It is often forgotten that Britain has had one of the best records in the Union on changing national law to fit with EU law.

One area in which Britain has made a critical contribution to European cooperation has been in foreign and security policy. Backed by the vast size of the European market – which now accounts for 30 per cent of global economic production – the EU member states have learned to work as one on global trade issues, have adopted common positions on a variety of headline international issues – such as the Israeli–Palestinian question and tensions between India and Pakistan over Kashmir – and have increasingly voted as a block in the UN General Assembly. They have not always been able to exert themselves militarily, however, because many prefer peaceful means to address disagreements, several member states (such as Finland and Ireland) are neutral, and the two major military powers – Britain and France – disagree on whether to defer to the NATO alliance and US leadership (Britain), or to take a more independent European line on security issues (France).

Where Britain long opposed attempts to promote greater European military integration, Tony Blair was sympathetic to the suggestion made in 1996 that the EU develop a defence and security 'identity' within NATO. The idea was that the Europeans would be able to mount peacekeeping or monitoring operations without necessarily looking for the support of the United States or other NATO member states; interested countries would contribute military forces that would come together under a joint command system. In 1999 the European Security and Defence Policy (ESDP) was announced, under which the EU would promote the 'Petersberg tasks' which had been agreed in 1992 and included humanitarian, rescue, peacekeeping and other crisis management operations.

A critical watershed in the development of the tripartite relationship between Britain, its EU partners and the United States was reached with the controversial US-led invasion of Iraq in 2003, designed to remove Saddam Hussein from power. While there had been an outpouring of British and European support and sympathy for the United States following the September 2001 terrorist attacks, the tide began to turn as the Bush administration shifted the spotlight of the 'war on terrorism' away from Afghanistan and towards Iraq. Bush claimed (and Blair agreed) that Saddam was building weapons of mass destruction, and was supporting the al-Qaeda terrorist network. Questions were raised about the lack of hard evidence, about the wisdom of setting a precedent of pre-emptive strikes, about how such an attack would fit with international law, about the extent to which such an attack would further destabilize an already unstable region, and about the real motives of the Bush administration.

As events unfolded in mid-2002, European leaders began withdrawing support from the Bush administration. The French equivocated, the Germans were positively hostile to American 'adventurism' (a position that was undoubtedly influenced by the closeness of the September 2002 German general election), while the conservative Berlusconi government in Italy gave its blessing. Meanwhile, the world was treated to the peculiar sight of Britain's Labour Prime Minister leading the chorus in support of a divisive policy pursued by a neoconservative American president. Forcefully arguing his case that Britain played a 'pivotal' role in world affairs, Blair gave vocal support to the Bush administration, analysts suggesting that at least part of his thinking was that it was better to be involved – and to have influence – than not to be involved and to have little or no say in a policy that might end up damaging Britain's interests (*The Economist*, 9 March 2002: 60).

But it was questionable how much influence Britain in fact had with US policy makers, and Blair's support for the invasion flew in the face of public opinion at home, as well as placing him at odds with many of his European partners. Polls at the time revealed that there was 70–90 per cent opposition to the invasion in every EU member state, and subsequent studies by Eurobarometer found high public support for common European foreign and security policies: according to Eurobarometer 68 (Spring 2008), 70 per cent of EU residents favoured a common foreign policy (including 46 per cent in the UK), and 76 per cent favoured a common European defence and security policy (including 53 per cent in the UK). As they prepared to vote in the 2016 EU referendum, 58 per cent of Britons favoured a common EU defence and security policy, and while only 46 per cent favoured a common EU foreign policy, they outnumbered the 40 per cent who opposed such an idea (Eurobarometer 85, Spring 2016).

The extent to which Britain has been bound in with its EU partners has been vividly illustrated by the effects first of the global financial crisis of 2007–10 and then by the eurozone crisis that broke in 2010. The British government could not make policy on the global financial crisis in isolation, having to instead work closely with its EU partners in developing a response on bailouts and aid to troubled parts of the economy. And while Britain may not have adopted the euro, its troubles inevitably impacted the British economy because of the extent of Britain's ties with the eurozone. Even hardened Eurosceptics realized that it was not in British interests for the euro to fail.

The dispute over Iraq helped encourage Britons to wonder anew about the Anglo-American special relationship, and to ponder in more depth – and even in the face of Brexit – the implications of closer foreign policy cooperation between Britain and the EU. Just as there has long been clear support for EU states working together on trade policy, so the widespread unpopularity within Europe of many US foreign policy positions has shifted governments and publics more towards the idea of common European policy positions. While the United States tends towards a uniquely American view of problems and their solutions, and has had an unfortunate inclination to use its enormous military power to achieve change without thinking through the longer-term political implications, Europeans take a more multilateral, universal and inclusive view of the world, and reject military options in favour of negotiation, encouragement and incentives. In spite of Brexit, Britain will likely continue to gravitate towards the European circle of influence, if for no other reason than a combination of its obligations to NATO and doubts about the wisdom of many US foreign policies.

The Changing Role of the British Military

Britain was once the pre-eminent military power in the world, and its history is peppered with great military leaders and celebrated victories that are at the heart of the mythology of British identity. From Edward III's decisive victory over the French at the Battle of Crécy in 1346 to Henry V's victory at Agincourt in 1415, to Sir Francis Drake and his defeat of the Spanish Armada in 1588, to the Duke of Marlborough (who never lost a battle and defeated the French at Blenheim in 1704), to Lord Nelson and the Duke of Wellington who between them contributed so much to ending Napoleon's aspirations for European hegemony, to General Bernard Montgomery who inflicted the first major defeat on the Nazis at El Alamein in 1942 the list is impressive, and the British are always quick to use anniversaries to roll out the ghosts of their military heroes as a means to celebrate past achievements. Of course there are also plenty of examples of military blunders and failures, but these are routinely overlooked, or occasionally turned to advantage: how many other countries could turn the Charge of the Light Brigade, when nearly 700 cavalrymen were mistakenly ordered to charge Russian artillery in the Crimea in 1854, into an example of glorious failure?

The Second World War may have been Britain's finest hour, but it also struck a blow to Britain's status as a great power, and it soon began to withdraw from its military commitments around the world, the Suez crisis of 1956 finally confirming its demotion to a second-rank power. It had played a leading role in the development of nuclear weapons during the closing years of the war, but was quickly overtaken by the United States, and while it still has an independent nuclear deterrent it is a relatively small one. From a time when British troops were committed all over the world to protect British interests and promote British policy, the British military by the 1970s was a shadow of its former self.

Emphasizing its reduced condition, it came perilously close in 1982 to failing in a minor war against an inferior enemy. On 20 April of that year, Argentina invaded the Falkland Islands (otherwise known as the Malvinas), a British possession in the south Atlantic since 1833, inhabited by less than 2,000 people. The Thatcher government responded by despatching a task force of 100 ships and 25,000 soldiers and sailors, supported by a small number of aircraft-carrier-based fighters. The troops fought valiantly, but resources were spread so thinly that the task force had to commandeer commercial ferries and luxury cruisers to transport soldiers, the Royal Navy lived in danger of sustaining crippling losses from a handful of French-made Exocet missiles fired by the Argentinean air force, and enough ships and helicopters were lost that the task force came close to losing the logistical support it needed to fight the war. But Britain prevailed, and the war ended with the surrender of Argentinean forces on 14 June.

Just before the Falklands War, there had been 320,000 personnel in the four branches of the regular forces: the Army, the Royal Air Force, the Royal Navy and the Royal Marines. The number went up slightly after the war but by 2001 had fallen to just under 211,000, a reduction of nearly one-third. It has since fallen to just over 197,000. Some of the slack was taken up by regular reserves, whose number increased over the same period by about one-third, to 282,000 before falling back. At the same time, defence spending as a percentage of GDP was more than halved between 1985 and 2015, falling from 5.1 per cent to 2.2 per cent.

Soon after coming to power, the Blair administration developed the Strategic Defence Review, aimed at outlining Britain's options in the period until 2015. Published in 1998, it was the first such study in 17 years and the first to consider the needs and possibilities of the post-cold war world (see Spear, 2000: 282–83). It concluded that there were no direct military threats to Britain, but that the end of the cold war had introduced instability and uncertainty, and that there was a variety of new non-military threats faced by Britain, including the potential proliferation of nuclear, chemical and biological weapons, organized crime and issues related to drugs, natural-resource issues and ethnic conflict. It argued that British forces would have to be ready to respond to a major crisis of a similar scale to the 1991 Gulf War, while being prepared for more extended commitments on a lesser scale such as peacekeeping and relief operations. It also concluded that Britain should have the capacity to commit small and highly trained groups of personnel into different situations at short notice.

Table 8.2   The British military

Personnel:	150,000 regular (Army, Royal Air Force, Royal Navy and Royal Marines) and 47,000 reserves and other. Total: 197,000
Nuclear warheads:	Less than 300, all sea-based, carried on four nuclear-powered submarines, no more than one of which is on patrol at any time with no more than 48 warheads
Aircraft:	724 aircraft, including 125 Panavia Tornado fighter-bombers, 132 Eurofighter Typhoons and about 370 helicopters (including Chinooks, Merlins, Pumas and Sea Kings)
Ships:	76 vessels, including 6 destroyers, 13 frigates, 4 nuclear-powered Vanguard class ballistic submarines armed with Trident missiles, and 7 fleet submarines armed with Tomahawk cruise missiles. Two new Queen Elizabethe class carriers are under construction
Defence spending:	2.2 per cent of GDP (2015)

Source: Mainly Ministry of Defence at www.gov.uk and related service websites (retrieved May 2017). Figures are for 2016.

Alongside its role in the conflicts in the Gulf in 1990–91 and in Serbia in 1999, the British military has been a key element in NATO rapid reaction forces, to which it has committed three aircraft carriers, 54 naval vessels, 12 nuclear-powered submarines, 55,000 troops and 140 aircraft. Meanwhile, it has been involved in UN peacekeeping operations in the Congo, Cyprus, East Timor and Georgia and international relief or evacuation operations in Angola, Eritrea, Mozambique, Rwanda and Somalia, as well as the following:

- After the breakdown of security in Sierra Leone in May 2000, and the taking hostage of UN peacekeepers by rebels, Britain deployed 4,500 troops to the war-torn country, and subsequently helped restore order and train a new army and police force.
- Britain contributed about 1,700 troops to the Stabilization Force (SFOR) set up to help implement the 1995 peace accords in Bosnia and Herzegovina, as well as police officers taking part in the UN International Police Task Force. It participates today in EUFOR Althea, the EU stabilization force which replaced SFOR in December 2004. It also made the biggest contributions (about 19,000 troops at its peak) to the NATO-led KFOR Kosovo Force, deployed in Kosovo in 1999 to help restore peace following the NATO attack on Serbia.

- Following its small supporting military role in the attack on the Taliban regime in Afghanistan, launched by the United States in the wake of the September 2001 terrorist attacks in New York and Washington, DC, Britain played the lead role in peacekeeping operations with second biggest commitment of personnel after the United States. The last British combat troops finally withdrew from Afghanistan in 2014, having sustained 453 casualties.
- Britain had the second largest commitment of troops to the invasion of Iraq, with 46,000 troops active at the height of operations in March/April 2003, the bulk based in and around the city of Basra in south-east Iraq. The British force had been reduced to just over 7,000 by mid-2006 and finally withdrew in 2009, having sustained 179 casualties.
- In March 2011 Britain became part of the UN-mandated effort to enforce a no-fly zone over Libya in the wake of the uprising against the Gaddafi regime.
- In 2014, Britain became part of the coalition formed to degrade and defeat ISIS, committing 1,300 personnel to training Iraqi troops and carrying out airstrikes against ISIS positions in northern Iraq and eastern Syria.

Another Defence Review in 2010, carried out in the wake of the global financial crisis, suggested a very different future for the British military. It resulted in significant cuts in spending and in personnel, the scrapping of several large weapons projects and a reduction in the ability of Britain to commit to large-scale military interventions such as those in Afghanistan and Iraq. It was telling that the government of the country which once had the world's most powerful navy took the decision to continue with the construction of two new aircraft carriers – the *Queen Elizabeth* and the *Prince of Wales* – at a combined cost of £5 billion (€6/$8 billion), even in the face of doubts that both vessels were needed. There was also speculation (initially denied by government officials) that France and Britain might share assets – including aircraft carriers – in order to help cut costs.

Much like other military powers, Britain is seen to face so-called 'asymmetric threats' such as terrorism and the threats posed by weapons of mass destruction. The new role of terrorism in international affairs was most graphically illustrated by the September 2001 attacks in the United States. Among the 2,753 victims of the destruction of the World Trade Center in New York were 66 British citizens, making the event the biggest single loss of British lives in an attack of its kind. The Blair administration provided diplomatic and moral support to the new 'war on terror' declared by US President George W. Bush, and Tony Blair himself became the most visible and active of national leaders in support of US policies. On 7 July 2005, the new brand of terrorism struck home

Illustration 8.2   The British Army in Afghanistan

The coffin of Royal Marine Sergeant John Manuel – killed by a suspected suicide bomber in Helmand Province, Afghanistan – is carried by pallbearers at his funeral. The British military has been active in multiple conflicts in recent years, including those in Afghanistan, Iraq, Sierra Leone and Libya.

when four separate bomb explosions in central London killed 52 people and injured more than 770. Two weeks later, four more attacks failed to materialize when only the detonators exploded. Then, in August 2006, news broke of a plot to use liquid explosives to blow up nearly a dozen airliners flying from Britain to the United States.

Terrorism continues to be a particular problem for Britain, as reflected in a number of recent incidents: a 2007 attack on Glasgow airport that injured five people, the 2013 murder of a British soldier in London, a 2015 knife attack on three people in London, and four incidents that took place within the space of three months in 2017. The worst of these was the bombing at an Ariana Grande concert in Manchester that left 22 dead and 120 injured. There was a resulting increase in revenge attacks against Muslims in Britain, including an incident in June 2017 when a van was driven into pedestrians near Finsbury Park Mosque in London, injuring ten people.

For some, Britain has become a target of such attacks mainly because of its support for US policies, which – if true – raises fundamental questions about the future of British defence policy. But the examples of Iraq, of the 'war on terror' and of Lebanon in July 2006 – when the Blair administration was unable to convince the Bush administration of the merits of calling for a ceasefire following the outbreak of hostilities with Israel – raise questions about whether the United States will ever really listen to Britain. Cox and Oliver (2006: 187) conclude that British ambivalence about the role of the EU in the world is matched only by unease about whether the United States will listen to British concerns. In defence policy, as in foreign policy, the exact location of Britain within Churchill's three circles of influence remains a troubling issue for debate. Had it remained within the EU, then it would doubtless have continued to try to balance obligations to its American and European partners. The changed relationship with the EU might have meant a move back to closer ties with the United States, but doubts about the directions taken by the Trump administration suggested that even within the Atlantic Alliance there was no longer the policy certainty that there once might have been.

Further Reading

Gowland, David (2016) *Britain and the European Union* (Routledge). The most recent study of Britain's troubled relationship with the EU, anticipating the fallout from the 2016 Brexit referendum.

Jackson, Ashley (2013) *The British Empire: A Very Short Introduction* (Oxford University Press). The *Very Short Introduction* treatment of this topic, offering a survey of the rise and fall of the British Empire in about 130 pages.

Kwarteng, Kwasi (2012) *Ghosts of Empire: Britain's Legacies in the Modern World* (Bloomsbury). An analysis of the way in which British imperialism helped shape many of the most troubling problems faced by the world today, with sections on Iraq, Kashmir, Burma, Sudan, Nigeria and Hong Kong.

McCormick, John (2017) *Understanding the European Union*, 7th edn (Palgrave). A brief survey of the EU, including chapters on its history, institutions and policies.

McKercher, B.J.C. (2017) *Britain, America, and the Special Relationship since 1941* (Routledge). An assessment of the ups and downs of the 'special relationship' from the Atlantic Charter to the present.

Conclusions

Britain today is a country darkened by dense clouds of doubt and uncertainty. In almost every respect – from the definition of Britishness to the state of its political and economic systems, to its social structure, to its place in the world – Britain is undergoing changes whose eventual outcome are hard to predict. The economic and social changes were already in place before June 2016, when British voters sent shockwaves throughout the world by opting in a national referendum to leave the European Union. A year later, an early general election that was designed to place the Conservative government in a stronger negotiating position on Brexit left it much weaker, and raised numerous troubling questions about the future of the British political system.

With its long history and many traditions, it is easy to think of Britain as stable and unchanging, and as forming the bedrock of the elements we associate with parliamentary government, capitalism and Western society. And yet nothing could be further from the truth. Few countries have gone through the kind of near-revolutionary changes that Britain has witnessed in the last three generations, evidence of which can be found everywhere: in the remodelling of the political system; in the upheavals that have altered the fortunes of the British economy; in the changes in the structure of British society; in the redefinition of the place of family, national identity, race and religion; in the changing views on the place of Britain in the world; and in the review of approaches to almost every area of public policy, from welfare to education, health care, transportation, economic issues and foreign affairs.

If there is anything that briefly sums up Britain and the British experience today, it is the idea of change. The people of Britain have had to become used to adjustment, innovation, diversity, reconstruction, novelty, revision, transition and transformation in almost every aspect of their lives:

- On the political front, the heritage of the parliamentary system can be traced back more than 800 years, giving Britain a political continuity that is virtually unmatched in the world. Yet the role and the powers of the monarchy, of the office of Prime Minister, of Parliament and of the bureaucracy have undergone fundamental change, as has the relationship among different levels of government, as have the values and preferences of British voters.

• On the economic front, Britain has had to make an adjustment that has taken it from being the pre-eminent economic and trading power in the world, the birthplace of the industrial revolution and the nursery of capitalism, through experimentation with competing approaches to managing the economy, to meeting the challenge of adjusting to both steady growth and rapid integration into the European marketplace, and most recently to having to respond to the triple blows of the global financial crisis, the eurozone crisis and the decision to leave the European Union. The scale and the variety of change have outpaced almost anything seen in the rest of Europe or North America.

• On the social front, the predictable patterns of the class system have become blurred, the meaning of 'British' has been redefined on the back of waves of immigration and questions about the future of the United Kingdom, and social relations have changed in the wake of the decline of the nuclear family, the growth of the middle class, a transformation of occupational structure, the growing gap between the rich and the poor, the ageing of the British population and worrying concerns about the health of the very fabric of British society.

This book has explored three key themes in the British experience. The first concerns the supposed decline of Britain, the debate about which has been an ongoing theme in assessments about Britain since at least 1945, possibly earlier. Naturally, a country that was once the world's pre-eminent political, economic, scientific and military power, but has since seen new competition for every quarter, has unavoidably declined. But there is a difference between the kinds of decline brought by wider change and the kinds of decline imposed on Britain by itself as a result of bad decisions or as a result of failures to adjust. To use a football analogy, many of Britain's problems have been own goals, as exemplified in its failure to build a stronger sense of national identity, to address pressing social needs, to modernize its system of government, and to reform its economy to meet new challenges. Then came the 2016 decision to leave the European Union, hailed by those who believe that it will open new opportunities but criticized by those who describe it as an appalling act of self-harm. It is still too early to know for sure which assessment is correct.

The second theme concerns the changes that will come to Britain in the wake of Brexit, assuming that it actually happens. Whether they have liked it or not, and many have not, the British have been further integrated into the networks that have pulled the states of Europe closer together since the early 1950s. European law permeates British law; European policy plays a central role in areas as diverse as agriculture, consumer protection, the environment, fisheries, trade, transport and working conditions; and Britain has become used to making its internal and external political and economic choices less in isolation and increasingly in concert with its EU partners. While membership of the EU has always been voluntary, even outside the EU it would be impossible for Britain to resist the gravitational pull of the continental European economic colossus. If for no other reason than to provide some global balance to the influence of the United States, and the new role of rising powers such as China and India, it is essential that Britain works out a better way of exerting its political, diplomatic and economic influence on the global stage.

The third theme concerns the meaning of Britain and the redefinition of its national identity. Externally, the British have had to adjust themselves to the idea that they are no longer a great power. From Suez to the collapse of the Berlin Wall, Britain was one of a group of middle-range powers that stood on the periphery of cold war disputes between the superpowers. Today, it is witnessing a review of its increasingly difficult relationship with the United States while facing the massive uncertainties of redefining its relationship with its EU neighbours. Fortunately, the angst of post-imperial decline has been replaced by greater congruence between reality and aspiration. Instead of frustrating itself by trying to punch above its weight, Britain has reached the point where it is more comfortable with its reduced role in the international system. The last edition of this book predicted that Britons would almost certainly see their country acting more closely in concert with their European neighbours in their relationship with the rest of the world, but that view has now been turned on its head.

Internally, the dominance of England over Scotland and Wales has declined. The last two generations have seen a newly assertive nationalism in all three countries that has raised questions about the future health of the union. Although peace now reigns in Northern Ireland, it is a troubled peace, compromised by ill feelings that will continue indefinitely to impact the way its different communities see each other. Meanwhile, new questions are asked about the prospects for independence in Scotland, and about the significance of the rise of English nationalism. Along the way, the definition of 'Britishness' continues to change as Britain becomes increasingly multicultural, and as Asian, Caribbean and African minorities are joined by waves of new arrivals from the Continent, coming either as asylum seekers or in the wake of eastward expansion of the EU. There is still much ground to be covered in the debate over the definition of 'Britain' and the 'United Kingdom'.

The changes that have come out of these three broad forces have been mixed. Overall, the British are healthier, wealthier and more self-sufficient than they were in 1945, they have rediscovered their competitive and entrepreneurial spirit, greater emphasis is given than perhaps ever before to merit and social equality, and there is much greater general awareness of the difficulties that society faces and how they might be addressed. But many problems remain, including poverty and social exclusion, racism, economic inequalities, public services of mixed quality, and crime. There is always a danger in focusing on short-term trends rather than taking the longer view, and there will always be a mixture of the good and the bad in such trends. But the short-term changes in Britain currently crowd out much consideration of where the country will be ten years from now, or a generation from now. Britain is currently faced by deep uncertainties in the wake of the Brexit decision, and many troubling questions remain about the health of British society. The last edition of this book commented that Britain was a dynamic and forward-looking society with a global influence that was remarkable for a country of its size. This edition must take the opposite view: that Britain has in many ways turned in upon itself, and that it will have to work hard to make sure that the political, economic and social changes it faces today work for the general and long-term good of the British people.

Britain Online

In terms of the number of websites available, and the proportion of people connected to the internet, Britain ranks among the highest in the world. This means that there is a wealth of information that can be found electronically, and the list that follows barely scratches the surface.

General

British Government: www.gov.uk
Office for National Statistics: www.ons.gov.uk

Society

National Health Service: www.nhs.uk/pages/home.aspx
Department of Health: www.gov.uk/government/organisations/department-of-health
Department for Education: www.gov.uk/government/organisations/department-for-education
Church of England: www.churchofengland.org
Church of Scotland: www.churchofscotland.org.uk
Equality and Human Rights Commission: www.equalityhumanrights.com
Ministry of Justice: www.gov.uk/government/organisations/ministry-of-justice
Law Society of England and Wales: www.lawsociety.org.uk
Home Office: www.gov.uk/government/organisations/home-office

Government

Royal Family: www.royal.gov.uk
Office of the Prime Minister: www.gov.uk/government/organisations/prime-ministers-office-10-downing-street

Houses of Parliament: www.parliament.uk
Supreme Court: www.supremecourt.uk
Scottish Parliament: www.parliament.scot
National Assembly for Wales: www.assembly.wales
Northern Ireland Assembly: www.niassembly.gov.uk
London Assembly: www.london.gov.uk
Local Government Association: www.local.gov.uk

Civil Society

Electoral Commission: www.electoralcommission.org.uk
European Parliament: www.europarl.europa.eu
Labour Party: www.labour.org.uk
Conservative Party: www.conservatives.com
Liberal Democrats: www.libdems.org.uk
Trades Union Congress: www.tuc.org.uk
Confederation of British Industry: www.cbi.org.uk
BBC: www.bbc.com
ITV: www.itv.com
The Times: www.thetimes.co.uk
The Independent: www.independent.co.uk
The Telegraph: www.telegraph.co.uk
The Guardian: www.theguardian.com
The Economist: www.economist.com

The Arts

National Theatre: www.nationaltheatre.org.uk
Royal Shakespeare Company: www.rsc.org.uk
British Film Institute: www.bfi.org.uk
Britmovie: www.britmovie.co.uk

Lifestyle

UK Sport: www.uksport.gov.uk
British Olympic Association: www.teamgb.com
Football Association: www.thefa.com

England and Wales Cricket Board: www.ecb.co.uk
World Rugby: www.worldrugby.org
Visit Britain: www.visitbritain.com

International

Foreign and Commonwealth Office: www.gov.uk/government/organisations/
    foreign-commonwealth-office
Ministry of Defence: www.gov.uk/government/organisations/ministry-of-
    defence
Department for International Trade: www.gov.uk/government/organisations/
    department-for-international-trade
The Commonwealth: www.thecommonwealth.org
European Union: www.europa.eu
North Atlantic Treaty Organization: www.nato.int

Bibliography

Ackroyd, Peter (2014) *Civil War: The History of England, Vol. III* (London: Macmillan).

Ahmad, Waqar (ed.) (2012) *Muslims in Britain: Making Social and Political Space* (Abingdon: Routledge).

Alcock, Pete and Margaret May (2014) *Social Policy in Britain*, 4th edn (Basingstoke: Palgrave).

Anderson, Benedict (2016) *Imagined Communities: Reflections on the Origin and Spread of Nationalism* (London: Verso).

Aughey, Arthur (2001) 'British Policy in Northern Ireland', in Stephen Savage and Rob Atkinson (eds) *Public Policy Under Blair* (Basingstoke: Palgrave).

Bagehot, Walter (1867) *The English Constitution* (London: Chapman and Hall).

Bale, Tim (2016) *The Conservative Party: From Thatcher to Cameron*, 2nd edn (Cambridge: Polity Press).

Bartle, John and Samantha Laycock (2006) 'Elections and Voting', in Patrick Dunleavy, Richard Heffernan, Philip Cowley and Colin Hay (eds) *Developments in British Politics 8* (Basingstoke: Palgrave Macmillan).

Baugh, Daniel (2011) *The Global Seven Years War, 1754–1763: Britain and France in a Great Power Contest* (Abingdon: Routledge).

Benn, Tony (1980) 'The Case for a Constitutional Premiership', *Parliamentary Affairs* 33(1), Winter: 7–22.

Billington, Michael (2007) *State of the Nation: British Theatre Since 1945* (London: Faber & Faber).

Booth, Alan (2001) *The British Economy in the Twentieth Century* (Basingstoke: Palgrave).

Brimblecombe, Peter (1989) *The Big Smoke: A History of Air Pollution* (London: Taylor & Francis).

Bryant, Christopher (2005) *The Nations of Britain* (London: Open University Press).

Budge, Ian, Ivor Crewe, David McKay and Ken Newton (2007) *The New British Politics*, 4th edn (Harlow: Longman).

Cahill, Michael (2010), *Transport, Environment and Society* (Maidenhead: Open University Press).

Childs, David (2012) *Britain Since 1945*, 7th edn (Abingdon: Routledge).

Clarke, Peter (2004) *Hope and Glory: Britain 1900–2000*, 2nd edn (London: Penguin).

Conboy, Martin (2005) *Tabloid Britain* (Abingdon: Routledge).

Cowley, Philip (2006) 'Making Parliament Matter?', in Patrick Dunleavy, Richard Heffernan, Philip Cowley and Colin Hay (eds) *Developments in British Politics 8* (Basingstoke: Palgrave Macmillan).

Cowley, Philip and Dennis Kavanagh (2016) *The British General Election of 2015* (Basingstoke: Palgrave Macmillan).

Cox, Michael and Tim Oliver (2006) 'Security Policy in an Insecure World', in Patrick Dunleavy, Richard Heffernan, Philip Cowley and Colin Hay (eds) *Developments in British Politics 8* (Basingstoke: Palgrave Macmillan).

Crane, Nicholas (2016) *The Making of the British Landscape* (London: Weidenfeld and Nicolson).

Crossman, Richard (1963) 'Introduction' to Walter Bagehot, *The English Constitution* (London: Fontana).

Crystal, David (2003) *English as a Global Language,* 2nd edn (Cambridge: Cambridge University Press).

Curran, James and Jean Seaton (2009) *Power Without Responsibility: Press, Broadcasting and the Internet in Britain*, 7th edn (London: Routledge).

Davie, Grace (2015) *Religion in Britain since 1945: Believing Without Belonging* (Oxford: Blackwell).

Davies, Alistair (2000) 'A Cinema In Between: Postwar British Cinema', in Alistair Davies and Alan Sinfield (eds) *British Culture of the Postwar* (London: Routledge).

Deacon, Russell (2012) *Devolution in the United Kingdom*, 2nd edn (Edinburgh: Edinburgh University Press).

Delreux, Tom and Sander Happaerts (2016) *Environmental Policy and Politics in the European Union* (London: Palgrave).

Dickens, Charles (1841) *The Old Curiosity Shop* (London: Chapman and Hall).

Douglas, Roy (2002) *Liquidation of Empire: The Decline of the British Empire* (Basingstoke: Palgrave Macmillan).

Edelman (2017) *Edelman Trust Barometer: Global Report*, Available at www.edelman.com/global-results (retrieved May 2017).

Edwards, Michael (2014) *Civil Society*, 3rd edn (Cambridge: Polity Press).

Evans, Eric J. (2013) *Thatcher and Thatcherism*, 3rd edn (Abingdon: Routledge).

Field, John (2017) *Social Capital*, 3rd edn (Abingdon: Routledge).

Fogle, Ben (2004) *The Teatime Islands: Adventures in Britain's Faraway Outposts* (London: Penguin).

Foley, Michael (2001) *The British Presidency*, 2nd edn (Manchester: Manchester University Press).

Fort, Tom (2006) *Under the Weather: The Story of Our National Obsession* (London: Century).

Fox, Kate (2014) *Watching the English: The Hidden Rules of English Behaviour* (London: Hodder and Stoughton).

Fox, Ruth (2014) Director of the Hansard Society, quoted in House of Commons, Political and Constitutional Reform Committee: Voter engagement in the UK. Fourth Report of Session 2014–15 (London: Stationery Office).

Fraser, Derek (2009) *The Evolution of the British Welfare State: A History of Social Policy since the Industrial Revolution*, 4th edn (Basingstoke: Palgrave Macmillan).

Gamble, Andrew (2009) *The Spectre at the Feast: Capitalist Crisis and the Politics of Recession* (Basingstoke: Palgrave Macmillan).

Gamble, Andrew (2016) 'What's British about British Politics?', in Richard Heffernan, Colin Hay, Meg Russell and Philip Cowley (eds) *Developments in British Politics 10* (London: Palgrave).

Garton Ash, Timothy (2001) 'Is Britain European?', in *The Guardian*, 22 February.

Garton Ash, Timothy (2004) *Free World: America, Europe and the Surprising Future of the West* (New York: Random House).

Geddes, Andrew (2013) *Britain and the European Union* (London: Palgrave).

George, Stephen (1998) *An Awkward Partner: Britain in the European Community* (Oxford: Oxford University Press).

Gillingham, John (2001) *The Angevin Empire*, 2nd edn (London: Edward Arnold).

Goldsworthy, Jeffrey (2010) *Parliamentary Sovereignty: Contemporary Debates* (Cambridge: Cambridge University Press).

Goldthorpe, John H. (2005) *Social Mobility and Class Structure in Modern Britain* (Oxford: Oxford University Press).

Grasso, Maria (2016) 'Political Participation', in Richard Heffernan, Colin Hay, Meg Russell and Philip Cowley (eds) *Developments in British Politics 10* (London: Palgrave).

Greer, Steven (2006) *The European Convention on Human Rights: Achievements, Problems and Prospects* (Cambridge: Cambridge University Press).

Hague, William (2004) *William Pitt the Younger: A Biography* (London: HarperCollins).

Hammerton, A. James (2005) *'Ten Pound Poms': Australia's Invisible Migrants* (Manchester: Manchester University Press).

Harris, John (2004) *The Last Party: Britpop, Blair and the Demise of English Rock* (London: HarperPerennial).

Hastie, Chris (2017) 'Grenfell's Tragedy is a Worldwide Truth: Fire is an Inequality Issue', in *The Guardian*, 11 July.

Hayward, Keith and Majid Yar (2006) 'The "Chav" Phenomenon: Consumption, Media and the Construction of a New Underclass', in *Crime Media Culture* 2:1, April, pp. 9–28.

Hazell, Robert (2006) *The English Question* (Manchester: Manchester University Press).

Heffer, Simon (1999) *Like the Roman: The Life of Enoch Powell* (London: Orion).

Heffernan, Richard (2006) 'The Blair Style of Central Government', in Patrick Dunleavy, Richard Heffernan, Philip Cowley and Colin Hay (eds) *Developments in British Politics 8* (Basingstoke: Palgrave Macmillan).

Higson, Andrew (2003) *English Heritage, English Cinema: Costume Drama since 1980* (Oxford: Oxford University Press).

Holt, Richard and Tony Mason (2000) *Sport in Britain 1945–2000* (Oxford: Blackwell).

Horrox, Rosemary and W. Mark Ormrod (2006) *A Social History of England 1200–1500* (Cambridge: Cambridge University Press).

Hughson, John (2016) *England and the 1966 World Cup: A Cultural History* (Manchester: Manchester University Press).

Hutchings, Peter (2009) 'Beyond the New Wave: Realism in British Cinema, 1959–63', in Robert Murphy (ed.) *The British Cinema Book*, 3rd edn (London: British Film Institute).

Johnson, Nevil (1999) 'The Constitution', in Ian Holliday, Andrew Gamble and Geraint Parry (eds) *Fundamentals in British Politics* (Basingstoke: Macmillan).

Jones, Bill and Philip Norton (2013) *Politics UK*, 8th edn (Harlow: Pearson Longman).

Jones, Ken (2016) *Education in Britain: 1944 to the Present*, 2nd edn (Cambridge: Polity Press).

Jones, Owen (2016) *Chavs: The Demonization of the Working Class* (London: Verso).

Jordan, Andrew and Camilla Adelle (eds) (2013) *Environmental Policy in the European Union*, 3rd edn (Abingdon: Routledge).

Kavanagh, Dennis, David Richards, Martin Smith and Andrew Geddes (2006) *British Politics*, 5th edn (Oxford: Oxford University Press).

Kavanagh, David and Philip Cowley (2010) *The British General Election of 2010* (Basingstoke: Palgrave Macmillan).

Kerr, Peter (2001) *Postwar British Politics: From Conflict to Consensus* (London: Routledge).

Kohn, Marek (2010) *Turned Out Nice: How the British Isles Will Change as the World Heats Up* (London: Faber and Faber).

Kuczera, Małgorzata, Simon Field and Hendrickje Catriona Windisch (2016) *Building Skills for All: A Review of England* (Paris: OECD).

Kumar, Krishan (2003) *The Making of English National Identity* (Cambridge: Cambridge University Press).

Kwarteng, Kwasi (2012) *Ghosts of Empire: Britain's Legacies in the Modern World* (London: Bloomsbury).

Kyle, Keith (2011) *Suez: Britain's End of Empire in the Middle East* (London: I B Taurus).

Lammy, David (2012) *Out of the Ashes: Britain after the Riots* (London: Guardian Books).

Leach, Robert, Bill Coxall and Lynton Robins (2011) *British Politics,* 2nd edn (Basingstoke: Palgrave Macmillan).

Leach, Robert, Bill Coxall and Lynton Robins (2018) *British Politics,* 3rd edn (Basingstoke: Palgrave Macmillan).

Lundestad, Geir (2003) *The United States and Western Europe since 1945* (Oxford: Oxford University Press).

Lundestad, Geir (ed.) (2008) *Just Another Major Crisis? The United States and Europe Since 2000* (Oxford: Oxford University Press).

Mangold, Peter (2006) *The Almost Impossible Ally: Harold Macmillan and Charles de Gaulle* (London: I B Taurus).

Marquand, David (1988) 'The Paradoxes of Thatcherism', in Robert Skidelsky (ed.) *Thatcherism* (London: Chatto & Windus).

Marr, Andrew (2017) *A History of Modern Britain* (London: Pan Books).

McCormick, John (2017) *Understanding the European Union*, 7th edn (London: Palgrave).

McKercher, B.J.C. (2017) *Britain, America, and the Special Relationship since 1941* (Abingdon: Routledge).

Middleton, Roger (2000) *The British Economy Since 1945* (Basingstoke: Macmillan).

Mitchell, David (2015) *Politics and Peace in Northern Ireland After 1998: Political Parties and the Implementation of the Good Friday Agreement* (Manchester: Manchester University Press).

Moran, Joe (2013) *Armchair Nation: An Intimate History of Britain in Front of the TV* (London: Profile).

Moran, Michael (2011) *Politics and Governance in the UK,* 2nd edn (Basingstoke: Palgrave Macmillan).

Moran, Michael (2017) *The End of British Politics?* (London: Palgrave Macmillan).

Morris, Marc (2012) *The Norman Conquest* (London: Windmill).

Mount, Ferdinand (2010) *Mind the Gap: The New Class Divide in Britain Now* (London: Short Books).

Mugglestone, Lynda (2007) *Talking Proper: The Rise and Fall of the English Accent as a Social Symbol,* 2nd edn (Oxford: Oxford University Press).

Norton, Philip (2010) *The British Polity*, 5th edn (New York: Longman).

Obelkevich, James and Peter Catterall (1994) 'Understanding British Society', in James Obelkevich and Peter Catterall (eds) *Understanding Post-War British Society* (London: Routledge).

Osborne, Roger (2013) *Iron, Steam and Money: The Making of the Industrial Revolution* (London: The Bodley Head).

Packer, Richard (2006) *The Politics of BSE* (Basingstoke: Palgrave Macmillan).

Paxman, Jeremy (2007) *The English: A Portrait of a People* (London: Penguin).

Phelps, Glenn and Steve Crabtree (2013) 'Worldwide, Median Household Income About $10,000', Available at http://news.gallup.com/poll/166211/worldwide-median-household-income-000.aspx (retrieved October 2017).

Pierre, Jon and Gerry Stoker (2000) 'Towards Multi-Level Governance', in Patrick Dunleavy, Andrew Gamble, Ian Holliday and Gillian Peele (eds) *Developments in British Politics 6* (Basingstoke: Palgrave).

Rackham, Oliver (2004) *Trees and Woodland in the British Landscape* (London: Phoenix Press).

Rawnsley, Andrew (1999) 'My Moral Manifesto for the 21st Century', in *The Guardian*, 4 September.

Reiff, K. and Schmitt, H. (1980) 'Nine second-order national elections: A conceptual framework for the analysis of European election results'. *European Journal of Political Research* Vol. 8, No. 1, pp. 3–44.

Reiner, Robert (2010) *The Politics of the Police*, 4th edn (Oxford: Oxford University Press).

Renwick, Chris (2017) *Bread for All: The Origins of the Welfare State* (London: Allen Lane).

Reynolds, David (2014) *The Long Shadow: The Legacies of the Great War in the Twentieth Century* (New York: W W Norton).

Richards, Jeffrey (1997) *Films and British National Identity: From Dickens to Dad's Army* (Manchester: Manchester University Press).

Richards, Eric (2004) *Britannia's Children: Emigration from England, Scotland, Wales and Ireland Since 1600* (London: Hambledon Continuum).

Riddell, Peter (1989) *The Thatcher Decade* (Oxford: Basil Blackwell).

Roberts, Alice (2015) *The Celts: Search for a Civilization* (London: Heron).

Roberts, Clayton, David Roberts and Douglas R. Bisson (2009) *A History of England*, 5th edn (Englewood Cliffs: Prentice-Hall).

Roberts, Richard (2008) *The City: A Guide to London's Global Financial Centre*, 2nd edn (London: The Economist).

Rosewarne, David (1984), 'Estuary English', in *The Times Educational Supplement*, 19, October.

Russell, Meg (2016) 'Parliament: A Significant Constraint on Government', in Richard Heffernan, Colin Hay, Meg Russell and Philip Cowley (eds) *Developments in British Politics 10* (London: Palgrave).

Sandbrook, Dominic (2009) *White Heat: A History of Britain in the Swinging Sixties* (London: Abacus).

Sanders, David (1997) 'Voting and the Electorate', in Patrick Dunleavy, Andrew Gamble, Ian Holliday and Gillian Peele (eds) *Developments in British Politics 5* (Basingstoke: Macmillan).

Saunders, Clare (2013) *Environmental Networks and Social Movement Theory* (London: Bloomsbury).

Savage, Mike (2015) *Social Class in the 21st Century* (London: Pelican).

Sargeant, Amy (2005) *British Cinema: A Critical and Interpretive History* (London: British Film Institute Publishing).

Seldon, Anthony and Peter Snowdon (2015) *Cameron at 10: The Inside Story 2010–15* (London: William Collins).

Shaw, George Bernard (2000) Pygmalion: A Romance in Five Acts (London: Penguin).

Shaw, Timothy M. (2007) *Commonwealth: Inter- and Non-state Contributions to Global Governance* (Abingdon: Routledge).

Simpson, Mark, Tracy Shildrick and Robert MacDonald (eds) (2006) *Drugs in Britain: Supply, Consumption and Control* (Basingstoke: Palgrave Macmillan).

Sloan, Stanley R. (2010) *Permanent Alliance? NATO and the Transatlantic Bargain from Truman to Obama* (New York: Continuum).

Smith, Adam (2008) *An Inquiry into the Nature and Causes of the Wealth of Nations* (Oxford: Oxford Paperbacks).

Smith, Martin J. (1999) *The Core Executive in Britain* (Basingstoke: Macmillan).

Soffe, Richard (ed.) (2003) *The Agricultural Notebook* (Oxford: Blackwell).

Spear, Joanna (2000) 'Foreign and Defence Policy', in Patrick Dunleavy, Andrew Gamble, Ian Holliday and Gillian Peele (eds) *Developments in British Politics 6* (Basingstoke: Palgrave).

Spencer, Colin (2011) *British Food: An Extraordinary Thousand Years of History* (London: Grub Street).

Stark, Steven D. (2006) *Meet The Beatles: A Cultural History of the Band that Shook Youth, Gender and the World* (New York: HarperCollins).

Storry, Mike and Peter Childs (eds) (2017) *British Cultural Identities*, 5th edn (Abingdon: Routledge).

Street, Sarah (2008) *British National Cinema*, 2nd edn (London: Routledge).

Talbot-Smith, Alison and Allyson M. Pollock (2006) *The New NHS: A Guide* (London: Routledge).

Tanner, Duncan (2002), 'Electing the Governors/the Governance of the Elect', in Keith Robbins (ed.) *The British Isles 1901–1951* (*The Short Oxford History of the British Isles*) (Oxford: Oxford University Press).

Thatcher, Margaret (1988) Speech to the College of Europe, Bruges, Belgium, 20 September.

Thomas, Robert (1999) 'Law and Politics', in Ian Holliday, Andrew Gamble and Geraint Parry (eds) *Fundamentals in British Politics* (Basingstoke: Macmillan).

Thorpe, Andrew (2015) *A History of the British Labour Party* (Basingstoke: Palgrave).

Turner, Alwyn W. (2014) *A Classless Society: Britain in the 1990s* (London: Aurum).

Walker, Alexander (2005) *Icons in the Fire: The Decline and Fall of Almost Everybody in the British Film Industry, 1984–2000* (London: Orion).

Wallace, William and Tim Oliver (2005) 'A Bridge Too Far: The United Kingdom and the Transatlantic Relationship', in David M. Andrews (ed.) *The Atlantic Alliance Under Stress: US–European Relations After Iraq* (Cambridge: Cambridge University Press).

Webb, Paul (2016) 'The Party System: Turbulent Multipartyism or Duopolistic Competition?', in Richard Heffernan, Colin Hay, Meg Russell and Philip Cowley (eds) *Developments in British Politics 10* (London: Palgrave).

Weight, Richard (2003) *Patriots: National Identity in Britain 1940–2000* (London: Pan Books).

Winder, Robert (2013) *Bloody Foreigners: The Story of Immigration to Britain* (London: Abacus).

Woods, Michael (2005) *Contesting Rurality: Politics in the British Countryside* (Aldershot: Ashgate).

Woodward, Antony and Robert Penn (2007) *The Wrong Kind of Snow; The Complete Daily Companion to the British Weather* (London: Hodder & Stoughton).

Young, Hugo (1999) *This Blessed Plot: Britain and Europe from Churchill to Blair* (Basingstoke: Macmillan).

Zurcher, Arnold J. (1958) *The Struggle to Unite Europe 1940–58* (New York: New York University Press).

Z/Yen Limited (2005) *The Competitive Position of London as a Global Financial Centre* (London: Z/Yen).

Index